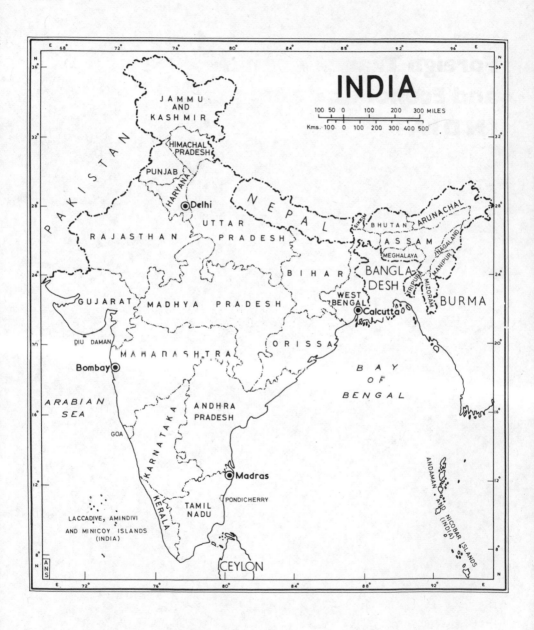

INDIA

100 50 0   100   200   300 MILES

Kms. 100   0   100 200 300 400 500

JAMMU
AND
KASHMIR

PAKISTAN

HIMACHAL
PRADESH

PUNJAB

HARYANA

⊙ Delhi

N E P A L

SIKKIM

BHUTAN

ARUNACHAL

RAJASTHAN

UTTAR
PRADESH

ASSAM

MEGHALAYA

NAGALAND

MANIPUR

BIHAR

BANGLA-
DESH

TRIPURA

MIZORAM

BURMA

GUJARAT

MADHYA   PRADESH

WEST
BENGAL

DIU DAMAN

M A H A R A S H T R A

O R I S S A

⊙ Calcutta

Bombay ⊙

ARABIAN
SEA

GOA

KARNATAKA

ANDHRA
PRADESH

B A Y
O F
BENGAL

⊙ Madras

KERALA

PONDICHERRY

TAMIL
NADU

LACCADIVE, AMINDIVI
AND MINICOY ISLANDS
(INDIA)

ANDAMAN AND NICOBAR ISLANDS
(INDIA)

CEYLON

Foreign Trade Regimes and Economic Development: INDIA

Foreign Trade Regimes and Economic Development:

*A Special Conference Series
on Foreign Trade Regimes
and Economic Development*

VOLUME VI

NATIONAL BUREAU OF ECONOMIC RESEARCH
New York   1975

INDIA

by **Jagdish N. Bhagwati**

MASSACHUSETTS INSTITUTE OF TECHNOLOGY

T. N. Srinivasan

INDIAN STATISTICAL INSTITUTE

DISTRIBUTED BY Columbia University Press
New York and London

NATIONAL BUREAU OF ECONOMIC RESEARCH

*A Special Conference Series on Foreign Trade Regimes
and Economic Development*

Library of Congress Card Number: 74–82374
ISBN for the series: 0–87014–500–2
ISBN for this volume:
Cloth: 0–87014–506–1
Paper: 0–87014–531–2

Printed in the United States of America
DESIGNED BY JEFFREY M. BARRIE

Relation of the Directors of the National Bureau to
Publication of the Country Studies in the Series on
Foreign Trade Regimes and Economic Development

The individual country studies have not passed through the National Bureau's normal procedures for review and approval of research reports by the Board of Directors. In view of the way in which these studies were planned and reviewed at successive working parties of authors and Co-Directors, the National Bureau's Executive Committee has approved their publication in a manner analogous to conference proceedings, which are exempted from the rules governing submission of manuscripts to, and critical review by, the Board of Directors. *It should therefore be understood that the views expressed herein are those of the authors only and do not necessarily reflect those of the National Bureau or its Board of Directors.*

The synthesis volumes in the series, prepared by the Co-Directors of the project, are subject to the normal procedures for review and approval by the Directors of the National Bureau.

To
H. G. Johnson
and
C. R. Rao

Contents

Tables

Figures

Co-Directors' Foreword

This volume is one of a series resulting from the research project on Exchange Control, Liberalization, and Economic Development sponsored by the National Bureau of Economic Research, the name of the project having been subsequently broadened to Foreign Trade Regimes and Economic Development. Underlying the project was the belief by all participants that the phenomena of exchange control and liberalization in less developed countries require careful and detailed analysis within a sound theoretical framework, and that the effects of individual policies and restrictions cannot be analyzed without consideration of both the nature of their administration and the economic environment within which they are adopted as determined by the domestic economic policy and structure of the particular country.

The research has thus had three aspects: (1) development of an analytical framework for handling exchange control and liberalization; (2) within that framework, research on individual countries, undertaken independently by senior scholars; and (3) analysis of the results of these independent efforts with a view to identifying those empirical generalizations that appear to emerge from the experience of the countries studied.

The analytical framework developed in the first stage was extensively commented upon by those responsible for the research on individual countries, and was then revised to the satisfaction of all participants. That framework, serving as the common basis upon which the country studies were undertaken, is further reflected in the syntheses reporting on the third aspect of the research.

The analytical framework pinpointed these three principal areas of research which all participants undertook to analyze for their own countries.

Subject to a common focus on these three areas, each participant enjoyed maximum latitude to develop the analysis of his country's experience in the way he deemed appropriate. Comparison of the country volumes will indicate that this freedom was indeed utilized, and we believe that it has paid handsome dividends. The three areas singled out for in-depth analysis in the country studies are:

1. *The anatomy of exchange control:* The economic efficiency and distributional implications of alternative methods of exchange control in each country were to be examined and analyzed. Every method of exchange control differs analytically in its effects from every other. In each country study care has been taken to bring out the implications of the particular methods of control used. We consider it to be one of the major results of the project that these effects have been brought out systematically and clearly in analysis of the individual countries' experience.

2. *The liberalization episode:* Another major area for research was to be a detailed analysis of attempts to liberalize the payments regime. In the analytical framework, devaluation and liberalization were carefully distinguished, and concepts for quantifying the extent of devaluation and of liberalization were developed. It was hoped that careful analysis of individual devaluation and liberalization attempts, both successful and unsuccessful, would permit identification of the political and economic ingredients of an effective effort in that direction.

3. *Growth relationships:* Finally, the relationship of the exchange control regime to growth via static-efficiency and other factors was to be investigated. In this regard, the possible effects on savings, investment allocation, research and development, and entrepreneurship were to be highlighted.

In addition to identifying the three principal areas to be investigated, the analytical framework provided a common set of concepts to be used in the studies and distinguished various phases regarded as useful in tracing the experience of the individual countries and in assuring comparability of the analyses. The concepts are defined and the phases delineated in Appendix A.

The country studies undertaken within this project and their authors are as follows:

Brazil	Albert Fishlow, University of California, Berkeley
Chile	Jere R. Behrman, University of Pennsylvania
Colombia	Carlos F. Díaz-Alejandro, Yale University
Egypt	Bent Hansen, University of California, Berkeley, and Karim Nashashibi, International Monetary Fund
Ghana	J. Clark Leith, University of Western Ontario

India   Jagdish N. Bhagwati, Massachusetts Institute of Tech-
                    nology, and T. N. Srinivasan, Indian Statistical Institute

Israel   Michael Michaely, The Hebrew University of Jerusalem

Philippines   Robert E. Baldwin, University of Wisconsin

South Korea   Charles R. Frank, Jr., Princeton University and The
                    Brookings Institution; Kwang Suk Kim, Korea Develop-
                    ment Institute, Republic of Korea; and Larry E. West-
                    phal, Northwestern University

Turkey   Anne O. Krueger, University of Minnesota

The principal results of the different country studies are brought together in our overall syntheses. Each of the country studies, however, has
been made self-contained, so that readers interested in only certain of these
studies will not be handicapped.

In undertaking this project and bringing it to successful completion, the
authors of the individual country studies have contributed substantially to the
progress of the whole endeavor, over and above their individual research.
Each has commented upon the research findings of other participants, and
has made numerous suggestions which have improved the overall design and
execution of the project. The country authors who have collaborated with us
constitute an exceptionally able group of development economists, and we
wish to thank all of them for their cooperation and participation in the project.

We must also thank the National Bureau of Economic Research for its
sponsorship of the project and its assistance with many of the arrangements
necessary in an undertaking of this magnitude. Hal B. Lary, Vice President-
Research, has most energetically and efficiently provided both intellectual and
administrative input into the project over a three-year period. We would also
like to express our gratitude to the Agency for International Development for
having financed the National Bureau in undertaking this project. Michael
Roemer and Constantine Michalopoulos particularly deserve our sincere
thanks.

JAGDISH N. BHAGWATI
Massachusetts Institute of Technology

ANNE O. KRUEGER
University of Minnesota

Preface

This study of India's trade and exchange rate policies is part of the NBER project described in the Co-Directors' Foreword. At the same time, as explained there, the organization and emphases in analysis have reflected our own views about what is important to examine and evaluate in the Indian economy.

In some ways, this work may be regarded as a sequel to *India: Planning for Industrialization*, by Bhagwati and Desai (see Chapter 1, note 1, below), which was finished some five years ago, just as the first effects of the June 1966 devaluation were being worked out. Our present work has managed to build on this earlier study, indeed freely drawing on it where useful; it is, however, self-contained and can be read on its own.

We have been helped in our analysis by a number of officials and economists in India. In particular, we should mention A. Vaidyanathan, Arun Ghosh, Manmohan Singh, K. G. Vaidya, and R. M. Honavar. Our thanks must go particularly to K. Sundaram for the material on the political effects of the 1966 devaluation (Chapter 10), V. R. Panchamukhi for working out the premium data and the ERP estimates (Chapter 13), Kirit Parikh for assistance in running the Eckaus-Parikh model program (Chapter 14), and Ashok Desai for surveying several firms on their research and development activities (Chapter 15).

As with other authors in the NBER project, we have benefited from the comments of other participants at the several conferences at which working drafts of our study were discussed. In addition, we should like to thank Mark Frankena, Jean Baneth, Neville Beharie, Solomon Fabricant, and Peter

K. Clark for helpful suggestions. The helpful comments of Anne Krueger have also led to many improvements in this study. Our greatest thanks go to Hal Lary of the National Bureau, who has read through successive drafts with the utmost care and thoroughness, far beyond the call of duty. His searching queries and patient prodding have resulted in a vastly improved manuscript.

For excellent and efficient research assistance, we thank B. M. Juyal, Asim Dasgupta, and, in particular, Chellamma Ramaswami and H. C. Sharma who put in sustained work. Parts of the manuscript were typed by Mehar Lal. The full draft has been typed by Katherine Eisenhaure, but for whose efficiency and cheerful cooperation we would have been totally lost between different drafts through the three-year period over which we were working on this book, and by Kris Beard, who worked on the final draft with equal efficiency. During the past year, while Bhagwati was Visiting Ford Research Professor at the University of California at Berkeley, the manuscript went through substantial revisions. The input provided by the university's secretarial facilities is gratefully acknowledged.

We should like to thank the *Economic and Political Weekly,* Bombay, for permission to reprint Chapter 10, which appeared there as the first of three installments during September 2, 9, and 16, 1972; the Oxford University Press for permission to quote and to use material from the Bhagwati and Desai volume mentioned above; and the M.I.T. Press for permission to reproduce tables 1.1, 3.1, and 3.2 from R. S. Eckaus and K. S. Parikh, *Planning for Growth* (1968).

Finally, we should record the caveat that our analysis was basically completed by October 1973. Most of the empirical results reported in this study were obtained, using published and unpublished (provisional) data which were available as of that date. At the time the page proofs were corrected (May 1975), revised data became available. The revisions, especially with respect to data on savings and investment, have been drastic and, in some instances, even the methodology of estimation has been changed. We have not been able to work with the new data at this late stage. However, we do not anticipate that our conclusions, particularly with respect to economic policy, will be changed in any major way. Needless to say, the events of 1971, leading to the dismemberment of Pakistan and the creation of Bangladesh, with all their economic consequences for 1972 and thereafter (e.g., India's refugee relief burden and her continuing aid to Bangladesh after the latter's creation), and the Declaration of Emergency in June 1975 have been major disturbances on the scene, whose long-term effects will not be clear for some time to come.

JAGDISH N. BHAGWATI
T. N. SRINIVASAN

Principal Dates and Historical Events in India

Political.

  I. *Constitutional events*
     Independence Day, August 15, 1947
     Republic Day, January 26, 1950

 II. *India's prime ministers*
     Jawaharlal Nehru, August 15, 1947–May 27, 1964
     Interim (Gulzarilal Nanda), May 27, 1964–June 9, 1964
     Lal Bahadur Shastri, June 9, 1964–January 11, 1966
     Interim (Nanda), January 11, 1966–January 24, 1966
     Mrs. Indira Gandhi, January 24, 1966–

III. *Wars*
     Indo-Chinese Conflict, October 20, 1962–November 21, 1962
     Indo-Pakistan Conflict, August 5, 1965–September 23, 1965
     Indo-Pakistan War, December 3, 1971–December 17, 1971

 IV. *General elections* (opening dates; first election ended February 1952)
     First general election, October 1951
     Second general election, February 24, 1957
     Third general election, February 16, 1962
     Fourth general election, February 15, 1967
     Fifth general election, March 1, 1971

Economic.

V. *Plans* (dates of formal adoption)
First Five-Year Plan (April 1, 1951–March 31, 1956), December 1952
Second Five-Year Plan (April 1, 1956–March 31, 1961), May 1956
Third Five-Year Plan (April 1, 1961–March 21, 1966), August 1961
Interim Annual Plans (April 1, 1966–March 31, 1969)
Fourth Five-Year Plan (April 1, 1969–March 31, 1974)

VI. *Industrial policy*
First Industrial Policy Resolution, April 6, 1948
Second Industrial Policy Resolution, April 30, 1956

VII. *Devaluations* (changes in rupees per U.S. dollar as a percentage of the older rates)
1949 devaluation (approximately 43.9 percent), September 20, 1949
1966 devaluation (approximately 57.5 percent), June 6, 1966

VIII. *Aid*
Formation of the Aid-India Consortium, 1958

IX. *Planning: Miscellaneous*
Formation of the Planning Commision, March 1950
Publication of
Professor Prasanta Mahalanobis's Second Plan Frame, March 1955
Draft Outline of Second Five-Year Plan, February 1956
Draft Outline of Third Five-Year Plan, June 1960
First Draft Outline of Fourth Plan (abortive), August 1966
Final Draft Outline of Fourth Plan, May 1970 (presented to Parliament May 18, 1970)
Approach to Fifth Plan, May 1972 (approved by National Development Council May 31, 1972)

Foreign Trade Regimes
and Economic Development:
INDIA

Part I

Introduction

Chapter 1

An Overview: 1950-70

In this volume we propose to examine India's foreign trade regime in its inter-action with domestic policies and objectives, so as to assess its efficiency and growth. Earlier analyses of India's trade and industrialization policies have focused largely on the criteria underlying the allocation mechanisms, both domestic and foreign, and have examined many of the principal, static ineffi-ciencies arising from these mechanisms.[1] The present study goes substantially beyond these issues in two major respects:

1. We examine at length the efficiency and outcome of the liberalization efforts represented by the June 1966 devaluation and the accompanying policy measures, thus casting light on the important issues raised by attempts at lessening the restrictive nature of the QR-regime and on the optimal methods of effecting a transition to a less restrictive foreign trade regime; and

2. We analyze at great length several issues relating to the growth effects of India's foreign trade regime, examining the impact on savings, innovation, inducement to invest, and other such effects which are correctly considered to be important in reaching an overall judgment on the desirability of the eco-nomic policy framework.

This chapter, which constitutes Part I, contains a broad description of the central economic and political characteristics of the Indian economy (such as industrial licensing and targeting under successive five-year plans), and a general review of the principal developments in economic indices (such as GNP, price level, foreign trade and agricultural production) since 1950. We then proceed to divide the period 1950–70, to which our analysis is confined, into several phases as defined by Bhagwati-Krueger for the NBER project,

3

whose main elements are spelled out at the beginning of this volume. Having then defined the phases, our study proceeds in Part II to a discussion of the "anatomy" of exchange control, concentrating on the period 1956–66. The purpose of this analysis is to indicate the methods of allocation and intervention in the foreign trade and payments sector practiced during this period by the government, and to trace their *economic* impact. The analysis concentrates here on the static efficiency effects of the foreign trade policies only in a general way; statistical analysis of the allocation effects as well as of differential returns to alternative acts of investment that follow from indiscriminate and automatic protection is deferred to later treatment along with the other growth effects of the regime. Part III presents an analysis of the period 1966–70, focusing on the outcome of the "liberalization episode" constituted by the June 1966 devaluation and associated policy changes. Finally, Part IV treats the growth effects of the foreign trade regime, taking the entire 1950–70 period as its canvas, and analyzes a number of possible linkages between India's economic performance and her foreign trade regime (taken in conjunction, of course, with her domestic economic regime).

THE INDIAN ECONOMY SINCE 1950

India became independent in 1947. By 1950, the country had formally initiated efforts at planning for accelerated growth consistent with the objective of social justice. This implied that a succession of five-year plans was to define the overall contours within which economic and social efforts were to be undertaken. The First Plan was to run from 1951 to 1956, with others following in continuous succession until a three-year interruption prior to the Fourth Plan.

The First Plan was essentially put together around a Harrod-Domar model. The emphasis of this approach, as is now well understood, is on *flow* analysis and the Plan therefore focused on fiscal policy aimed at raising domestic savings to the degree required by the projected investment levels that result from planned income expansion and the estimated marginal capital-output ratio. At the same time, the main thrust of the Plan was to build infrastructure. But the Second Plan (1956–61) was conceived around a *structural* model of the Feldman-Mahalanobis variety and this led to an emphasis on determining and controlling the pattern of investments, thus greatly reinforcing the tendency later imparted by the foreign exchange crisis that began with an overexpansion of investment in the first year of the Second Plan.[2] Thus the Second Plan witnessed the initiation and subsequent intensification of two basic pillars of policy that were strongly to influence the economic efficiency of the regime: (1) industrial targeting and licensing and (2) exchange control over all current transactions, resulting in the licensing of imports of capital goods, intermediates and consumer goods.

Indeed, in the analysis presented in this volume we will find that the interaction of these two licensing measures compounded disproportionately the inefficiencies that would have followed from the operation of either by itself, thus illustrating the point that it is not possible to analyze the effects of the foreign trade regime without taking fully into account the institutional mechanism at the domestic level as well. This emphasis on industrial and import licensing was to continue through the decade of 1956–66. Efforts to reduce its impact were undertaken through the early 1960s, and they were to culminate in the devaluation of June 1966 and in the associated policy changes that aimed at liberalizing the foreign trade regime. In view of their critical importance in assessing the efficiency of the foreign trade regime, the main features of the industrial licensing mechanism will be described in some detail below.

We should also note here, for later amplification, the importance of several other institutional features of the Indian economy: (1) a significant growth of public sector investment in areas outside of infrastructure; (2) a (less) significant growth of Indian trade with the Soviet bloc under bilateral agreements; (3) an increasing canalization of profitable imports, and partial handling-cum-subsidization of exports, by the government-owned State Trading Corporation; (4) a strict (*ex ante*) regulation, on a case-by-case basis, of the inflow of private foreign capital and technology into the economy; and (5) in contrast to many LDCs, the availability of an efficient administrative service, entrepreneurial talent and educated, skilled personnel for manning the projected investments. Before discussing these institutional features in detail, we review some of the major features of India's economic performance since 1950.

Basic Indices.

NATIONAL INCOME

According to the data on net national product presented in Table 1–1, the Indian economy seems to have grown, in real terms, at 3.5 to 4 percent per annum on the average during the first decade of planning, from 1950–51 to 1960–61, and then experienced a decline during the Third Five-Year Plan to an average rate of growth of about 2.5 percent. It is important to note that the end of the Third Five-Year Plan was attended by serious drought which led to an unprecedented decline in agricultural production, thus pulling down the overall rate of growth for the Third Five-Year Plan and for 1966–67.[3] A recovery in agricultural output brought a sharp rise in national income in the following year, followed by moderate though sustained rates of growth until a

TABLE 1–1

Net National Product, Total and Per Capita, 1950–51 to 1972–73

	Net National Product at 1960–61 Prices		Annual Growth Rates (percent)		Index Numbers (1960–61=100)	
	Total (Rs. billions)	Per Capita (Rs.)	Total	Per Capita	Total	Per Capita
(1)	(2)	(3)	(4)	(5)	(6)	(7)
1950–51	90.9	253.1			68.4	82.7
1951–52	93.1	255.1			70.1	83.4
1952–53	96.4	259.1			72.6	84.7
1953–54	102.6	270.8	3.7	1.8	77.3	88.5
1954–55	105.3	272.9			79.3	89.2
1955–56	108.9	277.1			82.0	90.2
1956–57	115.1	286.9			86.7	93.8
1957–58	113.2	276.9			85.2	90.5
1958–59	122.3	292.6	4.0	2.0	92.1	95.6
1959–60	124.5	292.2			93.7	95.5
1960–61	132.8	306.0			100.0	100.0
1961–62	137.3	309.3			103.4	101.1
1962–63	139.9	308.2			105.4	100.7
1963–64	147.7	318.3	2.6	0.4	111.2	104.0
1964–65	158.8	335.1			119.6	109.5
1965–66	150.8	310.9			113.5	101.6
1966–67	152.3	307.9	1.0	−1.0	114.7	100.6
1967–68	166.1	328.2	9.0	6.9	125.0	107.3
1968–69	171.5	331.1	3.3	0.7	129.2	108.2
1969–70	180.9	341.9	5.5	3.8	136.2	111.7
1970–71	188.6	348.6	4.3	2.0	142.0	113.9
1971–72	191.7	346.0	1.7	−0.7	144.4	113.1
1972–73	188.5	333.0	−1.7	−3.8	141.9	108.8

SOURCES: For the period 1950–51 to 1959–60, unpublished material made available to the authors. For 1960–61 to 1972–73, *Economic Survey,* Government of India, 1973–74.

new pronounced slowdown came with still another fall in agricultural production in 1971–72 and 1972–73.

POPULATION AND PER CAPITA INCOME

The growth of per capita income, as shown in Table 1–1, has been less than the growth of national income because population has grown. And the growth rate of population, as is clear from Table 1–2, has *accelerated* in the 1960s from its 1950s level. The percentage of urban population has marginally increased from 16 percent in 1951 to 18 percent in 1961 and presumably to 20 percent by 1971, so that the overwhelming bulk of the population continues to be rural.

TABLE 1–2

Population, Decennial, 1931–71

(millions)

	Total	Annual Average Increase (%)	Urban			Rural	
			Sub-total	Annual Average Increase (%)	Percent of Total	Sub-total	Annual Average Increase (%)
Census date (March 1)							
1931	279		33		12	246	
		1.34		2.6			1.1
1941	319		44		14	275	
		1.25		3.5[a]			1.0
1951	361		58[a]		16	303	
		1.98		3.1			1.7
1961	439		79		18	360	
		2.25		3.3			2.1
1971[b]	547		109[c]		20	439	

SOURCE: *Basic Statistics Relating to the Indian Economy: 1950–51 to 1970–71,* Government of India, Planning Commission, Statistics and Surveys Division, New Delhi.

a. The originally reported figure for urban population in 1951 was 62.4 million and this is the figure used here in calculating the percentage increase from 1941 to 1951. The 1951 figure, however, was subsequently adjusted downward when the 1961 census adopted a more rigorous definition of urban population. Figures for the earlier years have not been adjusted.

b. As of April 1.

c. Urban population for 1971 is estimated on the assumption of a further increase of 2 percentage points from 1961 in share of total population.

DOMESTIC SAVINGS

While the growth of national income, both absolute and on a per capita basis, has been modest, performance on the criterion of domestic savings effort was satisfactory during the period of the first three five-year plans (though the steady increase in the rate of saving has not been sustained since 1966, as we shall also see in Chapter 16).

Thus Table 1–3 shows that the savings rate, as a percent of NNP, went up from an average of 6.28 during 1950–52 to an average of 11.14 during

TABLE 1–3

Tax Revenue and Savings in India, 1950–51 to 1968–69

Year (1)	Tax Revenue as Percent of NNP[a] (2)	Domestic Savings as Percent of NNP[a] (3)
1950–51	6.92	7.30
1951–52	7.76	5.27
1952–53	7.22	5.11
1953–54	7.00	5.17
1954–55	7.91	6.17
1955–56	8.15	9.11
1956–57	8.30	8.13
1957–58	9.76	5.53
1958–59	9.15	5.64
1959–60	9.63	7.65
1960–61	10.98	9.21
1961–62	11.79	9.15
1962–63	13.33	10.08
1963–64	14.16	11.27
1964–65	13.42	10.12
1965–66	14.78	12.01
1966–67	14.33	9.87
1967–68	12.82	8.59
1968–69	13.51	n.a.

n.a. = not available.

SOURCE: *Estimates of National Product, 1948–49 to 1962–63* and *Estimates of National Product, Saving and Capital Formation, 1960–61 to 1971–72*, Government of India, Department of Statistics, Central Statistical Organization, New Delhi.

a. The post-1960–61 NNP figures are the revised series and the pre-1960–61 figures are the conventional series.

1964–66. A role in this improvement was played by tax policy: tax revenue as a percent of NNP also went up from less than 7 percent at the beginning of the period to more than 14 percent at the end of it. The contribution of the public sector to domestic savings has, however, not been fully commensurate with this tax effort, as official current expenditures have risen more rapidly than governmental savings. Indeed, the public sector contribution to the domestic savings effort seems to have reached a peak of 29.3 percent (Table 1–4) by 1964–65 and then declined later rather steeply, though the data on this phenomenon are rather tentative.

EXTERNAL RESOURCES

The inflow of external assistance to India has been low per capita, ranking India virtually at the bottom of the list of aid recipients.[4] By the criterion of aid in relation to GNP, India has fared a *little* better, for the simple reason that her per capita income is also at the tail end of the world distribution.

The data on external assistance to India as a percent of national income are given in Table 1–5. They underline the relatively small share of foreign aid in India's developmental effort; they also bring out clearly the abrupt fall in the role of foreign aid in her efforts since the peak reached in the mid-1960s.[5] While Table 1–5 shows aid utilizations, which differ from aid authorizations for well-known reasons, the conclusions we infer from it are sustained by the data on authorizations as well.

The role of private foreign investment in India has been even less important, given (1) the unwillingness of the Indian government to invite foreign investment uncritically, (2) the fact that the economy is so large that only a dramatic influx could possibly make the inflow large relative to national income, and (3) the outflow of capital from the older industries, principally tea.[6] Rather than burden the reader with detailed numbers, it should be enough to illustrate the rather small role of private foreign investment in Indian development by citing the figures for 1964–65. For this year, the gross inflow of portfolio plus direct investment into India was only about Rs. 1.02 billion, or slightly over .6 percent of the (conventional) NNP estimate for the year. And the net inflow, at Rs. 818 million was only a little over 0.5 percent of NNP.[7] Compared with the aid estimates in Table 1–5, the private inflow of all long-term capital was only about a seventh. The major investors on a country-of-origin basis were the United Kingdom, the United States and Japan, in that order, although the outstanding *stock* of private long-term capital was largely in British hands and has continued to be, given the heavy British investment in India before independence, the comparatively small inflow of private capital since, and the large British share in this inflow anyway. It should also be of some interest to note that, as of March 1967, the estimated distribution of private foreign capital in different sectors showed that manufacturing had 47.1

TABLE 1-4

Net Domestic Savings, by Source, 1960-61 to 1968-69

	1960-61	1961-62	1962-63	1963-64	1964-65	1965-66	1966-67	1967-68	1968-69
Distribution of net domestic savings (percent)									
Household sector	63.4	62.4	52.6	63.6	65.5	72.9	n.a.	n.a.	72.7
Private corporate sector	9.9	10.0	9.5	7.8	5.2	4.2	n.a.	n.a.	11.4
Public sector	26.7	27.6	27.9	28.6	29.3	22.9	n.a.	n.a.	15.9

n.a. = not available.

SOURCE: The 1960-61 to 1965-66 data from *Estimates of Saving in India, 1960-61 to 1965-66*, Government of India, Department of Statistics, Central Statistical Organization, New Delhi. The 1968-69 figure is in the Fourth Five-Year Plan.

TABLE 1-5

Utilization of External Assistance by India, as Percentage of Net National Product at Factor Cost, 1951–52 to 1969–70

	1951–52	1952–53	1953–54	1954–55	1955–56	1956–57	1957–58	1958–59	1959–60	1960–61
1. Loans	0.81	0.34	0.02	0.02	0.08	0.25	1.06	1.78	1.27	1.39
2. Grants	0.04	0.12	0.16	0.10	0.28	0.35	0.30	0.19	0.26	0.22
3. Assistance under P.L. 480/665, etc.	—	—	—	—	0.05	0.45	1.01	0.74	0.75	1.39
4. Total aid	0.86	0.47	0.19	0.11	0.40	1.05	2.37	2.71	2.28	3.01

	1961–62	1962–63	1963–64	1964–65	1965–66	1966–67	1967–68	1968–69	1969–70
1. Loans	1.60	2.02	2.21	2.38	2.37	0.41	0.47	0.39	0.37
2. Grants	0.15	0.10	0.09	0.10	0.16	0.06	0.03	0.03	0.01
3. Assistance under P.L. 480/665, etc.	0.61	0.81	1.05	1.07	1.14	0.2?	0.20	0.09	0.09
4. Total aid	2.37	2.93	3.35	3.55	3.67	0.69	0.71	0.52	0.48

NOTE: The 1960–61 to 1969–70 estimates are for the revised NNP series. The 1966–67 to 1969–70 aid estimates are at the post-devaluation exchange rate.

SOURCE: *Economic Survey*, annual issues 1966–73, Government of India, Ministry of Finance, Department of Economic Affairs, New Delhi.

percent; services, 23.9 percent; petroleum, 16.8 percent; plantations, 11.4 percent; and mining, 0.9 percent.[8]

PRICE LEVEL

The Indian economy has also been somewhat atypical, during 1950–1966, in that its price increases have been moderate over the period as a whole. This is clearly evident in the wholesale price index in Table 1–6, which shows the 1965–66 price index at 147.0 with base 1950–51, indicating a simple annual rate of increase of only 3 percent.[9]

On the other hand, this remarkable stability began to disappear after 1962–63. The rise in defense expenditure following the Sino-Indian border war of 1962 and the two serious agricultural droughts during 1965–66 and 1966–67 had much to do with this; and the subsequent moderation of the price increases to trend level during a recessionary period has again given way to serious price rises since 1972–73, reflecting partly the refugee and defense burdens arising from the Bangladesh crisis and also another bad harvest which afflicted the Indian economy (as well as the Soviet and the Chinese economies) during 1972–73.[10]

PRODUCTION STRUCTURE

The importance of agricultural production in explaining the post-devaluation performance of exports and the price level is intuitively seen also by noting at this stage that agriculture has continued to play an important role in the production structure of the economy during the entire period of our study. Thus Table 1–7 shows that agriculture and allied activities continued during the 1960s to provide approximately half of net domestic product measured in current prices. On this basis there would seem to have been no significant decline in the role of agriculture in the Indian economy. This result is partly attributable, however, to the greater increase in agricultural prices than in those of other sectors. At constant (1960–61) prices the shares in NDP in 1969–70 were 43.7 percent for agriculture and allied activities, 22.9 percent for industry, 15.9 percent for trade and transport and 17.5 percent for services.

AGRICULTURAL PRODUCTION

We may further note that according to the 1971 census, nearly 70 percent of the workers were employed in agriculture. Agriculture is the dominant supplier of wage goods and raw materials for the production of wage goods. It also accounts for more than a third of India's exports.

It is thus of importance for the reader to keep in view the major aspects of India's agricultural performance during the period of our study. In particular, it should be noted that, from the viewpoint of production trends, the period through 1964–65 must be distinguished from the subsequent period for two

TABLE 1–6

Index Numbers of Wholesale Prices, 1950–51 to 1970–71

| | 1950–51 = 100 | | | 1961–62 = 100 | | | |
| | Food Articles | Manu-factured Articles | | Agricul-tural Com-modities | Food Articles | Manufac-tures | All Com-modities |
Year (1)	(2)	(3)	General (4)	(5)	(6)	(7)	(8)
1950–51	100.0	100.0	100.0	—	—	—	—
1951–52	96.7	115.5	105.5	—	—	—	—
1952–53	88.9	96.8	89.4	—	—	—	—
1953–54	94.8	95.8	93.6	—	—	—	—
1954–55	84.1	97.4	87.0	—	—	—	—
1955–56	77.0	96.5	82.7	—	—	—	—
1956–57	90.9	102.9	94.2	—	—	—	—
1957–58	94.6	104.6	97.0	—	—	—	—
1958–59	102.4	104.9	101.0	—	—	—	—
1959–60	105.8	108.1	104.7	—	—	—	—
1960–61	106.7	119.9	111.7	—	—	—	—
1961–62	106.8	122.6	111.9	100.0	100.0	100.0	100.0
1962–63	112.1	124.7	114.4	102.3	106.5	102.6	103.8
1963–64	121.6	126.9	121.0	108.4	115.4	104.8	110.2
1964–65	142.1	132.9	136.6	130.9	135.4	109.0	122.3
1965–66	150.0	144.4	147.0	141.7	144.6	118.1	131.6
1966–67	177.7	157.8	171.1	166.6	171.1	127.5	149.9
1967–68	215.3	160.2	190.2	188.2	207.8	131.1	167.3
1968–69	205.6	163.2	188.0	179.4	196.9	134.4	165.4
1969–70	—	—	—	194.8	196.8	143.5	171.6
1970–71	—	—	—	201.0	203.9	154.9	181.2

NOTE: The blanks represent unavailable estimates.

SOURCES: *Basic Statistics Relating to the Indian Economy, 1950–51 to 1968–69,* Government of India, Planning Commission, Statistics and Surveys Division, New Delhi. *Economic Survey: 1970–71,* Government of India, Ministry of Finance, Department of Economic Affairs, New Delhi.

TABLE 1-7

Net Domestic Product by Sector of Origin in Current Prices, 1960–61 to 1969–70

(Rs. billions)

Sector	1960–61	1962–63	1963–64	1964–65	1965–66	1966–67	1967–68	1968–69	1969–70
1. Agriculture and allied activities	68.21 (51.0)[a]	71.97	83.57	102.14	99.45	120.11	151.40	145.02	156.14 (49.7)
2. Industry	26.88 (20.1)	32.06	37.05	40.94	43.84	47.96	52.56	55.96	62.67 (19.9)
a. Mining and quarrying	1.44 (1.1)	1.78	2.04	2.04	2.34	2.52	2.90	3.16	3.39 (1.1)
b. Large-scale manufacturing	10.71 (8.0)	12.98	15.18	16.86	18.39	19.70	20.41	21.92	24.83 (7.9)
c. Electricity, gas and water supplies	0.68 (0.5)	0.87	1.09	1.28	1.44	1.77	2.00	2.43	2.66 (0.8)
d. Small-scale manufacturing	7.85 (5.9)	9.42	10.82	11.82	12.25	13.25	14.60	15.56	16.94 (5.4)
e. Construction	6.20 (4.6)	7.01	7.92	8.94	9.42	10.72	12.65	12.89	14.85 (4.7)
3. Trade and transport	18.70 (14.0)	22.13	24.92	29.25	31.65	36.97	42.01	44.45	47.94 (15.3)
a. Transport and communications	5.69 (4.3)	7.19	7.87	8.56	9.30	10.34	11.34	13.13	14.33 (4.6)
b. Trade, storage, hotels and restaurants	13.01 (9.7)	14.94	17.05	20.69	22.35	26.63	30.67	31.32	33.61 (10.7)

4. Services	19.87 (14.9)	23.65	26.54	29.76	32.92	36.32	40.36	43.93	47.57 (15.1)
a. Banking and insurance	1.58 (1.2)	2.24	2.49	2.88	3.41	3.62	4.16	4.59	5.04 (1.6)
b. Public administration and defense	5.38 (4.0)	6.68	7.78	8.90	9.89	10.99	12.47	13.93	15.02 (4.8)
c. Real estate and ownership of dwellings	3.86 (2.9)	4.47	5.28	5.62	5.96	6.38	6.59	7.00	7.29 (2.3)
d. Other services	9.05 (6.8)	10.26	10.99	12.36	13.66	15.33	17.14	18.41	20.22 (6.4)
Net domestic product at factor cost	133.66 (100.0)	149.81	172.08	202.09	207.86	241.36	286.33	289.36	314.32 (100.0)

SOURCE: *Estimates of National Product, 1960–61 to 1969–70*, Government of India, Department of Statistics, Central Statistical Organization, New Delhi.

a. Figures in parentheses represent percentage share of NDP.

reasons that critically affect the latter: (1) new technology—the so-called "Green Revolution" based on new varieties of foodgrains—began to spread from 1965–66 on; and (2) there were two unprecedented droughts in 1965–66 and 1966–67. The consequences of the droughts clearly dominate the effect of the Green Revolution so that the annual compound (semi-log trend) growth rate of agricultural output is 3.2 percent for 1949–50 to 1964–65 but falls drastically if we include the two drought years. It should be noted, however, that even when we exclude those years and extend the period to 1969–70, the annual compound growth rate is slightly lower at 2.9 percent, though the decline is imperceptible (from 3.0 to 2.9 percent) in the case of foodgrains (to which the Green Revolution is really relevant).[11] Thus the Green Revolution, at best, seems to have arrested a possible decline in *foodgrain* production but has not been effective in eliminating a slight decline in the overall trend growth rate in *agricultural* production.

We may also note that this growth rate has been the result of both area extension and growing yield per hectare, the two factors contributing in equal measure to the growth rate of total production. Moreover, the aggregate picture conceals divergent performances by different commodities. The new technology had its impact primarily on wheat. The estimated rate of growth of wheat production was thus 4 percent per annum during 1949–50 to 1964–65 but increases to 5.1 percent when the period is extended to 1969–70. The contribution of yield growth was 1.3 percent per annum in the former period but turns out to be 2.4 percent per annum over the longer period. Thus the new technology has accelerated the growth of yield per hectare and hence that of total output of wheat.

SHIFTING STRUCTURE OF INDUSTRIAL PRODUCTION

Two things are notable about the performance of the industrial sector during the period of our study. First, the growth rate of this sector exceeded that of the agricultural sector and also accelerated through the three five-year plans. The index number of industrial production (Table 1–8) shows a compound, annual rate of growth of 5.75 percent in the First Plan, nearly 7.5 percent in the Second and close to 8 percent in the Third. The post-1966 performance has been less satisfactory because of the industrial recession which set in during 1966–67 and continued through 1969–70. This phenomenon is analyzed at length in connection with the June 1966 devaluation discussed in Chapter 8.[12]

Second, the structure of industrial production has gradually shifted away from a preponderant role for consumer goods production to a growing role for capital goods and intermediates. During 1951–63, for example, the relative shares in terms of gross value added, gross output at factor cost and gross output at market price, declined steadily for consumer goods, rose steadily

TABLE 1–8

Index of Industrial Production, 1951–72

(1960 = 100)

Year	Weight	Consumer Goods Industries 37.25	Capital Goods Industries 11.76	Intermediate Goods Industries 25.88	Overall Index
1951					58.7
1952					60.8
1953					62.0
1954					66.3
1955					71.9
1956					77.9
1957					80.7
1958					82.1
1959					89.2
1960		100.0	100.0	100.0	100.0
1961		106.6	118.0	105.8	109.2
1962		108.0	153.0	113.6	119.8
1963		110.4	170.0	122.9	129.7
1964		118.6	206.1	132.2	140.8
1965		127.5	244.2	140.1	153.8
1966		131.3	210.1	136.7	152.6
1967		125.7	205.3	139.7	151.4
1968		131.9	210.3	148.2	161.1
1969		145.3	214.0	154.4	172.5
1970		154.7	224.6	158.8	180.8
1971		159.7	224.3	160.4	186.1
1972		168.2	243.5	171.2	199.4

NOTE: The weights shown apply to the series starting with 1960. Index numbers by end-use categories are not available for earlier years. The overall index shown above for years prior to 1960 (originally based on 1951 as 100) has been linked to the new index, based on 1960, in that year.

SOURCES: *Reserve Bank of India Bulletin,* November 1960, June 1961, June 1970, December 1972 and December 1973.

for capital goods and remained steady at around 35 to 40 percent for intermediates and raw materials.[13] Furthermore, by using alternative measures of
import substitution and by carefully distinguishing among them, Padma Desai
has shown that all measures underline the following conclusions: (1) for the
period 1951–63, import substitution in the capital goods sector predominates;
(2) the First Plan, however, was characterized by relatively substantial import
substitution in the consumer goods sector; and (3) the Second Plan, with its
emphasis on investment in heavy industries, registered the lowest import substitution in the consumer goods sector and the highest in the capital goods
sector.[14] These conclusions must carry over into the Third Plan as well, as is
evident if one examines the industrial production index during 1961–66: with
1960 = 100, it stands at 244.2 for capital goods industries, 140.1 for intermediate goods industries and 127.5 for consumer goods industries for 1965.[15]

FOREIGN TRADE

We will have occasion later to analyze the foreign trade sector intensively. Here, in this broad overview of the Indian economy, we confine ourselves to a very general and brief description of the major features of India's
trade performance and policies.

Import Licensing. Throughout the period under study, imports have
been licensed. The proportion of licenses going to traders (the *Established
Importer* licenses) has steadily diminished (from over 61 percent of all licenses
issued in 1951–52 to less than 3 percent in 1970–71) and the proportion
going directly to producers (the *Actual User* licenses for intermediates and the
Capital Goods licenses for equipment) has now taken over the bulk (more
than half) of available imports. The licensing has further been characterized
by numerous restrictions on import specification, transferability and "indigenous clearance" to protect domestic suppliers of import-substitutes. Finally,
the licensing has varied in degrees of restrictiveness. It was rather light during
the First Plan, intensely severe during the Second, somewhat less so during
the Third (except in the last two years), and perhaps equally so since then.
It may be noted that import licensing has been operated, virtually throughout
the period since the Second Plan, in conjunction with industrial licensing over
much of the Organized Industrial Sector.

Exports. India has not merely a rather low ratio of exports to national
income;[16] her share in total world trade has also been falling through the
period of our study, as Table 1–9 highlights, and is now less than one-third as
large as it was in the years immediately following World War II.[17] The composition of Indian exports has remained heavily biased toward "traditional" items
such as tea, jute manufactures and cotton fabrics, these three items alone
accounting for a quarter of India's export earnings as late as 1970–71. But
new, "non-traditional" exports such as engineering goods, chemicals and allied
products have grown in the 1960s to over 10 percent of India's total exports.[18]

TABLE 1–9
India's Exports and Share of Total Value of World Exports, 1948–70

Calendar Year (1)	World Exports (U.S. $ millions) (2)	Indian Exports (U.S. $ millions) (3)	Indian Exports as Percentage of World Exports (4)
1948	53,300	1,363	2.6
1949	53,900	1,309	2.4
1950	55,200	1,146	2.1
1951	74,800	1,611	2.2
1952	72,400	1,295	1.8
1953	73,400	1,116	1.5
1954	76,400	1,182	1.5
1955	83,200	1,276	1.5
1956	92,600	1,300	1.4
1957	99,300	1,379	1.4
1958	94,800	1,221	1.3
1959	100,600	1,308	1.4
1960	113,400	1,331	1.2
1961	118,600	1,387	1.2
1962	124,700	1,403	1.1
1963	136,000	1,631	1.2
1964	152,600	1,749	1.2
1965	165,400	1,686	1.0
1966	181,400	1,606	0.89
1967	191,200	1,612	0.84
1968	213,700	1,760	0.82
1969	244,900	1,835	0.75
1970	280,500	2,026	0.72

SOURCES: *International Financial Statistics*, Supplement to 1966–67 issues, March 1968, October 1973, International Monetary Fund.

Imports. The structure of imports has been shifted almost exclusively toward capital goods, intermediates and raw materials, the only consumer goods imported in any significant quantity being foodgrains. Import licensing has been used for this purpose; and the shift from EI to AU and CG licensing is also clearly linked to this phenomenon of the drastic decline of consumer goods imports. Table 1–10 quantifies the picture as of 1966–67 to 1968–69: the only consumer goods imports, other than food, come under the non-food

TABLE 1–10

Imports by Category, 1966–67 to 1968–69

(U.S. $ millions)

	1966–67	1967–68	1968–69
Food[a]	868	691	449
Non-food	1,903	1,986	2,096
(1) Machinery and equipment	363	289	265
(2) Maintenance imports	1,393	1,508	1,612
(a) Components and spares	415	402	434
(b) Raw materials and intermediates			
(excluding metals)	733	852	948
(c) Metals			
(i) Iron and steel	131	142	115
(ii) Non-ferrous	114	119	119
(3) Others	146	191	218
Total imports	2,771	2,677	2,545

SOURCES: Government of India, Ministry of International Trade, Office of the Chief Controller of Imports, New Delhi.

International Financial Statistics, May 1961, May 1971, December 1962, October 1967, November 1972, August 1973, International Monetary Fund.

a. Food here consists only of cereals and cereal preparations. A small amount of food and edible products is included in item 3 (others).

item (3) and these clearly were at most 5 to 8 percent of total imports by the late 1960s.[19]

Trade and Current Balance. In a QR-regime, the trade balance is of little intrinsic significance while the potential deficit (which is suppressed) and the resulting premia on imports are more important concepts. The Indian trade balance has been constantly negative for the simple reason that external resources have come in as aid and long-term investment and that the balance on invisibles account is both relatively small and again negative. The trade deficit has, in fact, been of the order of $700 to $1300 million, and the current account deficit of the order of $750 to $1500 million during 1961–62 and 1967–68 but has declined thereafter (along with aid flows generally). Thus during 1968–69, 1969–70 and 1970–71, the trade deficit was estimated at $497, $238 and $424 million, respectively, and the current account deficit at $676, $437 and $632 million, respectively.

Foreign Exchange Reserves. These estimates may be compared with the foreign exchange reserves position portrayed in Table 1–11. Note that the foreign exchange position became "thin" after the First Plan, the reserves being virtually halved during 1957 when the balance of payments crisis erupted with the onset of the Second Plan. The decline continued sporadically through the late 1960s.[20]

Key Institutional Features.

We now add a brief description of some of the basic institutional features of India's economic and political structure. An understanding of these features is essential if the reader is to put the analysis in this volume into proper perspective.

INDUSTRIAL TARGETING AND LICENSING

Beginning with the Second Plan, the practice of setting industrial targets became common, and subsequent plans have set out detailed targets for capacity and production in the Organized Industrial Sector.

In addition, the system has been characterized by comprehensive industrial licensing. Licensing has been wider in scope than targeting for the simple reason that it has extended to finer product classification; it has also had to contend with applications to create capacities in areas and in products that were not anticipated in the plan documents. Except for exemptions granted later during the period of our study, both in terms of the exemption limit on size of investment and in terms of exemption by industrial classification of the applicant, industrial licensing has been comprehensive.

The industrial licensing system has been operated alongside the import licensing system in that any expansion of capacity or altogether new investment has required both CG import licenses and industrial licenses through the bulk of the period since industrial licensing began with the Second Plan. This accounts for the important point, made later in this study, that the relaxation of industrial licensing in the late 1960s did not manage to change the restrictiveness of the economic regime because import licensing did not change in substance.

Industrial licensing has also been applied in an extremely detailed manner in relation to its intended purpose. Thus augmentation of capacity by marginal addition of equipment (even for the sake of achieving balance among the various branches of a plant), product diversification and other such responses to changing market conditions that would be normal in an efficient industrial environment have been constrained by the way industrial licensing has functioned.[21]

It should also be noted that a principal objective of the industrial licensing system was to prevent further concentration of economic power in large concerns. In practice, efforts to reach this objective were to be frustrated because the smaller entrepreneurs generally could not invest as much in the aggregate, or in the targeted industries, as contemplated under the Plans; and also

TABLE 1-11

India's Gold and Foreign Exchange Reserves, 1951–72

(U.S. $ millions)

End of Period (1)	Official Gold (2)	Official Foreign Exchange (3)	Official Reserves of Gold, Foreign Exchange and SDRs (2)+(3) (4)	IMF Gold Tranche Position (5)	Overall Reserves (4)+(5) (6)	Use of IMF Credit (7)	Net Position (6)−(7) (8)
1951	247	1,697	1,944	—	1,944	−72	1,872
1952	247	1,549	1,796	—	1,796	−72	1,724
1953	247	1,615	1,862	—	1,862	−72	1,790
1954	247	1,620	1,867	—	1,867	−26	1,841
1955	247	1,619	1,866	15	1,881	—	1,881
1956	247	1,188	1,435	28	1,463	—	1,463
1957	247	695	942	—	942	−173	769
1958	247	475	722	—	722	−177	545
1959	247	567	814	—	814	−132	682
1960	247	423	670	—	670	−63	607
1961	247	418	665	—	665	−188	477
1962	247	265	512	—	512	−292	220
1963	247	360	607	—	607	−298	309
1964	247	251	498	—	498	−154	344
1965	281	319	599	—	599	−287	312

Year						
1966	243	364	608	—	608	−361	247
1967	243	419	662	—	662	−456	206
1968	243	439	682	—	682	−374	308
1969	243	683	926	—	926	−240	686
1970	243	698	985	—	985	−10	975
1971	264	699	1,124	—	1,124	—	1,124
1972	264	566	1,098	—	1,098	—	1,098

NOTE: The figures include SDRs worth $44 million, $161 million and $268 million for 1970, 1971 and 1972, respectively.
SOURCE: *International Financial Statistics*, International Monetary Fund.

because it became clear that the bureaucratic system of administered allocations was as disproportionately accessible to larger business houses with their
connections and muscle as the market system was in view of their greater access
to finance. Ultimately, by the late 1960s, the government was to shift to a policy
under which the Large Industrial Houses, so designated, were to have their
investments confined to the so-called "core" (generally heavy) industries.
Under the same policy, a nationalized banking system was to encourage the
expansion of the small-scale sector and a Monopolies and Restrictive Practices
Commission was to be set up to watch out for and check the expansion of
monopoly and concentration in Indian industry and to examine related issues.
As we shall see, none of these changes, which were designed to permit and
prompt the expansion of the Large Industrial Houses in approved (core)
sectors, so as not to hinder the task of expanding *overall* investment in the
economy, were really successful and for this reason, among others, industrial
investments were to be slack in the late 1960s.

PUBLIC SECTOR

Among the most important institutional features of the Indian economy
are the large share and continuing expansion of the public sector in overall, as
in industrial, investments. This phenomenon is of particular importance as the
impact of trade and exchange rate policies on allocation and production decisions within the public sector cannot be totally decisive: we should also take
into account the ability of these investments to survive the market test owing
to implicit subsidies (as when the public sector enterprises do not have to show
"normal" profits). In practice, the difference between private and public sector
performance does not go particularly beyond this. The reason is simply that
the policy of automatic protection for domestic investments, whether public or
private, has served to make the market test of survival more or less irrelevant
for weeding out inefficient firms and industries; thus the additional impairment
of the market mechanism, implied by the public sector not having to turn in
"normal" profits, adds little of substance to this basic weakness of the Indian
economic regime.[22]

The share of the public sector in total Indian investment has been estimated at over 46 percent for the First Plan, over 61 percent for the Second
and over 58 percent for the Third. The public sector's share in Organized
Industrial Sector investment has consistently run well over half of the total
during this period. Within the industrial sector, furthermore, the government
has invested significantly in heavy industry: steel, oil refineries, heavy electrical
and heavy engineering being the major areas. The distribution by sector of
cumulated investment in public sector projects during 1965–66 registered
40.62 percent for steel, 20.29 percent for engineering, 9.11 percent for chemicals, 12.22 percent for petroleum and 7.49 percent for mining and minerals. The

remaining 10.29 percent was accounted for by financial institutions, shipping, aviation and miscellaneous activities.[23] The government has also sought, through two Industrial Policy Resolutions, to reserve certain "key" industrial sectors for public sector investment (e.g., steel); but in practice these restrictions have been treated with some flexibility.

CONTROL OF INFLOW OF TECHNOLOGY AND INVESTMENT

We should next note the strict regulation of the inflow of technology and investment by the government throughout the period of our study. The "technical collaboration agreements" between Indian entrepreneurs and foreign sellers of technology have had to be approved and the royalty terms carefully screened and sanctioned. At the same time, clearance has been required for all equity investment, whether in joint ventures or in subsidiaries (which are generally disapproved in favor of joint ventures). This clearance has involved not merely the whole gamut of import and industrial licensing but also the additional restrictive criteria relating to royalty terms on associated technical transfers and to areas of permissible investment. In this regard, the Indian economy has again been characterized by more stringent restrictions on the inflow of technology and investments than the economies of many other developing countries seeking external capital.[24]

STATE TRADING CORPORATION

The foreign trade of India is not exclusively in the private sector. This is true not merely in the sense that there are public sector enterprises whose current output is also being exported. It is rather that the State Trading Corporation, established in 1956, has come to handle a substantial volume of both import and export trade. It directly engages in trade and also occasionally permits private traders to effect deals, subject to the corporation's approval and commission, in commodities otherwise traded by the STC alone. By 1965, this trade was about 5 percent of total Indian trade. Thus, the role of the STC is not very significant; but it needs to be kept in view, especially as the STC has been a vehicle for channeling lucrative imports of some scarce commodities and also for subsidizing the exports of some other commodities through STC's absorption of losses on export sales. Two other corporations, of relatively minor importance, are the Minerals and Metals Trading Corporation (constituted in 1963) and the Metal Scrap Trade Corporation (constituted in 1964).

TRADE AGREEMENTS

India has not been averse to conducting trade under bilateral trading agreements, not merely with the Soviet bloc but also with other developing countries. Trade with the Soviet bloc in particular has steadily increased. Thus, exports to the bloc were about 5 percent of total Indian exports during the Second Plan but grew to nearly 16 percent during the Third Plan and have steadily increased since. Nonetheless, the overwhelming bulk of Indian trade continues outside the Soviet bloc and outside the framework of bilateral agreements. Moreover, it is well known that both India and her trading partners conduct bilateral trade with keen attention to international prices, so that such trade presents no serious complication to the present analysis (nor do the operations of the State Trading Corporation discussed above).[25]

POLITICAL STRUCTURE

Since independence in 1947, India has been a parliamentary democracy and has enjoyed remarkable political stability. The government has witnessed long periods of firm leadership, with only three Prime Ministers in more than twenty-five years. The dominance of one party, the Congress party, through the bulk of the period has also increased political stability. The only interruption in this unparalleled record of political equilibrium was the struggle that broke out over the prime ministership when Mrs. Indira Gandhi succeeded Mr. Lal Bahadur Shastri. This upheaval led to the eventual bifurcation of the Congress party and the near-decimation of the faction that became the so-called "old Congress" before the "new Congress" emerged under Mrs. Gandhi's firm leadership.

The main thrust of the political leadership has been toward ideological positions identified with that nebulous word, socialism. This has implied attention to objectives such as the prevention of concentrated economic power and land reform, objectives which have not been pursued with the keenness that attends their affirmation in the country. The opposition parties have been on both left and right, ranging from laissez-faire Swatantra and backward-looking Jan Sangh to varying shades of revisionist and non-revisionist Communist parties eternally splintering and bickering. None of them have managed to pose a sustained and serious challenge to the ruling Congress party whose economic and political philosophy is fairly étatist and centrist.

The country is federal, with the central government overseeing state governments in as many as seventeen states.[26] The Congress party has generally managed to rule in the states as well, but not always and, in recent years, even less often. But even when the Congress party has had extensive control of the state governments, center-state frictions have not been reduced, for regional pulls tend to cut across party identifications.

Internationally, the country has experienced continuing problems on its borders with Pakistan and China. There have been three wars with Pakistan and one with China, and the burden of defense expenditure has been estimated at 3 percent of GNP since the 1962 war with China.

PHASES: 1950–70

Having given the reader an overview of the important institutional features of and the key economic-performance indicators for the Indian economy, we are now in a position to delineate the different phases (as defined in Appendix A) in the Indian foreign trade regime. And we propose to analyze the Indian economy in terms of the periods defined by these phases, in contrast to the customary analysis in terms of the five-year plans. The phases which we distinguish are identified in Figure 1–1, which also traces several of the major economic variables relevant to the delineation of the phases.

1950–56 (Phase IV).

This period corresponds roughly to the period of the First Plan. It was characterized by good harvests and hence a satisfactory agricultural expansion of nearly 5 percent per year. The index of agricultural production (1949–50 = 100) went from 90.5 in 1950–51 to 120.8 in 1956–57 for foodgrains and from 95.6 in 1950–51 to 124.3 in 1956–57 for all commodities. Indian exports fell as a percentage of world exports, remaining relatively stagnant in absolute value after the Korean War peak, and import demand balanced this off to result in a roughly equilibrated exchange rate which put little pressure on the QR-framework that had been inherited from the Second World War. The foreign exchange reserve position thus remained comfortable and official reserves remained close to $1.9 million through this period. There was no evidence of high import premia, systematic allocations of imports and industrial licenses and associated economic policies of the kind that were to spring up in the next period.

In a predominant sense, therefore, we can characterize this period as corresponding to Phase IV of the Bhagwati-Krueger schema. The convertibility was not total, the QR-regime was not fully absent and so Phase V, as defined, was not really present. On the other hand, the QRs were *not* systematically designed to adjust the international accounts and their scope was severely limited: they were, almost literally, left over from the Second World War and the machinery for administering them had not been dismantled.

1956–62 (Phase I).

By contrast, the period extending approximately from 1956 to 1962, broadly synchronizing with the Second Five-Year Plan, was characterized by the imposition of a QR-regime in the strong sense, provoked by a severe balance of payments crisis in early 1957. This was also a period of a shift in the investment pattern to manufacturing industry and to heavy industry as

FIGURE 1–1

Selected Macroeconomic Indicators for India, 1950–70

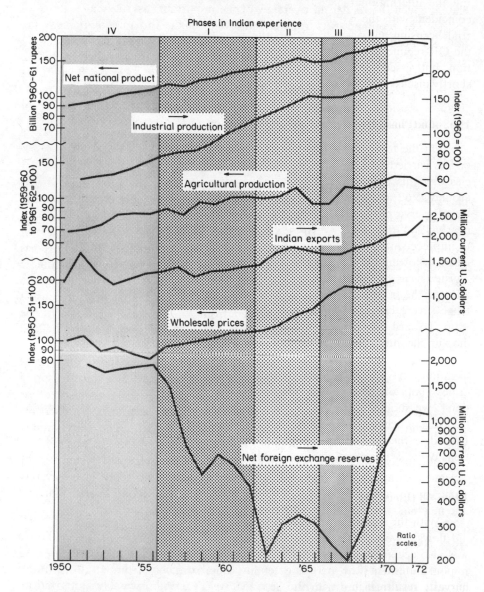

well,[27] imposition of strict industrial licensing,[28] accrual of significant aid flows, a rise in the domestic rate of saving, a severe reduction in foreign exchange reserves and a continuing stagnation in export performance (implying a falling ratio of exports both to GNP and to world exports).

Clearly, the period is somewhat easily characterized as Phase I, in terms of extensive and intensive emergence of the QR-regime as a method of adjusting the international accounts. At the same time, it should be noted that, coincident with the balance of payments rationale, the introduction of industrial licensing and industrial targeting simultaneously implied a rationale for the QR-regime which rested rather on the objective of selective industrialization, buttressed by QR-regime-generated, automatic protection—as we shall shortly discuss in Part III.

1962–66 (Phase II).

On the foreign payments front, the situation described above was more or less carried into the period 1962–66, with one significant exception which classifies this period as Phase II: export subsidization was begun in earnest around 1962 and intensified through the period on a whole range of exports.

Reserve position continued to be "thin"; aid flows were stabilized up to nearly 1964–65; QRs remained severe (the premia on imports, however, rose to unprecedented levels around late 1965 and early 1966 with the suspension of aid following the Indo-Pakistan War in late 1965); and export performance registered a significant improvement (until 1965 when a major drought affected the traditional exports adversely). Industrial licensing also continued to be severe but, toward the end of the period, efforts were made to loosen it up. Toward the end, the government also steadily deployed import duties to mop up the import premia.

This period can be broadly characterized as one involving "partial liberalization" in view of the export subsidization and growing resort to import duties (both of these policies involving therefore a growing, *de facto* devaluation); we should also note the halting moves toward more liberal industrial licensing procedures. These moves were to culminate in our "Liberalization Episode": the June 1966 devaluation and the accompanying import liberalization. We will thus characterize this period as Phase II.

1966–68 (Phase III).

With the 1966 devaluation and import liberalization (based on enlarged aid flows), we can identify the beginning of a third phase. The devaluation was also accompanied by an elimination of export subsidies and reduction of import duties. As it turned out, this period was afflicted by a second disastrous harvest, resulting in price increases and an adverse impact on traditional exports, and subsequently by an industrial recession. This liberalization episode, in consequence, was ill-starred for economic reasons. These difficulties were further compounded by the acute political pressure brought by aid donors for this change of policies—as we discuss in Chapter 10. Thus, for several reasons explored in Part IV in depth, Phase III did not lead to a Phase IV of yet further loosening up of the QR-regime and its attendant effects, but rather to a relapse, by 1968–69, into Phase II.

1968–70 (Phase II).[29]

By 1969–70, the liberalization appeared to have been largely reversed. The import premium was back to 30 to 50 percent on the average, export subsidies had been reinstated and were up to high levels, industrial de-licensing had amounted to little (especially because of continuing QRs), automatic protection with QRs was still the order of the day, and the picture looked very similar to (though marginally better than) that obtaining during 1962–65. The system had not really moved into Phase IV effectively but had rather relapsed into Phase II. In this sense, the liberalization episode had failed; it had also failed politically for the reason that exogenous developments (e.g., price rises due to drought) plus foreign pressures had (erroneously) discredited, in the political and public eye, such a liberalizing package and hence diminished the likelihood of its being tried again.

The delineation of the (approximate) phases in the Indian economy, as defined above, now enables us to proceed to the following analysis:

1. characterize the "anatomy of exchange control" for Phase I and Phase II, the former and the latter periods being similar in their import regimes but different in that exports were subsidized during the latter Phase; this is the subject of our analysis in Part II;

2. analyze in Part III the "liberalization episode" of 1966–68, beginning more or less with the June 1966 devaluation, determine the conditions that governed its outcome and draw lessons therefrom; and

3. examine in Part IV the overall growth effects of the foreign trade regime (broadly defined to include the exchange rate policy plus the *framework* of domestic policies such as industrial licensing), to determine whether the QR-regime contributed to India's rather unsatisfactory economic performance or improved it.

NOTES

1. For a comprehensive analysis along these lines see Jagdish N. Bhagwati and Padma Desai, *India: Planning for Industrialization* (London: Oxford University Press, 1970). This study, commissioned by the Organization for Economic Cooperation and Development, is part of a series on industry and trade in some developing countries edited by Ian Little, Tibor Scitovsky and Maurice Scott.

2. For a detailed discussion of the economic theory and techniques underlying the successive plans, consult J. Bhagwati and S. Chakravarti, "Contributions to Indian Economic Analysis: A Survey," *American Economic Review,* Special Supplement, 1970.

3. See Figure 1–1 for index numbers tracing the course of agricultural production over the period since 1950–51.

4. See Bhagwati and Desai, *India,* p. 181, for documentation and details.

5. The issue of whether foreign aid helped retard the domestic savings effort will be discussed in Chapter 16 where we reach the conclusion that there is little evidence for such a view. Note also that in Table 1–5 aid is being converted into rupees at post-devaluation prices from 1966–67.

6. For details, consult M. Kidron, *Foreign Investment in India* (London: Oxford University Press, 1965).

7. These estimates are taken from the *Reserve Bank of India Bulletin,* August 1969.

8. *Ibid.* This original source provides further breakdowns by direct and portfolio investments as well as by branches and "foreign controlled rupee companies."

9. For some of the *caveats* in interpreting this index, especially with regard to biases downward when prices are moving up, see Bhagwati and Desai, *India,* p. 76.

10. Our analysis, however, will stop around 1971–72 for reasons stated in the Preface.

11. These and other estimates in our discussion in this section are based on T. N. Srinivasan, "The Green Revolution or the Wheat Revolution?" in *Comparative Experience of Agricultural Development in Developing Countries of South East Asia since World War II* (Bombay: Thacker and Co. for the Indian Society of Agricultural Economics, 1972). More details and analysis are given there.

12. The index of industrial production during 1965, 1966, 1967, 1968 and 1969 was 153.8, 152.6, 151.4, 161.1 and 172.5, respectively, as estimated in mid-1972 and reported in the *Reserve Bank of India Bulletin.*

13. For detailed analysis, see Padma Desai, *Import Substitution in the Indian Economy* (Delhi: Hindustan Publishing Corporation, Jawahar Nagar, 1972). The data refer to the Organized Industrial Sector which is defined to include all establishments except those employing fewer than ten workers using power or fewer than twenty without power.

14. *Ibid.* See also an original paper by the same author, "Alternative Measures of Import Substitution," *Oxford Economic Papers* (November 1969), for a theoretical analysis of the rationales that may underlie the different measures.

15. In view of excess capacity in various industries and the tendency to deny imported inputs to consumer goods industries in times of abnormal foreign exchange stringency, the relative expansion of consumer goods *investments* may seem slightly understated if one tries to infer it from the relative expansion of consumer goods *production.*

16. This ratio, for example, was 4.8 percent in 1960–61. By a Chenery-type regression technique, however, it can be argued that India's exports are no smaller than what her size would indicate to be the "on-the-line" level. See J. Bhagwati and J. Cheh, "LDC Exports: A Cross-Sectional Analysis," in *International Economics and Development,* ed. Luis Eugenio de Marco (New York: Academic Press, 1972).

17. The interaction among external factors, domestic policies and export performance will be examined in later parts of this study.

18. If we include fish, art silk fabrics and iron and steel exports as well, the share rises to nearly 20 percent in 1970–71. The major traditional export commodities include coir yarn and manufactures, tobacco, leather and leather manufactures, coffee, iron ore, manganese ore and mica.

19. This shift of the import structure so that consumer goods imports are seriously reduced is typical of the postwar trend in many LDCs. See J. Bhagwati and C. Wibulswasdi, "A Statistical Analysis of Shifts in the Import Structure in LDCs," *Bulletin of the Oxford University Institute of Statistics* 34 (May 1972).

20. The reserves had recovered by 1972 to nearly $1 billion. This period, however, is beyond the scope of our study.

21. Some of these constrictive features were to be relaxed after 1965, as noted in Chapter 4. For fuller details of the licensing system until that time, consult Bhagwati and Desai, *India*, pp. 231–248.

22. While the additional impact on inefficiency in allocation may be marginal, the same is not true of the impact on savings. Thus, the early hope of Indian economists that growing public sector investments would generate public savings to support growing investment in the economy has not been realized.

23. The information in this section comes from *Annual Reports of the Working of Industrial and Commercial Undertakings of the Central Government*, Government of India, Ministry of Finance, New Delhi.

24. We do not discuss in this volume the rationale of these restrictions and whether, on balance, they helped or hurt the economy. Several works are now available on the theme of technology and foreign investment in the Indian economy, both for the private and for the public sectors: Bhagwati and Desai, *India;* Kidron, *Foreign Investments;* V. N. Balasubramanyam, *International Transfer of Technology to India* (New York: Praeger, 1972); Padma Desai, *The Bokaro Steel Plant* (Amsterdam: North-Holland Publishing Co., 1972).

25. See Asha Datar, *India's Economic Relations with the USSR and Eastern Europe, 1953–1969* (Cambridge: Cambridge University Press, 1972); reviewed by Padma Desai in *Economic Journal* (September 1973), pp. 976–979.

26. The number of states has increased over time owing to linguistic demands for the bifurcation of existing states and for other parochial reasons of one kind or another. In addition to the seventeen states in 1972–73, there were twelve "Union Territories" during 1972.

27. We have already discussed the estimates of import substitution in these areas during successive plan periods. See also Desai, *Import Substitution*.

28. We have indicated the main outlines of industrial licensing. For a more intensive analysis, see Bhagwati and Desai, *India*, pp. 231–248.

29. Although our analysis stops in 1970 because of data lags, Phase II has continued and indeed was intensified at least until 1973 by the economic stress of the events that led to the creation of Bangladesh in 1972.

Part II

The Anatomy of Exchange Control

Chapter 2

Import Control Policy: Criteria for Allocation and Effects

This chapter considers the methods of administering imports that were generally in vogue during the period 1956–66. These methods were modified in favor of more flexibility in the period since 1966, but by 1969–70 the QR-regime had *de facto* regressed in the direction of the earlier methods reviewed here with only modest improvements.

We intend to describe the criteria used in the allocation of imports and to discuss their general economic implications.[1] More detailed statistical analysis of the implications for allocation of investments and capacity underutilization will be deferred until Chapter 13 in Part IV; later chapters in Part IV will also be addressed to an analysis of the QR-regime.[2] In the next chapter, we complement our analysis of the anatomy of import control with an analysis of the anatomy of export promotion until 1966 and its broad economic implications. And Chapter 4 brings together several of the partial, halting measures taken before the June 1966 devaluation to soften the restrictiveness of exchange and industrial licensing.

CRITERIA FOR ALLOCATION OF FOREIGN EXCHANGE

We begin this chapter with a description and analysis of the criteria of allocation used in India, as part of the import and exchange control policy during 1956–66, to divide up the available foreign exchange among competitive users. These methods, which involved essentially the operation of a tight regime of import (and complementary exchange) restrictions, were put into operation especially after the 1956–57 exchange crisis.

Organization and Procedures.

The import and exchange policy regime, throughout this period, aimed at comprehensive, direct control over foreign exchange utilization. Thus administrative decisions had to be made over the allocation of foreign exchange for practically all uses in the economy. For the overwhelming bulk of imports, the government (except for a beginning in this direction after the budget in 1965) did not explicitly aim at using tariffs either to siphon off the resulting import premia or to regulate imports via the price mechanism, the only well-known exceptions being crude rubber, pulp and waste paper, cotton and kerosene. Reliance on the direct allocative mechanism was thus almost complete during this period.

The allocation of permissible imports was broadly by two administrative categories: private sector and public sector. Further, there was an important operational distinction between imports of raw materials, spares and components as against imports of capital goods and equipment. The allocation of different permissible imports by these categories among industries, and further still by firms and plants, was carried out by an elaborate administrative machinery which evolved through the period. Since the details of this evolution are of little economic significance, we confine ourselves here to describing the system as it was at its peak, around 1965, when it began to be "liberalized" gradually into the somewhat major changes that came with the devaluation of the rupee in June 1966.

For every six months, April 1 to September 30, and October 1 to March 31, the Foreign Exchange Budget Branch of the Department of Economic Affairs in the Ministry of Finance would prepare its estimate of available foreign exchange for the six-month period. When the first charge expenditures such as debt repayments and Embassy expenditures had been netted out, the residual estimate of available foreign exchange would have to be allocated among different users. Food, fertilizers, petroleum, oil and lubricants (POL) and defense would normally be pre-empted first.

The administrative allocation, at the next stage, was essentially at three points: (1) an allocation was earmarked for the different public sector undertakings, for both raw materials and equipment, and was assigned to the ministries within whose domain they lay; (2) the Iron and Steel Controller would get a bulk allocation; and (3) the Economic Adviser, Ministry of Commerce, would get a bulk allocation for the private sector's imports of raw materials, spares and components (excluding, among other things, iron and steel, newsprint and POL).

The industry and unit-wise allocations, under each of these heads, involved a variety of bodies. Frequently, the same unit would receive import allocations from different agencies: iron and steel from the Iron and Steel Controller, non-ferrous metals from the corresponding ministry department, other inputs from the bulk quota of DGTD (Directorate General of Technical Development) in the Ministry of Industry, and so on.

The licensing procedures, through which each unit had to process all imports, involved three license-*issuing* authorities: (1) The Chief Controller of Imports and Exports (CCI&E), (2) The Iron and Steel Controller (I&SC), and (3) The Development Officer (DO), Tools, Development Wing of the Ministry of Commerce and Industry. Except for iron and steel (cleared by the I&SC), and certain types of machine tools (licensed by the DO), the CCI&E controlled the issuance of all other licenses.

The licenses issued by the CCI&E, which constituted the main bulk, were divided into the following categories: (1) *established importers* (EI); (2) *actual users* (AU); (3) *new-comers* (not covered by EI and AU); (4) *ad hoc* (covering items such as State Trading Corporation imports); (5) *capital goods* (CG); (6) *heavy electrical plant* (HEP); (7) *export promotion,* given as import entitlements to exporters in specific schemes; (8) *miscellaneous categories*: such as *Railway Contract* (relating to orders placed by the Railways), *Replacement Licenses* (to replace defective or unsuitable imports) and *Blanket Licenses* (mainly for POL).

The procedures followed for each category of licenses, and the authorities involved in the process, reflected two major criteria: (1) the principle of "essentiality"; and (2) the principle of "indigenous non-availability." Thus imports, in terms of *both* magnitude and composition, were to be permitted under each category only if some designated agency of the government had certified that they were "essential" (as inputs or equipment for production). At the same time, some agency had to clear the imports from the viewpoint of indigenous availability: if it could be shown that there was domestic production of the imports demanded, then the imports were not permitted (regardless of cost and quality considerations). Thus, in addition to the license-*issuing* authority, there was a "sponsoring" agency certifying "essentiality" and a "clearing" agency for "indigenous clearance."

For *public sector* applications, the procedures were basically similar. Paradoxically, the procedures were even more complex at times—as when the sanction of the Department of Economic Affairs had to be obtained, *in addition* to indigenous clearance and essentiality certification, for many applications for raw material imports. Besides, in certain cases, the project authorities themselves had the authority to grant indigenous clearance and essentiality certificates. But these and others were, by and large, differences of detail.

Principles and Criteria of Allocation.

The allocation of foreign exchange among alternative claimants and uses in a direct control system such as that just described would presumably be with reference to a well-defined set of principles and criteria based on a system of priorities. In point of fact, however, there seem to have been few such criteria, if any, followed in practice. We shall examine, in particular, the allocations arising from AU licensing.

There are basically two questions of economic significance which need to be asked here: (1) how were allocations by industry decided? and (2) how were these allocations further divided up among the constituent firms or units? We shall examine each of these questions in turn.

ALLOCATIONS BY INDUSTRY

As far as the allocations by industry were concerned, it is clear that the sheer weight of numbers made any meaningful listing of priorities extremely difficult. The problem was Orwellian: all industries had priority and how was each sponsoring authority to argue that some industries had more priority than others?

It is not surprising, therefore, that the agencies involved in determining allocations by industry fell back on vague notions of "fairness," implying *pro rata* allocations with reference to capacity installed or employment, or shares defined by past import allocations or similar other rules of thumb.

ALLOCATIONS BY UNIT

The principles and criteria adopted for further subdividing industrial allocations among constituent firms or units were equally without any rationale other than the spreading-out evenly of a scarce resource on a "fair" and "equitable" basis. There was a great variety of norms used, with significant possibility and occasional exercise of discretion. But the overwhelming bias of the system was toward some form of "equitable" allocations and cuts therein. This conclusion holds, not merely for the DGTD but also for small-scale sector allocations, the scheduled industries not on the books of the DGTD and the other classes of import applicants.

Quality of Information for Assigning Priorities.

As we have already noted, numerous authorities were involved in the licensing procedure: sponsoring bodies, authorities granting indigenous clearance and actual license-issuing authorities. Each such authority presumed to act on some set of priorities, in principle, and therefore had to have reasonable information so as to enable it to exercise its functions meaningfully.

Although it was impossible to have a meaningful, well-defined set of priorities at any level in this bureaucratic machine, except in relation to overriding matters such as defense, no allocations were ever made without intensive scrutiny and examination of individual applications at each stage in the bureaucracy. The quality of the information on which these examinations and ensuing decisions were presumably based can be inferred from what is known about (1) the small-scale sector applications and (2) the working of the DGTD concerning imports.

SMALL-SCALE SECTOR

The State Directorates of Industries were the authorities which were supposed to process the import applications in the first instance and to attach Essentiality Certificates (ECs). While considerable time was indeed taken in granting these ECs, the quality of the information on which the relevant decisions had to be made was poor.[3]

DGTD

The case of the DGTD was hardly any better, despite its obvious advantages over the Directorates in charge of the small-scale sector. It is well known, for example, that capacity as well as capacity utilization data, both of which ostensibly were taken into account in making unit-wise allocations, are bad. Similarly, with respect to those units which must seek indigenous clearance from the DGTD, the DGTD directorates frequently maintained incomplete records of the indigenous suppliers, did not have sufficient information in adequate detail on what these suppliers could produce and of what quality, did not distinguish adequately between the mere fact of the existence of an indigenous supplier and the availability of the supply to an individual purchaser, and thus ended up occasionally withholding sanction even for critical imports.

The DGTD not merely tried to secure indigenous clearance prior to permitting imports but even seemed to determine the quantitative mix of permissible imports in many cases. Clearly the DGTD had, in the nature of the case, no capacity to form reasonable judgments on this issue in the absence of very detailed information on plant conditions—something that was automatically ruled out when we see that the DGTD carried on its book (1965) over 5,000 units.

Priority in Favor of the Small-Scale Sector.

While, however, clear criteria for the allocation of imports among alternative uses were generally conspicuous by their absence and the informational basis for decision-making was exceptionally weak, it might be contended that certain broad priorities were pursued by the authorities. Thus, a typical defense of the import control system was that it was the only way of ensuring that supplies went on a "fair and equitable" basis to "small" entrepreneurs. This is not an argument for economic efficiency; but it is a valid argument for income redistribution *if* alternative ways of subsidizing the smaller entrepreneurs are not feasible.

But it is extremely difficult to take this defense of the import control system seriously. In point of fact, there is reason to conclude that the control system discriminated against the small-scale sector, as when import cuts in face of a sudden accentuation of the foreign exchange shortage fell relatively more acutely on the small-scale sector and much less on the (well-connected) larger firms. It does not follow, of course, that the small-scale sector would have either secured greater allocations or been more competitive if it had had to purchase imports in a free market. On the other hand, it does cast doubt on the usual claim that the import control system made the small-scale sector better off than under the alternative import regimes.[4]

Foreign Exchange Saved from Being Spent on Consumption.

It might be contended that the import policy regime was directed at preventing scarce foreign exchange from being "frittered away" on consumer goods and that this general priority was strictly maintained by the import-licensing authorities. It is certainly true that, over the period of our study, direct imports of consumer goods were slashed. This was reflected in the steady reduction of EI licenses and the growth of AU licenses granted to producers. However, two important points concerning this question need to be made.

1. While imports of manufactured consumer goods indeed went down, it is pertinent to note that these were frequently offset by growth in domestic production of the same and other consumer manufactures. In the present context, where we are discussing the allocation of "maintenance" imports (i.e., imports of raw materials and intermediates), the following further point needs to be noted.

2. The maintenance imports necessary to support current production of domestic consumer goods industries were not negligible. Hazari has worked out estimates of the direct and indirect import requirements of consumption in India, divided by these two groups. He finds, for the years 1961–62 and 1963–64, that the proportion of *total* imports which went to support the level of consumption of "luxuries" was 7.6 and 8.5 percent, and that of "necessities" was 28.7 and 32.9 percent, respectively.[5]

In any event, it seems that, irrational as it may be to seek to prohibit imports of "inessential" consumer goods while permitting their production domestically, even such an objective could have been as readily achieved, with none of the other detrimental effects of a full-fledged control system embracing all transactions, by a selective set of prohibitive tariffs or quotas on specific items sought to be excluded from imports.

Corruption and Frustration of Apparent Priorities.

We have noted that the import control system worked on (1) incomplete and unsystematic information and (2) lack of any discernible economic criteria. Further, whatever limited allocational aims it may have had were frustrated, in varying degrees, by the corruption that inevitably arose from the large premia on imports under the control system.

There are essentially two different kinds of illegality which the control system generated: (1) since imports were remunerative in general, there were innumerable bogus claims to import license entitlement under the existing rules of allocation; and (2) since numerous restrictions obtained with respect to transferability of imports and import licenses, black markets arose to transact such illegal traffic. It has not been possible for us to quantify any of these illegal transactions in a meaningful manner, but there is little doubt that they existed widely.[6] We should also note that these illegal transfers of imports often must have served to increase economic efficiency by reducing the irrational inflexibility that the legal restrictions on transferability entailed.

ECONOMIC EFFECTS OF IMPORT CONTROLS

What were the economic consequences of these methods of allocating foreign exchange in India's QR-regime? While we consider the consequences for resource allocation and capacity utilization, and the growth effects on savings, research and development, quality of production, inducement to invest and other aspects of India's economic performance in Part IV, we note here several other, mainly adverse, effects. In particular, we will consider: (1) delays, (2) administrative and other expenses, (3) inflexibility, (4) lack of coordination among different agencies, (5) absence of competition, (6) inherent bias in favor, *ceteris paribus,* of industries with imported, as distinct from domestically produced, inputs, (7) anticipatory and automatic protection afforded to industries regardless of costs, (8) discrimination against exports and (9) loss of revenue.

Delays.

The working of any system of allocation will take a certain amount of time. Even if a free foreign exchange market were to operate, the participants in the market would have to expend time, for example, in acquiring information about availabilities of different kinds of foreign exchange. In principle, the administrative system of allocations need involve no significant increase in time, and hence in "delays," over a price system under which scarce foreign exchange is rationed out in the market: the introduction of priorities would, in principle, be equally time-consuming in both cases, though the procedure would be different, since the price system would involve administrative decisions as to tax and subsidy incentives whereas the control system would involve administrative decisions as to quotas.

In practice, however, the exchange control system seems to degenerate into an inordinately time-consuming allocational device. There are essentially three reasons for this. (1) In a situation of general scarcity of foreign exchange, the definition of priorities becomes exceptionally difficult, as we have seen earlier, and the system ends up having to accommodate all conceivable demands on some "equitable" basis, while making a pretense of administering priorities, this pretense frequently taking the form of collection of yet more information from applicants and time taken in "scrutinizing" it and "arriving at an informed decision." Delays become, sociologically, the "conspicuous" substitute for exercise of priorities by the bureaucracy. (2) Equally important, the multiplication of the bureaucratic apparatus leads inevitably to files failing to move quickly and decisions being delayed because procedures are time-wasting. As we shall see shortly, much of the delay to which the Indian import-control system was subject can be put down to the inefficiency of administrative procedures. For example, where indigenous clearance had to be obtained by the DGTD from two or more other directorates, these were to be sought sequentially rather than simultaneously. (3) Finally, some significance must be attached, in explaining delays under the Indian allocation system, to the fact that, with files often moving from the bottom to the top in the Indian administrative system, they often fail to move until appropriate graft is paid to the lower-level clerks. If all graft were paid promptly, there should be no delay on this account; but newcomers and honest applicants are unlikely to conform readily to this widespread practice, hence delays occur on this count in the system as well.

Administrative and Other Costs.

The elaborate bureaucratic machinery for operating the licensing mechanisms undoubtedly involved direct costs as also the costs resulting from the necessity for actual and potential entrepreneurs to maintain elaborate and frequent "contacts" with the licensing authorities. Admittedly, alternative allocation mechanisms also must necessitate "administrative" and information-gathering costs. But the specific type of "command" mechanism involved in the Indian QR and industrial licensing regimes added to these costs by mak-

ing necessary expenditures to ensure "file-pushing" by bribe-seeking bureaucrats at lower levels, for example. It is highly dubious, for example, that
the considerable growth of Indian Airlines traffic into Delhi from the major
industrial cities such as Calcutta and Bombay and the growth of the license-
allocating bureaucracy in Delhi and elsewhere are anything but a net cost
attributable to the regime. And if we could only disentangle (as we cannot)
the job expansion in the bureaucracy which has resulted from the licensing
machinery, much of the enormous expansion of current governmental expenditures during 1956–71 may turn out to be a net cost of the regime.

Inflexibility.

The twin principles of "essentiality" and "indigenous non-availability"
also imparted considerable inflexibility to the pattern of utilization of imports.
This occurred via a rigid itemization of permissible imports, frequently by
specified value for different items, both for AU and EI licenses.

At the same time, the theoretical premise that AU allocations were
being made on the basis of well-defined priorities at the detailed industry
level led the authorities to rule out legal transferability of the licenses among
the different industries; and bureaucratic logic took the inevitable next step
and eliminated transferability even among units within the same industry,
thus making AU licenses (legally) *altogether* non-transferable by the licensee
units. Needless to say, none of the imports under the AU licenses were allowed
to be legally resold either (but were occasionally sold in the black market,
of course).

The rigid pattern of permissible imports (only occasionally adjusted
through changing the contents of the lists by discretionary action) and the
non-transferability of the AU licenses and imports thereunder were bound to
create inflexibility leading to economic inefficiency because:

1. the *total* AU allocations to individual units were neither made by
well-defined priorities nor based on assessment of reasonably accurate and
analyzed information, but were mostly based on notions of "fair sharing"
with occasional injection of "pragmatism" and "judgment of cases on merits";

2. the *itemized* breakdowns were based on (a) indigenous non-availability which, as we have noted, was assessed with inaccuracy by the responsible bodies such as the DGTD, and (b) these bodies' assessment of the
optimal mix of imported inputs, which again was more on an administrative
and *ad hoc* basis than on any recognizable criterion of economic efficiency; and

3. there is considerable uncertainty about the availability of foreign exchange, leaving aside the general unpredictability of the entire economic
situation, so that no "optimal mix" of inputs laid down in advance (even if
worked out on the basis of well-defined criteria, accurately gathered avail-

able information and explicitly assumed future developments) can hope to be optimal *ex post,* thus requiring flexibility in the matter of the input-mix and transfers of inputs from one set of users to another.

Yet another implication of the inflexibility arising from the non-transferability of import licenses might have been an excessive holding of inventories by Indian firms. Indian inventories, especially the raw materials and intermediates held, compare unfavorably with those of firms in similar industries elsewhere. However, other factors on the Indian scene probably explain these large inventories. For example, interest rates in the Organized Industrial Sector are quite low, thus making inventory-holding relatively inexpensive; on the other hand, it is not clear that the relevant Indian interest rates (real or nominal) have been significantly lower than abroad. Lower efficiency in transport (and shortage thereof) would also make inventory-holding more valuable. Furthermore, inventory holdings, including raw materials and intermediates, appear to have declined (as a proportion of output) generally through the period of our study, for many industries.[7] Hence, while it makes *a priori* sense to argue that, *ceteris paribus,* an import control regime of the Indian type would tend to inflate inventory holdings, it would not be correct to argue that the empirical analyses currently available support this hypothesis.

Lack of Coordination among Different Agencies.

The multiplicity of agencies dispensing imports further accentuated the difficulty in procuring desired imports on the part of the applicants. For example, the typical unit under DGTD jurisdiction would get its share in the bulk allocations by the Economic Adviser to the DGTD and would *also* get allocations of iron and steel from the I&SC's office as well as non-ferrous allocations from decisions made by the corresponding department (which, in turn, got bulk allocations for this purpose). Unfortunately, coordination of these allocations, either in initial allocations or in cuts therein, does not appear to have been a routine matter.[8]

Absence of Competition.

In addition, the import allocation system in force had virtually eliminated the possibility of competition, either foreign or domestic. Foreign competition was ruled out because of the principle of "indigenous availability": every item of indigenous production, no matter how much its cost of production exceeded the landed c.i.f. price, was automatically shielded from competition through imports, indeed the onus being put on the buyer to show conclusively that he could not procure the item from indigenous producers.

At the same time, the possibility of domestic competition was, in turn, minimized by the combination of CG licensing (concomitantly with other industrial licensing provisions) and the method of AU licensing on a "fair-share" basis among rival firms in an industry. Strict CG and industrial licensing eliminated free entry by new firms as well as efficiency-induced expansion by existing firms. And the fact that each firm was entitled to its "share" of AU licenses, and no more, ensured that the efficient firms could not even (legally) enlarge output from existing capacity by competing away the scarce imports from less efficient firms.

Thus, all forms of effective competition, potential and actual, were virtually eliminated from the industrial system. The effects, therefore, were (1) to eliminate incentives to reduce costs per unit of output (as the penalty for sloppy operations was no longer incapacity to survive against more efficient rivals) and (2) to prevent production from being concentrated in the most efficient units (and industries).

Bias in Favor of Industries Using Imported Inputs.

Under the actual-user system of allocation of imports, combined with the principle of indigenous non-availability, it may be expected that the *quantum* of import allocations would, *ceteris paribus,* tend to be inversely related to the availability of indigenously produced inputs.

But this, in turn, would lead to a bias in the effective incentive provided to the processes using relatively more imported inputs: they would be able to get relatively greater allocations of imports under AU licenses and hence obtain these inputs at import-premium-*exclusive* prices (which would include only the explicit tariff duty) whereas the other industries would have to buy import-substitute, indigenous items at premium-*inclusive* prices (since these items would fetch a price equal to the c.i.f. prices plus the import premium). The effective incentive given to the former industries or processes would thus be greater, other things being equal. And, while it may fortuitously be the case that some of these industries may require relative subsidization on economic grounds, there is no gainsaying the fact that the import system in India gave rise to these differential incentives purely as an incidental side effect.

Anticipatory and Automatic Protection to Industries.

Another significant impact of the Indian import policy, under which the principle of indigenous availability was used to exclude or restrict imports in favor of purchase of domestic import-substitutes, was that protection was automatically extended to all industries regardless of cost, efficiency and comparative advantage. This automatic protection was further fully to be anticipated by every producer, merely as long as he was willing to make his capacity and production known to the relevant agencies (e.g., the DGTD) in charge of "indigenous clearance."

The influence of this policy on the pattern of industrial investments that emerged through the period must have been considerable. It is clear that the policy of anticipatory and automatic protection that inhered in the working of import policy served to divorce market-determined investment decisions from any guidelines that international opportunity costs (with suitable modifications) might have otherwise provided.

Discrimination against Exports.

Our analysis of the import-control policy would be incomplete if we were not to mention the rather obvious fact that such a system discriminates against exports. The effective export exchange rate, on the average, was inevitably less than the effective import exchange rate (Table 2–1); and this was the case at the level of each industry also, until (from around 1962) the initiation and later intensification of significant export subsidization schemes began to redress, though not restore, the balance (and, in some cases, must have even led to a net subsidization rate in excess of the import rate).

Again, one of the important side effects of the principle of indigenous availability was that exportable items which therefore had to be manufactured with inferior-quality domestically produced inputs and capital equipment were, in turn, faced with enhanced difficulties in the highly competitive international markets. This was particularly the case with the new exports in the engineering industries, which in any case faced serious difficulties in cultivating foreign markets almost from scratch.

Further, since there was little flexibility for getting more inputs through bidding in the market, in view of the restrictive character of the import policy, and capacity also could not be expanded owing to equally stringent controls on entry, industries which needed flexibility in production in order to get hold of large foreign orders, whenever available, found themselves unnecessarily handicapped.

Clearly, from the beginning of the Second Plan until late 1964, the entire industrial licensing and import policy was unfavorable to manufacturing exports largely because it was devised with a substantially inward-looking bias.

Loss of Revenue.

Another noteworthy and obvious effect of the import-control system was the inevitable loss of revenue that it involved in passing the profits on scarce imports on to the private sector.

TABLE 2–1

EERs, PLD-EERs and PPP-EERs for Indian Exports and Imports during 1950–71

Year (1)	I^t (2)	I_t^p (3)	EER (4)	Imports		
				PLD-EER (5)	PPP-EER (6)	

Year (1)	I^t (2)	I_t^p (3)	EER (4)	PLD-EER (5)	PPP-EER (6)
1950	0.823	0.773	5.58	6.79	8.78
1951	0.906	0.911	5.46	6.02	6.61
1952	0.793	0.909	5.56	7.01	7.71
1953	0.786	0.876	5.69	7.24	8.27
1954	0.752	0.873	5.78	7.69	8.81
1955	0.691	0.891	5.66	8.19	9.19
1956	0.775	0.923	5.56	7.17	7.77
1957	0.821	0.954	5.42	6.60	6.92
1958	0.838	0.960	5.37	6.41	6.67
1959	0.872	0.966	5.43	6.23	6.45
1960	0.929	0.975	5.41	5.82	5.97
1961	0.950	0.987	5.61	5.91	5.99
1962	0.961	0.996	5.76	5.99	6.02
1963	1.000	1.000	6.06	6.06	6.06
1964	1.105	1.010	6.19	5.60	5.55
1965	1.195	1.032	6.63	5.55	5.38
1966	1.338	1.060	9.23	6.90	6.51
1967	1.539	1.063	9.02	5.86	5.52
1968	1.531	1.078	8.97	5.86	5.43
1969	1.563	1.121	9.06	5.80	5.17
1970	1.660	1.168	9.45	5.69	4.88
1971	1.723	1.222	9.70	5.63	4.61

(continued)

TABLE 2-1 (concluded)

	Exports								
	α = 0		α = 0.05		α = 0.10			α = 0.20	
Year	EER	PLD-EER	EER	PLD-EER	EER	PLD-EER	EER	PLD-EER	PPP-EER
(1)	(7)	(8)	(9)	(10)	(11)	(12)	(13)	(14)	(15)
1950	4.39	5.33	4.46	5.42	4.53	5.50	4.67	5.67	4.40
1951	4.17	4.61	4.24	4.68	4.31	4.75	4.44	4.90	4.35
1952	4.30	5.43	4.37	5.51	4.44	5.60	4.53	5.78	5.21
1953	4.42	5.62	4.49	5.71	4.56	5.80	4.71	5.99	5.27
1954	4.43	5.89	4.50	5.98	4.57	6.07	4.70	6.25	5.45
1955	4.47	6.46	4.54	6.57	4.61	6.67	4.75	6.88	6.11
1956	4.54	5.86	4.62	5.96	4.69	6.06	4.85	6.26	5.76
1957	4.54	5.53	4.69	5.71	4.84	5.89	5.14	6.26	5.97
1958	4.59	5.48	4.75	5.67	4.91	5.86	5.22	6.23	5.94
1959	4.65	5.34	4.77	5.47	4.89	5.61	5.13	5.88	5.62
1960	4.67	5.03	4.85	5.22	5.02	5.41	5.38	5.79	5.60
1961	4.68	4.92	4.85	5.11	5.03	5.29	5.38	5.66	5.57
1962	4.70	4.89	4.88	5.08	5.06	5.26	5.41	5.63	5.59
1963	4.75	4.75	4.93	4.93	5.12	5.12	5.49	5.49	5.49
1964	4.75	4.30	4.94	4.47	5.12	4.64	5.50	4.97	5.05
1965	4.75	3.98	4.94	4.14	5.13	4.29	5.51	4.61	4.79
1966	6.79	5.08	6.95	5.20	7.12	5.32	7.44	5.56	5.93
1967	6.78	4.41	6.95	4.52	7.12	4.63	7.47	4.85	5.22
1968	7.08	4.62	7.25	4.74	7.43	4.85	7.78	5.08	5.58
1969	7.15	4.57	7.34	4.70	7.54	4.82	7.92	5.07	5.73
1970	7.20	4.34	7.39	4.45	7.57	4.56	7.93	4.78	5.64
1971	7.18	4.16	7.38	4.28	7.57	4.40	7.95	4.63	5.65

NOTES: 1. EER = Effective Exchange Rate. This is calculated for exports by taking into account the export duties and dividing the figure for duties collected by total exports and so deriving the average duty rate for exports in each year. As for export subsidies, on non-traditional exports, we will see later in this volume that these were given in various ways and are impossible to quantify with any degree of accuracy. Hence we have taken three subsidy rates (α) at 5, 10 and 20 percent to arrive at subsidy-inclusive EERs. We would argue that the EERS up to 1962 are best treated as ones not involving any subsidy; the 1962–64 are probably best taken as involving 5 percent subsidy; 1964–65 as involving 10 percent subsidy; and 1965–66 as involving 20 percent subsidy. Since the revival of subsidy after the June 1966 devaluation took a little time, it is best again to think of the transition through export subsidy rates at 5, 10 and 20 percent through the years 1966 to 1971.

2. I_t and I_t^p are the Indian wholesale price index and the (import-share) weighted partner-country wholesale price index, respectively.

3. PLD-EER is obtained by deflating the EER by I_t.

4. PPP-EER for imports is obtained by multiplying the PLD-EER by I_t^p. For exports, an alternative price index, reflecting partner-country weights in *exports*, was constructed and similarly utilized.

5. EER for imports takes into account only the average tariff rate, computed as the duty collected divided by total imports. It excludes the premium on imports. This premium has been difficult to obtain with any degree of reliability because of the enormous number of (non-transferable) import licenses involved: as we have discussed in Chapters 2 and 3. It may be noted here that the import premia have often been close to 100 percent during most of the 1960s.

SOURCES: *International Financial Statistics*, December 1969, July 1971, 1972 Supplement, January 1973, International Monetary Fund. *Direction of Trade*, annual issues, 1950–53, 1954–57, 1958–62, 1960–64, 1966–70, International Monetary Fund. *Statistical Yearbook*, 1972, United Nations. *Basic Statistics Relating to the Indian Economy*, 1950–51, 1966–67, 1950–51 to 1968–69, 1950–51 to 1970–71, Government of India, Department of Statistics, Statistics and Surveys Division, New Delhi. *Explanatory Memorandum of the Central Government Budget*, annual issues from 1952–53 to 1973–74, Government of India, Ministry of Finance, New Delhi.

(1) Where the imports were channeled through traders, as with EI licenses, there is little reason to doubt that the import premium fully reflected the scarcity value of the items. It may therefore be expected that, if the government had channeled these imports through its own agencies *or* auctioned them off *or* levied suitable tariffs, the scarcity premium would have accrued to it as revenue.[9]

(2) For the AU imports, it may again be expected that the entrepreneurs who obtained them would nonetheless proceed to charge for their outputs the prices that the market would bear. Hence, the effect of raising tariffs by the "implicit" premium on AU licenses, for example, would not generally have been to affect the price of the outputs but merely to cut into the profits that accrued to the entrepreneurs purely as a result of access to scarce inputs. However, under cost-plus pricing, this result would not follow and it could not be argued that there was a simple loss-of-revenue effect thanks to the import-control system. In view of the fact, however, that several import premia got seriously reduced without there being a significant rise in final prices, subsequent to the devaluation of June 1966, we are inclined to argue that profit maximization, rather than cost-plus, seems to be a better approximation to the behavior of Indian firms.[10]

Distributional Impact.

We may finally touch on two important "distributional" questions that have been raised in defense of the direct-allocational system of import regulation used in India.

1. It has, for example, been argued that the method of AU allocations such that each unit gets *some* share of the scarce imports ensures that employment is not eliminated in inefficient units which would, under an alternative (market) system, fail to bid successfully for the imports. Concerning this argument, we may quote what one of us wrote elsewhere.[11]

> This argument, however, assumes that the increase in employment in the efficient firms which get more inputs under the [market system] is less than the decrease that accompanies the failure of the inefficient to get exchange (which may be true if the inefficient firms are labour intensive). It should also be remembered that a policy that creates extra real income will promote greater capital formation and employment in the longer run.

2. The other argument is superficially more difficult to dispute. It relates to the fact that *regional* constraints in a country such as India make it impossible to leave allocations of scarce imports (and materials) to the market. Since value is attached by each state to production and investment in themselves, it is not possible to take the position that allocations should be by

economic criteria alone and that income transfers should be made as compensation to the states that do not attract inputs or investments. In short, the problem of allocating resources in a federal country such as India involves economic solutions similar to those that would have to be provided in customs unions or free-trade areas among sovereign countries where constraints have to be provided in the shape, for example, of the distribution of manufacturing investments as a whole among the constituent countries.

But if this is indeed the case, the question again is whether the "subsidization" of the states that are likely to "lose" in a system of market-ruled allocations of AU imports should be undertaken through an import-control regime with all the disadvantages we have discussed or whether it is not more sensible to achieve the politically required allocations among regions or states by direct subsidization policies, such as differential corporation taxes among regions, which would at the same time permit the import policy to be run on sounder lines. We have little doubt, in the light of our analysis, that this latter would be very much the better course.

NOTES

1. This chapter draws on the more detailed analysis in Bhagwati and Desai, *India,* pp. 281–334. It may be read in conjunction with Part IV for a continuous and comprehensive analysis of the total economic impact of India's import control methods.

2. See Chapters 6, 7 and 9 for further discussion of export policies and performance since the June 1966 devaluation. Chapter 14 deals with the economic implications of an improved export performance (made possible by a change in India's QR-regime) within the framework of a multi-sector, multi-period planning model.

3. For evidence see the *Report of the International Perspective Planning Team on Small Industries* (1963) and the *Report of the Raj Committee on Steel Control* (1963). While their critical observations mainly concerned the distribution of scarce domestic materials, there is no reason to expect that the allocation of *import* licenses by state directorates was any more systematic or informed.

4. For a discussion of the discrimination against the small-scale sector that is intrinsic to the operation of the import control mechanism, see Bhagwati and Desai, *India,* pp. 281–311.

5. B. R. Hazari, "The Import Intensity of Consumption in India," *Indian Economic Review,* October 1967.

6. We were unable to successfully use the partner-country-data comparison technique to detect faked invoicing of imports or exports. For a discussion of this technique and the problems in using it, see the contributions by Bhagwati, Richter and Morgenstern in J. Bhagwati, ed., *Illegal Transactions and International Trade: Theory and Measurement* (Amsterdam: North-Holland Publishing Co., 1974).

7. Note, however, that a declining ratio of inventories to output with reduced foreign exchange under the QR-regime does not *necessarily* contradict the hypothesis that such reduction under the QR-regime leads to a higher ratio than such reduction without a QR-regime.

8. It is arguable, of course, that coordination procedures may have led to more delays; but we doubt this and rather think that sequential clearances are likely to have been more dilatory.

9. Indeed, this is what it sometimes, but all too infrequently, tried to do when it transferred the import trade in certain high-premium commodities to the State Trading Corporation, as with caustic soda. However, even with STC imports, frequently the STC did not charge the buyers full premium.

10. Of course, the post-devaluation situation was also characterized by a significant increase in availability of imports for AU licensing, thanks to foreign aid, and soon thereafter large-scale recessionary tendencies also reduced the demand for imports. However, the immediate import effect in the three months after the devaluation was not affected by these complications and does seem to support the conclusion in the text.

11. J. Bhagwati, "Indian Balance of Payments Policy and Exchange Auctions," *Oxford Economic Papers* (February 1962).

Chapter 3

Export Policy and Performance, 1951-66

The preceding analysis of import control may now be complemented by the analysis of export policy, to fill out the total picture of the anatomy of the trade and exchange rate regime in India.[1] Our analysis will embrace the period 1951–66 although our main focus will be on the sub-period 1956–66. From the viewpoint of the anatomy of export policy, it is useful to think of this sub-period as divided into Phase I: 1956–62, and Phase II: 1962–66. The former period is characterized by an essentially passive export policy; the latter by a growing attempt at export subsidization to offset the effects of the overvaluation of the exchange rate.

We shall begin with a brief analysis of export performance during Phase I, but extend the period back to Phase IV, 1951–56, so as to draw on earlier work by Manmohan Singh.[2] Then, in considering Phase II, we shall draw on the work of Bhagwati and Desai and throw into sharp relief the criteria of export subsidization and the economic efficiency thereof. This period represents an ideal research area for understanding the anatomy of export subsidization in the context of an overvalued parity. The reader may further be reminded that in the present volume we extend the analysis of export policies and performance to the post-1966 period in chapters 6, 7 and 9 in Part III, while also examining the economic implications of improved export performance in the framework of a computable planning model in Chapter 14 in Part IV.

EXPORT POLICY AND PERFORMANCE
DURING THE 1950s: PHASES IV AND I

The onset of the QR-regime and Phase I, during the Second Plan virtually from its first year 1956–57, is now known to have been accompanied by a significant deterioration in India's export performance. During the First Plan, in Phase IV, the value of Indian exports had collapsed from its Korean War peak in 1951 and had stagnated; and this stagnation continued until 1961, implying a falling Indian share in world exports and a falling ratio of exports to GNP.

This picture is only filled out, rather than substantially altered, if we examine the behavior of export volumes and prices separately over the period. Table 3–1 contains these estimates. These indicate strongly that the First Plan period (Phase IV), while it showed *on the average* an improvement over the previous three years' average export performance, largely achieved this thanks to the large price gain during the two Korean War boom years, 1951 and 1952. On the other hand, there is a continuous though mild improvement in the average export *volume* since 1952, which is masked in the value figures because of the post-Korean War decline in prices. As against this, the Second Plan period (Phase I) shows stagnation in both average prices and volume. For the decade as a whole, leaving out the Korean War boom, the stagnation in both average price and volume is quite striking.[3]

The picture that emerges from the aggregate behavior of export values, volumes, and prices is reflected in the performance of individual commodities. Table 3–2 shows the breakdown of Indian exports by principal commodities through this decade. Table 3–3, containing estimates of the linear regression equation $x = a + bt$ (with x as the export value and t as time) fitted to the data on each item for 1952–53 through to 1960–61, shows that, except for cashew kernels, iron ore and coffee, there is no upward trend of statistical significance to be found in the export performance of any of the commodities.

Further, if we examine the principal export commodities, many of them exhibit not merely a dismal rate of growth of earnings; they are also characterized by a falling share in the world market. We note here that, in five major export items adding up to over 50 percent of total export earnings—jute manufactures, tea, cotton textiles, vegetable oilseeds and oils and unmanufactured tobacco—there was a discernible, and at times considerable, reduction in India's share in world trade.[4]

The detailed analysis, by commodities, of India's faltering export performance through the 1950s by Manmohan Singh has led Bhagwati and Desai to conclude that, except for a few items such as iron ore, this decade's stagnation of export earnings is to be largely attributed to domestic policies which

TABLE 3–1

Export Earnings, Volume and Price Indices, 1948–66

Calendar Year	Value of Indian Exports (U.S. $ Millions) (1)	Export Value Index (1958 = 100) (2)	Export Price Index (1958 = 100) (3)	Export Volume Index (1958 = 100) (4)
1948	1363	112	90	124
1949	1309	107	90	119
1950	1146	94	98	97
1951	1611	132	143	96
1952	1295	106	117	89
1953	1116	91	100	92
1954	1182	97	102	94
1955	1276	104	100	105
1956	1300	106	101	101
1957	1379	113	101	110
1958	1221	100	100	100
1959	1308	107	100	107
1960	1331	109	109	101
1961	1387	114	111	105
1962	1403	115	106	112
1963	1631	134	106	126
1964	1749	143	106	134
1965	1686	138	112	124
1966	1606	132	111	119

SOURCE: *International Financial Statistics,* Supplement to 1966–67 issues, March 1968, International Monetary Fund.

frequently led to falling shares in India's traditional exports and an inadequate expansion of new exports (in the absence of any export promotion on that front).[5] This analysis is also supported broadly by our aggregative regression analysis in Chapter 14 which underlines the role of domestic production and availability (and hence of the price paid to producers which is a function of the effective exchange rate on exports) in explaining the exports of important, traditional items such as tea and jute textiles, and the probable role of the 1966 devaluation in explaining the improved performance of the new, non-traditional exports.

Bhagwati and Desai have made a notional calculation of the loss of export earnings that followed from the failure to maintain export shares. As-

TABLE 3-2

India's Export Earnings from Principal Commodities, 1951–52 to 1960–61

(Rs. millions)

	1951–52	1952–53	1953–54	1954–55	1955–56	1956–57	1957–58	1958–59	1959–60	1960–61
1. Total exports	7,288.9	5,723.0	5,261.6	5,884.7	6,038.5	6,130.3	5,845.2	5,531.9	6,299.0	6,329.4
Commodity composition										
2. Jute manufactures	2,697.3	1,289.2	1,137.6	1,237.8	1,182.5	1,188.1	1,109.2	1,011.5	1,090.0	1,317.2
3. Tea	939.4	808.6	1,021.6	1,477.4	1,091.4	1,451.4	1,136.5	1,296.9	1,290.9	1,235.9
4. Cotton fabrics	521.5	620.6	636.4	633.1	566.3	629.6	584.7	454.8	641.5	576.5
5. Vegetable oils	236.1	255.4	48.9	200.2	343.5	155.9	105.9	63.7	148.1	85.4
6. Iron ore	10.0	37.0	58.2	42.1	62.7	93.1	118.6	96.5	145.9	170.3
7. Manganese ore	156.9	217.6	242.7	129.2	107.2	258.1	297.0	136.4	119.9	140.6
8. Mica	132.1	90.1	79.9	67.2	83.7	87.7	86.6	95.8	100.4	101.5
9. Unmanufactured tobacco	161.4	130.3	110.2	117.6	106.5	124.8	146.3	146.8	135.3	146.1
10. Coffee	5.5	13.9	14.6	76.4	14.9	66.9	67.3	78.9	63.3	72.2
11. Cashew kernels	90.5	129.8	109.9	107.0	129.2	145.3	151.6	158.5	160.5	189.1
12. Manufactured leather	250.2	201.1	249.7	205.8	225.2	209.7	209.2	188.6	304.5	248.5
13. Spices	291.7	205.9	162.0	104.3	93.1	78.0	80.1	80.1	144.6	166.4
14. Coir yarn and manufactures	102.8	71.6	81.5	84.5	89.4	96.9	82.8	82.1	88.6	90.0
15. Raw cotton	136.7	193.3	94.0	101.9	296.9	134.6	90.8	166.2	100.6	70.0
16. Lac	148.7	74.4	67.6	105.5	117.1	94.6	68.5	57.0	62.9	63.2
17. Raw wool	49.0	84.1	58.7	86.1	97.3	104.0	110.8	96.6	122.1	77.2
18. *Subtotal (2–17)*	5,929.8	4,422.9	4,173.5	4,776.1	4,606.9	4,918.7	4,445.9	4,210.4	4,719.1	4,750.1

NOTE: Statistics relate to Indian fiscal years beginning 1 April.
SOURCE: Statistics published by the Director-General of Commercial Intelligence and Statistics, Calcutta. Reproduced from Bhagwati and Desai, *India*, p. 372.

TABLE 3–3

**Linear Regression Equations for Export Volume and Price
Indices and Selected Export Earnings, 1948–61**

Item Regressed on Time (Equation: $x = a + bt$) (1)	Period (2)	Unit (3)	Estimated Coefficients and Their Standard Errors	
			Constant Term (a) (4)	Regression Coefficient (b) (5)
1. Value of Indian exports	1948–61	Rs. millions	1,289.11 (78.33)	1.80* (9.87)
2. Value of Indian exports	1951–61	Rs. millions	1,319.98 (87.94)	−1.62* (12.97)
3. Value of Indian exports	1953–61	Rs. millions	1,149.39 (45.10)	25.83 (8.01)
4. Export price index	1948–61	1958 = 100	119.42 (7.63)	−1.54* (0.96)
5. Export price index	1951–61	1958 = 100	118.27 (7.95)	−1.77* (1.17)
6. Export price index	1953–61	1958 = 100	97.33 (2.39)	1.07 (0.42)
7. Export volume index	1948–61	1958 = 100	88.58 (3.11)	1.44 (0.39)
8. Export volume index	1951–61	1958 = 100	91.61 (3.56)	1.41 (0.52)
9. Export volume index	1953–61	1958 = 100	98.89 (4.30)	1.02* (0.76)
10. Jute manufactures	1952–61	Rs. millions	1,220.07 (73.65)	−9.28* (13.09)
11. Tea	1952–61	Rs. millions	1,017.74 (145.08)	36.69* (25.78)
12. Cotton fabrics	1952–61	Rs. millions	635.33 (42.48)	−8.32* (7.55)
13. Vegetable oils	1952–61	Rs. millions	230.75 (67.95)	−14.88* (12.08)
14. Iron ore	1952–61	Rs. millions	11.51 (11.93)	16.02 (2.12)
15. Manganese ore	1952–61	Rs. millions	222.54 (52.29)	−7.87* (9.29)
16. Mica	1952–61	Rs. millions	74.17 (5.85)	2.79 (1.04)
17. Unmanufactured tobacco	1952–61	Rs. millions	109.60 (8.78)	3.94 (1.56)

(continued)

TABLE 3-3 (concluded)

Item Regressed on Time (Equation: $x = a + bt$) (1)	Period (2)	Unit (3)	Estimated Coefficients and Their Standard Errors	
			Constant Term (a) (4)	Regression Coefficient (b) (5)
18. Coffee	1952–61	Rs. millions	15.65 (15.91)	7.28 (2.83)
19. Cashew kernels	1952–61	Rs. millions	99.46 (9.08)	8.57 (1.61)
20. Manufactured leather	1952–61	Rs. millions	201.62 (25.56)	5.06* (4.54)
21. Spices	1952–61	Rs. millions	146.47 (35.23)	−4.53* (6.26)
22. Coir yarn and manufactures	1952–61	Rs. millions	78.31 (4.65)	1.39* (0.83)
23. Raw cotton	1952–61	Rs. millions	184.61 (51.77)	−9.18* (9.20)
24. Lac	1952–61	Rs. millions	96.02 (14.92)	−3.41* (2.65)
25. Raw wool			76.56 (12.94)	3.28* (2.30)
26. Subtotal (10–25)	1952–61	Rs. millions	4,420.41 193.55)	27.55* (34.39)

NOTE: Values of the regression coefficient marked with an asterisk are not significant at the 5 percent level of significance.

SOURCE: Rows 1–9 calculated from Table 1–1; rows 10–26 calculated from Table 3–2. Reproduced from Bhagwati and Desai, *India*, p. 373.

suming the 1948–50 shares for the major commodities—jute manufactures, tea, cotton textiles, groundnuts, linseed oils and oilseeds and tobacco—and assuming that unit values and world volumes would not have changed from the observed levels each year, they have worked out the hypothetical earnings that would have accrued to India. They treat these as somewhat optimistic estimates, as it is probable that attempts by India at maintaining her share (in jute and tea, in particular) would, in many cases, have tended to depress the unit values.[6]

Their resulting estimates are reproduced in Table 3–4. They are quite striking. The overall improvement in feasible export earnings, over the ten years 1951–60, comes for these five commodities to around 16.5 percent of the actual performance. If we add to the estimated improvement of Rs.5,740 million a rough estimate of the potential improvement in three other items—

coffee, manganese ore and leather—we get close to an overall figure of about Rs.6,200 million.[7]

In Chapter 14, we shall examine how far policies resulting in such an improved export performance might have helped improve also India's economic performance. Immediately, however, we proceed to analyze the salient features of the export promotion efforts mounted during 1962–66, the period which constituted Phase II.

EXPORT POLICY AND PERFORMANCE FROM 1962 TO 1966: PHASE II

The policy of neglect of the export sector was rationalized later as "export pessimism." It characterized Phase I during the Second Five-Year Plan and was to give way during the Third Five-Year Plan to an escalating policy of export subsidization. By 1966, the subsidies embraced a large fraction of India's exports and included substantial rates; the period 1962–66 was thus clearly Phase II. The total export performance during this period improved in consequence of these subsidies and as a result of an expansion of trade with the socialist bloc (Table 3–5).

The success of the subsidies in countervailing the effects of the overvalued exchange rate and promoting exports was obvious in relation to the emerging exports of new manufactures and did much to counter the export pessimism which partly underlay the Second Plan but was also largely the product of that Plan's poor export performance.

But, while the subsidization reduced the average degree of overvaluation, one of its remarkable features was that it was as selective, chaotic and cost-unconscious as the process of automatic protection for import substitution. Thus, the subsidization was relatively energetic; but it was *not* efficient in the neoclassical sense and, as many instances of value-subtraction (at international prices) strongly underlined, wasteful in consequence.

In this section, therefore, we describe briefly the methods of export subsidization and analyze their efficiency implications. In particular, our discussion will indicate why the June 1966 devaluation was announced: essentially to enable the government to sweep away the chaotic and inefficient pattern of subsidization and replace it with the uniform and stable export incentive implied by the devaluation.

Policies of Export Subsidization.

Export subsidization policies took essentially two major forms: (1) fiscal measures, and (2) import entitlement schemes (which entitled exporters to premium-carrying import licenses). In addition to these measures, which

TABLE 3–4

Estimation of Expansion of Export Sales If Volume Shares Were Maintained at 1948–50 Levels

Commodity (1)	1951 (2)	1952 (3)	1953 (4)	1954 (5)	1955 (6)	1956 (7)	1957 (8)	1958 (9)	1959 (10)	1960 (11)	1951–60 Total (12)
(A) Jute manufactures											
A.1: Hypothetical incremental export earnings (in Rs. millions)	323.06	154.66	170.00	147.75	172.29	207.85	202.03	242.78	329.50	408.74	2,358.66
A.2: A.1 as a percentage of actual export earnings	13.44	9.47	15.36	12.17	13.92	18.47	17.58	23.58	29.75	32.55	
(B) Tea											
B.1: Hypothetical incremental export earnings (in Rs. millions)	58.53	62.29	0.40	275.49	265.21	47.43	192.47	138.68	167.22	290.12	1,497.84
B.2: B.1 as a percentage of actual export earnings	6.23	7.70	0.03	18.64	24.29	3.26	16.93	10.69	12.95	23.47	
(C) Cotton textiles											
C.1: Hypothetical incremental export earnings (in Rs. millions)	76.11	86.31	26.05	Negative	Negative	37.08	Negative	42.05	Negative	254.12	521.72
C.2: C.1 as a percentage of actual export earnings	8.06	11.64	4.08			5.95		7.29		36.84	
(D) Unmanufactured tobacco											
D.1: Hypothetical incremental export earnings (in Rs. millions)	Negative	Negative	Negative	41.66	38.39	21.35	65.53	8.78	47.39	51.36	274.46
D.2: D.1 as a percentage of actual export earnings				35.42	36.04	17.10	44.79	5.97	35.02	35.15	

(E) Groundnuts and oil										
E.1: Hypothetical incremental export earnings (in Rs. millions)	Negative	Negative	40.07	164.60	Negative	70.57	153.50	138.89	59.87	94.85	722.35
E.2: Hypothetical incremental export volume as a percentage of actual export volume			228.08	152.12		163.93	10,762.50	445.00	82.39		438.18
(F) Linseed and oil										
F.1: Hypothetical incremental export earnings (in Rs. millions)	26.94	Negative	16.96	179.76	Negative	Negative	57.58	17.02	26.98	39.62	364.86
F.2: Hypothetical incremental export volume as a percentage of actual export volume			66.40	257.89		1,700.00	208.39	54.30	102.62		437.68
Total of A–F										
Total hypothetical incremental export earnings (in Rs. millions)	484.64	303.26	253.48	809.26	475.89	384.28	671.11	588.20	630.96	1,138.81	5,739.89
Total hypothetical incremental export earnings (in Rs. millions) as a percentage of total actual export earnings from these commodities	10.65	9.76	8.56	22.06	14.47	10.82	21.76	19.77	18.78	31.21	16.45

SOURCE: Calculated on the basis of average volume shares in 1948–50, from pp. 15, 38, 57, 74, 75, 99, 101, and 130, of M. Singh, op. cit. The hypothetical incremental export earnings for jute manufactures, tea, cotton textiles, and unmanufactured tobacco are derived by first multiplying the 1948–50 volume shares by the volume of world trade and then multiplying the result by the unit price of exports i.e., Indian export earnings divided by Indian export volume. For groundnut and linseed oil, the hypothetical incremental export *volume* is first derived on the basis of 1948–50 shares; the hypothetical incremental export earnings are then derived by multiplying this incremental volume with the unit price of all oil and oilseed exports. The export value figures of tea, unmanufactured tobacco, groundnut and oil, and linseed and oil are on a financial year basis. Reproduced from Bhagwati and Desai, *India*, p. 392.

TABLE 3–5
Exports by Major Destinations, 1956–57 to 1960–61 and 1961–62 to 1965–66
(Rs. millions)

Destination	Average		Change	% Change on Second Plan Total	% of Total Change
	Second Plan	Third Plan			
Socialist countries	357	1,133	+776	217.37	49.11
W. Europe	2,323	2,383	+60	2.58	3.79
(E.E.C. therein)	(467)	(574)	(+108)		
(E.F.T.A. therein)	(1,759)	(1,702)	(−57)		
Asia and Oceania	1,597	1,900	+304	19.04	19.25
(Japan therein)	(303)	(554)	(+250)		
Africa	475	522	+47	9.89	2.95
(U.A.R. therein)	(109)	(160)	(+51)		
Americas	1,286	1,679	+393	30.60	24.90
(United States therein)	(928)	(1,311)	(+384)		
Total	6,037	7,617	1,580	26.17	100.00

SOURCE: *Basic Statistical Material Relating to Foreign Trade, Production and Prices,* Volume XIII—Part II, Government of India, 1967. Reproduced from Bhagwati and Desai, *India,* p. 397, with minor corrections and expression of percentages to two decimal places.

improved the direct profitability of export sales, there were also some promotional activities, in the form, for example, of budgetary appropriations for market development, which indirectly raised the profitability of foreign sales to domestic producers and traders.

FISCAL MEASURES

Among the fiscal measures which the export drive was based on were: (1) exemptions from sales taxes on final sales and refunds of indirect taxes, domestic and customs, on inputs; (2) direct tax concessions; (3) outright subsidies; and (4) rail freight concessions.

1. Exemptions and refunds from indirect taxes (sales, customs and excise) were generally made available to Indian exporters, although their incidence was not always as intended owing to dilatory procedures and inefficiencies. These exemptions, refunds and rebates applied to both imported components and to exported outputs.

Drawbacks of import duties were introduced for raw materials used in exported finished articles (including art silk fabrics, cars, dry radio batteries, electric fans and cigarettes) in 1954. Rebates of excise duty were announced in 1956, with immediate applicability to the raw materials used in exported ready-made apparel, tents, and sugar products and to direct exports of cotton and silk fabrics produced on powerlooms. The scope of both these measures was considerably enlarged during the 1960s, though several inefficiencies of procedure and insufficient accessibility to the drawbacks and rebates persisted through the ensuing years. The exemptions from *sales* taxes raised even more difficulties in practice.

While no breakdown of the refunds, rebates, and drawbacks actually earned on different export items is available, it is estimated that the refund of excise duties in 1963–64 was around Rs. 58 million.

2. More important were the *direct* tax concessions, which had been made in three successive budgets. The first, and somewhat hesitant, step was taken with the 1962 budget which gave a non-discriminatory tax concession to exporters. Apart from its non-selectivity, the subsidy was characterized by its being calculated on profits from exports (with the tax rate being fixed thereon at 45 percent instead of the standard 50 percent).

The 1963 budget added a different kind of tax incentive. It was both selective and related, not to profits, but directly to the f.o.b. value of exports— at 2 percent thereof.

The 1965 budget took the further striking step of giving selective concessions, described as tax credits, at *different* rates to different industries. The rates went up to as far as 15 percent and were extended to a larger number of industries. Yet, in relation to the import entitlement schemes which are discussed below, the incentives were relatively small and confined to a small range of exports.

3. In addition to the tax concessions granted through the budget, which therefore must be classified as subsidy equivalents, there were two other major forms of subsidization in the system: (a) open, cash subsidy by budgetary appropriation for sugar; and (b) disguised cash subsidy, in the shape of losses incurred by the STC on exports of certain commodities, which were "financed" by profits on other (essentially import) trade.

4. With respect to rail freight concessions, as early as 1960 the Ministry of Railways had agreed to grant reductions in freight rates to selected commodities for transportation between specified destinations. The commodities covered ranged from motor vehicle batteries and oil pressure lamps to textile machinery and bicycles: they were essentially non-agriculture-based manufactures whose exports were a recent phenomenon.

An examination of the eligible routes and corresponding concessions indicates that the intention was to offset the transport cost "disadvantage" to exporters, even sometimes to the point of providing progressively concessional rates as distance increased (as with manganese ore)! As the export drive intensified, this aspect of rail freight concessions was to have more appeal for the authorities in charge of export promotion, despite its obvious contradiction of economic logic. The notion that transport costs may reflect real costs to the economy and the fact that, if anything, the "shadow" freight rates were almost certainly higher than those charged on a non-concessional basis, seem to have concerned none of the authorities in charge of the export drive.

In addition to these direct fiscal measures, involving explicit or implicit subsidization of exports, at budgetary expense, there were also (a) budgetary grants for promotional activities, such as the Market Development Fund, under which the activities of the numerous Export Promotion Councils were financed along with research exhibitions and market surveys geared to export expansion, and (b) special allocations of scarce items at controlled prices, including priority access to rail space and allocations of domestic materials, such as iron and steel, which constituted effective subsidization insofar as these facilities and materials, if purchased at (black) market prices, would have been otherwise more expensive.

IMPORT ENTITLEMENT SCHEMES

While the export promotion measures deployed by the Indian Government had, therefore, numerous aspects (including outright subsidies and tax concessions), the principal instrument of export promotion soon became the import entitlement schemes, under which eligible exporters received import licenses, fetching high import premia, *pro rata* to the value of exports effected. By early 1965 the import entitlement schemes already had a very considerable coverage.

The rates of import entitlements. Even a cursory examination of the rates schedules for import entitlements under the export promotion schemes (as, for example, for engineering and chemicals) shows that wide variations existed in these rates for different products. When the criterion used for fixing these rates was sought, governmental declarations seemed to yield definitive answers. Take, for example, a typical statement:[8]

> The most important feature of these schemes is that a specified percentage of the f.o.b. value of exports is allowed to be used for importing raw materials and components required in the production of the export products or a group of allied products. The import entitlement is generally determined on the basis of twice the import content subject to a maximum of 75 per cent of the f.o.b. value of exports.

Two central principles seemed to emerge from these and other declarations: (1) the import entitlement would not exceed 75 percent of f.o.b. export value; and (2) the import entitlement would, subject to the preceding constraint, equal only twice the value of import content.

As it turned out, however, neither of these principles appears to have been taken seriously since the intensification of the export drive began during 1963. Why were they so clearly flouted? It appears as though the authorities initially thought that some uniform incentive should be provided and this uniformity was thought to be present in the rule of twice-the-import-content on the ground that each exporter could thus earn one extra import-content to produce one more unit for domestic sale. Of course, this does not at all mean a uniform *ad valorem* incentive to export for all commodities covered by such a scheme; but that does not appear to have been appreciated. At the same time, the ceiling of 75 percent of f.o.b. value appears to have been imposed for any or all of the following reasons: (1) the schemes were supposed to yield net foreign exchange for non-exporting industries and hence entitlements in excess of 100 percent seemed ruled out; (2) an excessive entitlement might encourage over-invoicing of exports; and perhaps (3) larger entitlements would result in "throw-away" exports.

The general flouting of the 75 percent ceiling and the twice-the-import-content rule appears to have been a reflection of the shift in practice to the notion that the value of exports must generally be maximized and that uniformity of the kind implicit in the twice-the-import-content rule, as well as any ceiling on the entitlements, must not be taken so seriously as to impede the export drive. These attitudes were evident also in the growing number of concessions granted for rail transport and the accelerating clamor even for (economically) perverse rules under which the concessional rates would be linked directly with the distance over which the goods must be carried. We shall revert to this point later, when we evaluate the economic effects of the entitlement schemes.

Permissible imports. Unlike some exchange retention schemes, the import entitlement schemes did not permit free use of the entitlements. Invariably, a list of authorized imports was issued. An analysis of these lists and accompanying official declarations shows several features.

1. The imports allowed were claimed to be direct inputs into the industries covered by the exports promotion scheme in question. This was generally correct; but there were important qualifications:

(a) Since different industries were frequently grouped together into a single scheme, the directness of the importable inputs, as far as any *one* industry was concerned, could not be considered to be really maintained by the scheme.

(b) Similarly, from the viewpoint of the exporting manufacturer, if he was a multi-product manufacturer and the different products had interchangeable materials, the directness of the imported inputs into the exported product surely did not rule out in practice their use for manufacture of the other unexported products within the same firm.

(c) Moreover, as many materials (especially chemicals) go into a large range of industries, thus straddling different export promotion schemes, and as the legal transferability of entitlements frequently occurred via traders, it is only natural that *illegal,* inter-scheme transfers also occurred from time to time.

(d) Finally, the "directness" principle was openly flouted eventually by the introduction of the special dryfruits scheme under which *ad hoc* licenses were given to exporters of diverse items (including chemicals and engineering products) to import high-premium-yielding dryfruit. This scheme amounted of course to nothing but an indirect method of cash subsidization and no pretense could be made of dryfruit being a direct input into the exported items.

2. There were, further, occasional changes of items in permissible imports of materials and components. There appears to have been a conflict between the interests of the exporters and those of the domestic producers of materials competing with imports. Exporters sought to include high-premia materials, whereas domestic producers of these materials opposed this because inclusion in the permissible imports list would reduce their profits. In a sheltered market these conflicts assumed economic significance, and the occasional shifts in items on the import list seemed often to reflect the relative bargaining positions of the pressure groups involved rather than significant changes in objective economic conditions.

3. In the beginning, the use of entitlements was further restricted to the import of materials, spares and components, while the import of capital goods for replacing or extending capacity was excluded. This restriction was probably prompted by a desire not to disrupt Capital Goods (Import) Control (CGC), although of course there was no reason why permission to import equipment could not be allowed, subject to prior approval by CGC. Yet another reason may have been that the influential policy-makers really regarded the entitlement schemes as more or less breaking the bottlenecks to exports arising from inability to use *current* capacity because of scarcity of imported materials and did not fully appreciate the subsidy aspect of the schemes or the possibility that expansion of capacity in the export industries itself might be desirable from the viewpoint of export promotion. These restrictions, however, were gradually reduced and, in some cases, altogether eliminated, so that it became customary eventually to have large proportions of the entitlement specified as expendable on imports of equipment.

Transferability of import entitlements. While import entitlements had earlier been subjected to extremely stringent restrictions concerning transferability and sale, they eventually became more readily saleable although several restrictions continued. Several variants of transferability were employed in the different schemes.

A typical formula, widely used, permitted the entitlement to be transferred by the exporter, who might be a trader or a manufacturer-exporter, to other manufacturers covered by the *same entitlement scheme*. Among other variants the transferability of the engineering scheme, for example, was restricted within each of *three* groups: (1) general engineering and electrical manufactures; (2) machinery and transport equipment; and (3) non-ferrous semis, alloys and fully processed manufactures. In fish products, handicrafts, processed goods, leather and leather manufactures, silk fabrics and ready-made silk garments, again the transferability of imports was confined to other exporters within the scheme and does not appear to have been extended to all manufacturers. For dyes and chemicals entitlements in art silk exports, on the other hand, transferability extended even to units in cotton and woolen textiles.

Premium on entitlements. Thus import entitlements were generally transferable within a scheme and could earn whatever premium cleared the market at any point of time. Occasionally, indeed not infrequently, ceilings were imposed on the chargeable premium.

In the bulk of the entitlements issued, the effective subsidization to any exporter depended on the premium on the entitlements (in addition, of course, to the entitlement rate itself).[9] In practice, the segmentation of the different entitlement markets meant that the level of the premium varied from commodity to commodity. Besides, the premium varied over time, within each market. The factors which must have determined the premium included the restrictiveness of the permissible imports list, the entitlement rate, the leakage into prohibited sales and expectations about the current and future inflow of entitlements into the market.[10]

Changes and variability in the export incentive offered by the entitlements schemes. So far we have considered the questions of the fixation of entitlement rates, the transferability of the entitlements and the premium on entitlements. From this, it is easy to infer the effective subsidy which was available, at a single point of time, on export sales to an atomistic exporter. But the question remains whether this export incentive tended to be variable, with the effective subsidy on exports changing from time to time.

There is little doubt that the export incentives were variable under the entitlement schemes, although it is difficult to quantify this variability accurately in view of the paucity of reliable information for many schemes. There were three major reasons why such variability arose:

1. changes in the *coverage* of the schemes
    (a) products were included and/or excluded from period to period; and
    (b) exports to certain areas were excluded and/or their entitlements were changed from time to time;

2. changes in entitlement for *given* products, arising from changes in formula used or revised notions about the incentives, from time to time; and

3. changes in the premium on the entitlements, arising from:

(a) revisions in rules governing the transferability of entitlements; or

(b) changes in the coverage of the items for whose import the entitlements could be used; or

(c) inevitable, periodic shifts in the premium which entitlement licenses (with given coverage and transferability) enjoyed in the market; or any combination of all of these factors.

In conclusion, the Indian export promotion policies were based essentially on the entitlement schemes which applied by 1965–66, in significant degree, to nearly 60 percent of Indian export earnings, although the magnitude of export subsidization they involved was unforeseeably discriminatory in incidence among the different items.[11]

Economic Effects of Import Entitlement Schemes.

We now turn to an analysis of the main economic features and consequences of these import entitlement schemes, which (as noted) constituted the bulk of India's export subsidization effort until the June 1966 devaluation. To begin with, in contrast to the simple exchange retention schemes of countries such as Pakistan, the Indian schemes had the following, almost unique features:

1. the number of entitlement rates was very large and subject to occasional change;

2. by and large, the entitlement rates were below 100 percent of export value;

3. the market for the (transferable) entitlements was segmented by export promotion schemes;

4. the premium on entitlements showed fluctuations in the different, segmented markets;

5. the list of permissible imports excluded consumer goods;

6. the value of exports covered by the scheme, on the most liberal interpretation which would include tea and coffee exports, amounted to around 80 percent of the total Indian exports and to around 60 percent on more restricted assumptions; and

7. the value of imports coming under entitlements was throughout less than 5 percent of the *total* value of imports (including aid-financed imports).

The import entitlement schemes, set in the framework of an overvalued exchange rate, were undoubtedly a useful improvement on a situation where otherwise exports were being seriously discriminated against. But the essential question is whether these were an *efficient* way of countering the effect of the overvaluation of the exchange rate on exports. The analysis that follows in this chapter is addressed to this question and seeks to establish the inefficiency of such schemes.

As the Indian import entitlement schemes were characterized by considerable segmentation, differential rates and non-transferability resulting in differential premia, we shall analyze the efficiency of these schemes (1) on the hypothetical assumption that these markets and rates were unified and (2) on the more realistic assumption that the markets and rates were differentiated. We will, in fact, be arguing that these schemes were basically an inefficient way of simulating the working of a flexible exchange rate system; and that these inefficiencies were compounded by the differential nature of the effective subsidization granted under the Indian regime.

Subsidy Aspects per se

Among the several, significant effects of the Indian import entitlement schemes, omitting (as we have noted) the aspect of differential rates and selectivity in general, we shall note the following main features: over-invoicing of exports; revenue effect; self-limiting export promotion; instability of the incentive offered; utilization of foreign exchange allocations explicitly for creating incentives; and welfare effects.

Over-invoicing of exports. Insofar as the import entitlement schemes constituted subsidy measures, they gave rise to an incentive, *ceteris paribus,* to over-invoice exports: an incentive that would be eliminated under a straightforward, direct adjustment of the exchange rate (which would obviate the need to subsidize exports to counter the disincentive offered to exports by the overvaluation of the exchange rate).[12]

We must note here that the incentive to over-invoice led some exporters, especially (though not exclusively) in sectors such as plastics and art silks, to send out shoddy goods with faked, higher-price declarations, which were cleared in foreign markets at "what they could fetch." At a time when India's immediate and long-term export drive had to rest increasingly on the export of manufactures (and, for that matter, quality and complex manufactures by and large), the building up of goodwill was quite important. This was precisely what was jeopardized by the practitioners of over-invoicing. We shall soon see that the instability of the incentive offered by the entitlement schemes, combined with the differential incidence of the benefits on the numerous, different items, accentuated this phenomenon by encouraging the entry into the export trade of roving traders, in search of quick profits, whose primary objective was short-run, immediate profit maximization.

Revenue effects. An argument frequently advanced in India in favor of the import entitlement schemes, as a method of export subsidization, as against direct subsidization, is that these schemes finance themselves: the subsidy is paid by the users of the import licenses. However, insofar as this is the case, it would be equally open for the authorities to levy such a tax directly on imports and to finance therewith a direct subsidy on exports. Hence, the argument in favor of the entitlement schemes must rest on the illusion that taxation of imports may be feasible if disguised but not otherwise. Such an illusion may well exist, but we doubt its plausibility and have seen no evidence in support thereof.

Besides, we may note that if we were to compare a regime with an over-valued exchange rate combined with entitlement schemes for export, with an adjusted exchange rate, the revenue effect would have been against the former regime for the simple reason that imports exceeded exports approximately by the amount of the net aid inflow which was quite considerable.

Self-limiting nature of the subsidy.   Further, the entitlement schemes con-trasted unfavorably with direct, *ad valorem,* subsidies in another respect. Whereas *ad valorem* subsidies apply the incentive equally at all levels of export (and concomitant prices), the entitlement schemes build into their structure an important feature which reduces the incentive with the value of exports achieved.

This self-limiting aspect, implying that the more successful the scheme is in increasing exports, the less the incentive to export *at the margin,* arises from the fact that the incentive rests crucially on the entitlement premium (once the entitlement rate is fixed). If export value increases, thanks to the entitlement schemes, import entitlements entering the market will proportion-ately increase, thus tending to push the premium down. But the lower the premium the lower also the incentive, at the margin, on exports.

An *ad valorem* subsidy instead would maintain the full incentive. A flexible exchange rate or suitable devaluation, on the other hand, would have effects similar to an *ad valorem* subsidy, except for the incremental cost of imported and import-competing inputs which would operate with respect to the import side.

Instability of the incentive.   A related feature of such export subsidization schemes is the additional source of instability that they constitute, in view of the fact that the premium on entitlements would vary, in contrast to an *ad valorem* export subsidy. Moreover, as we have already noted, the frequent changes in the premia brought about by changing rules concerning permissible imports and transferability, for example, as also frequent changes in the en-titlement rates themselves, constituted further elements of instability in the operation of the entitlement schemes in India.

Utilization of foreign exchange allocations for creating export incentives. The economic consequences and inefficiencies that we have just discussed arose primarily from the fact that the entitlement schemes operated by divert-ing the allocations of premium-fetching imports, by way of economic reward and incentive, to exporters. Among the other effects of such a policy, we may now note two in particular.

(1) The system may have resulted in foreign exchange being allocated to industries (which albeit were induced thereby to export) for non-priority use. For example, if imports of luxury goods were permitted under the entitlements schemes, and this was merely to provide a high-premium incentive for export, and the import of luxury goods was otherwise intended to be prohibited, this could well be regarded as a *minus* factor in the evaluation of the entitlement schemes (from the point of view of this policy). On the other hand, if the government did not seek to prohibit imports of these luxury goods or if they were merely diverted from established importers to import entitlements, the foreign exchange used (*via* the entitlements) on importing these luxury goods could not be properly regarded as "misallocation" from the viewpoint of socially declared objectives. Thus, for example, the Pakistan bonus scheme has permitted imports of consumer goods (including luxury goods), but so has their general, import licensing policy.

On the other hand, the Indian entitlement schemes, as we have noted, followed exclusively the principle of exclusion of consumer goods. Where, however, the leakage into non-priority allocations may be alleged to have occurred is in industries such as art silk where the *total* foreign exchange allocations (AU plus import entitlement licenses), as a result of the export incentive taking the form of import entitlements rather than *ad valorem* subsidies, may have been greater than otherwise. In the absence of any statistical evidence on AU licenses by sector-of-use (for any length of time, for this industry), it is impossible to arrive at any reasonably firm conclusion on this question.

(2) Another effect of the use of foreign exchange allocations for promoting exports, in the Indian context, was quite favorable (although it would have ceased to be so under an adjusted exchange rate which could obviate the reliance on strict import controls and the resulting inflexibility). Until these entitlement schemes were operating, there was practically no legal way of getting hold of foreign exchange in order to break expensive bottlenecks and unforeseen demands. The entitlement markets thus served to introduce a much needed flexibility in an otherwise excessively inflexible system.

While this basic advantage to the economy, arising from the introduction of legal accessibility to scarce imports (albeit with restrictions, but still significant), was considerable, many exporters who were interviewed argued that the entitlement schemes, in view of their granting such access to imports, were also a superior, more effective way of sustaining an export drive than *ad valorem* financial subsidies. (1) It was argued that *flexibility* of access to foreign exchange was a considerable advantage, which would not be available if the subsidy was a financial one; and that their export performance would have been affected adversely by the replacement of these schemes by financial subsidies.[13] (2) It was further argued that the vast majority of exporting producers exported just enough to get the amount of foreign exchange for maintaining full capacity utilization in their plants and that their motivation in exporting was *not* to increase overall profits but to expand capacity utilization; and hence the export drive would suffer by the replacement of entitlement schemes by purely financial incentives. (3) Finally, it was also claimed that, with foreign exchange not otherwise available in a free market, it was possible that firms which might find it attractive to export on being given a financial incentive to do so, might not be in a position to produce at all for export (the assumption, of course, being that their AU allocations were meager).

While these beliefs were strongly held, only the last argument has some element of logic in it. The first argument is fallacious because any advantage following from flexibility can generally be quantified and the corresponding incentive provided through fiscal subsidies.[14] As for the second argument, there is little evidence of Indian firms following a policy of output, rather than profit, expansion. The very fact that many firms were known to sell their entitlement licenses, at least at the margin, indicates that the force of this argument is not considerable. The last argument, based on the fact that firms restricting themselves to legal purchases would not be able to produce for export, but would have to confine themselves to diverting existing production to exports, has some plausibility. Even in this case, however, we have to allow for the fact that incremental export earnings would be released into the economy and hence could be used eventually for augmenting production for exports. We are thus left essentially with the argument that the entitlement schemes introduced flexibility into the import regime, undoubtedly resulting in sizable gains via the breaking of costly bottlenecks.

Other welfare effects. We may now consider other more direct welfare effects associated with the fact that the entitlement schemes involved a departure from unified exchange rates. As already noted, an *ad valorem* subsidy on exports would help, in an overvalued exchange rate situation, to reduce the discrimination against exports. On the other hand, a system under which export subsidization is combined with an overvalued exchange rate involving import controls differs significantly from a system where the exchange rate is altered to equilibrium levels and thus implies a unified exchange rate policy.

Thus, in the Indian-type import regime, we have already observed that imports were partly allocated on an AU basis and hence the effective rate on these imports was the parity plus the relevant tariff. On the other hand, insofar as other inputs were purchased from the market, the effective import rate on these included the import premium as well. Thus, as we shall argue at length in Chapter 13, there followed non-unified exchange rates and un-predictably different and bizarre incentives for resource allocation.

In this situation, the introduction of even a unified export subsidy would have perpetuated the continuation of non-unified exchange rates, while helping to reduce the overall disincentive to exports. But, in fact, such a subsidy would give rise to the possibility of losses arising from the effective export rate for a commodity *exceeding* the effective average import rate on its inputs. Such a situation could lead to the possibility mentioned earlier that the process would yield "value subtracted" at international prices.

SELECTIVITY OF THE SUBSIDIZATION

In point of fact, many of the inefficiencies resulting from the entitlement schemes were compounded by the selectivity with which they were adminis-tered and from which we have so far been abstracting.

Undoubtedly, in an ideal world, one should want to make rational departures from unified exchange rates. There are, in fact, a vast number of grounds on which we can argue for optimal intervention in the shape of trade tariffs and subsidies and tax-cum-subsidies on production, consumption, and factor-use.

However, the Indian export subsidization schemes involved policy inter-vention in a selective manner, with little economic rationale. As argued earlier, the principle apparently aimed at in the beginning was the supply of one more unit of "import-content," in addition to "replacement," as the economic incentive for export promotion. The equivalent *ad valorem* subsidy, therefore, would have varied among different export commodities and, con-verted into different *ad valorem* rates of import entitlements for different com-modities, it did. The effective export subsidy further varied among commodi-ties because, for administrative reasons and as a result of notions about priorities in some undefined sense, the entitlement licenses could be marketed, as we have already seen, only within segmented markets and hence carried differential premia.

In point of fact, toward 1965–66, the principle of export subsidization had clearly begun to veer around to the proposition that exports should be maximized—although, we should not forget that, on many *traditional* exports which were outside the range of such export subsidization, domestic absorp-tion continued to create difficulties in the way of more successful export promotion.

The principle of maximizing exports, which became fairly widespread among the newer manufactures, was practiced by a continuous tendency to-ward raising the effective subsidization. Also, for example, it became gener-ally possible to ask the Ministry of International Trade for *ad hoc* entitle-ments, for chemical and engineering exports, to make up for any ostensible

difference between the domestic sale price of a product and its supposed
f.o.b. export price plus the subsidy normally available through drawbacks,
fiscal tax concessions, and entitlements. In addition, we have also noted how
transport freight concessions were sought, and sometimes granted, to com-
pensate for "transport cost disadvantage" to products manufactured in the
hinterland. The fact that transport involves a real cost to the economy and
hence must be accounted for, instead of being compensated for, was apparently forgotten in the general strategy of pushing out any and all of the new
exports in particular.

Thus, the policy of export promotion generally adopted during the
Third Plan period, ending in the devaluation of June 1966, can best be
described as having ultimately become one of indiscriminate export promotion, with even a perverse bias toward fixing the subsidy inversely to the
competitive strength of the exportable commodity. This system had its counter-
part in the indiscriminate protection that import policy furnished to domestic
industries.

It is thus difficult to escape the conclusion that, while the Third Plan
witnessed a major shift toward export subsidization, export promotion policies were inefficiently designed and implemented. These policies were to
be subjected to change in the direction of greater efficiency with devaluation in June 1966. We discuss these changes in Part III. But first we proceed,
in the next chapter, to discuss the other measures, such as use of import
duties to mop up premia, which were also undertaken during the latter part of
Phase II, prior to the June 1966 devaluation and associated policy changes.

NOTES

1. The discussion in this chapter is an abridged version of Bhagwati and Desai,
India, pp. 371–467.
2. Manmohan Singh, *India's Export Trends* (Oxford: Clarendon Press, 1964).
3. The regression equation $x = a + bt,$ fitted to the price and volume indices for
the periods 1948–61, 1951–61 and 1953–61 confirms the statistical significance of this
stagnation. The estimated equations are reproduced in Table 3–3.
4. Singh, *Export Trends.*
5. Bhagwati and Desai, *India,* p. 394.
6. On the other hand, the "negative" entries in Table 3–4 show that the 1948–50
average was by no means the highest feasible share, even in the ensuing decade, for
cotton textiles, tobacco, groundnut, and linseed oilseed and oils.
7. Bhagwati and Desai, *India,* pp. 394–395.
8. *Annual Report, 1963–64,* Government of India, Ministry of International Trade,
New Delhi, p. 14.
9. Here, as elsewhere, we are referring only to the incentive provided an individual,
atomistic exporter under the entitlement schemes. It would be incorrect to generalize the
argument to the point of saying that therefore the replacement of such a scheme by an
identical *ad valorem* export subsidy would produce equivalent real effects.

10. For example, the premia rose severely for these licenses during May–June 1965, when the import policy announcement was delayed and the removal of the entitlement schemes was widely expected. This happened again in the months prior to devaluation in June 1966.

11. For further evidence in support of this conclusion, see Bhagwati and Desai, *India,* pp. 428–430. The figure of 80 percent there exceeds the figure of 60 percent here because it includes nearly negligible entitlements given to items such as tea and jute.

12. Whether over-invoicing would be worthwhile would depend, of course, on the relative values of the black market foreign exchange rate and the degree of export subsidization. In India, the incentive to over-invoice was clearly present in many cases.

13. This assertion, of course, is an important indictment of the import control regime and the inflexibility it entailed.

14. We presume that necessary production would be feasible under the export subsidy solution.

Chapter 4

Liberalization Efforts Prior to 1966

As we pointed out in the preceding chapter; the Indian economy may be characterized as going through Phase II during the 1962–66 period. Export subsidization was steadily and energetically undertaken to reduce the degree and the consequences of the overvaluation of the exchange rate. In addition, the period was characterized by a steady attempt at unifying the import duties which had been increasingly deployed to mop up the import premia on the QR-regime-administered allocations of foreign exchange, and by attempts at streamlining the industrial licensing system so as to reduce, though not to eliminate (in the nature of the case) its adverse effects on efficiency and distributive justice. In many ways, and not just in the matter of export subsidization, this period was one of growing attempts to reduce the adverse impact of Phase I-type policies. Thus, we could well describe our Phase II as a period of partial and halting efforts at liberalization, as contrasted with the preceding period, 1956–61, which witnessed the imposition and consolidation of the QR-regime.

In this chapter, before we proceed to discuss the June 1966 devaluation which constitutes our liberalization episode, and which we analyze intensively throughout Part III of this study, we note the major aspects of these other reforms at removing the worst aspects of the Phase I regime.

INCREASING USE OF TARIFFS

From 1962–63 onward, import duties were used with increasing frequency to mop up the import premia which the QR-regime was generating.[1] Table 4–1

TABLE 4-1
Average Incidence of Import Duties, 1962–67
(Rs. millions)

Item	1962–63	1963–64	1964–65	1965–66	1966–67 (April–May 1966)	June 1966 to March 1967
Total imports	11,315	12,229	13,490	13,940	2,271	16,746
Deduct non-dutiable imports, viz.,						
(i) Food	1,443	1,796	2,821	3,091	644	5,080
(ii) Fertilizers	297	376	329	448	92	875
(iii) Crude petroleum	302	462	272	349	29	335
(iv) Hides and skins–raw and salted	28	34	31	24	2	15
(v) Newsprints	69	69	74	62	10	108
(vi) Books	30	34	41	32	5	36
	2,168	2,771	3,569	4,006	781	6,448
Dutiable imports (estimates)	9,147	9,458	9,921	9,935	1,490	10,298
Total net import duty revenue	2,347	3,261	4,030	5,473	924	3,926
Average import duty on dutiable imports, %	25.7	34.5	40	55	62	38

Source: Department of Economic Affairs, Ministry of Finance; at request. Reproduced from Bhagwati and Desai, *India*, p. 472.

summarizes this trend, showing that the average import duty (collected on dutiable imports) rose steadily up to the devaluation when, concurrently with the parity change, many duties were revised downward.[2]

The vast majority of these tariff increases were selective and differential, although some reliance was placed on across-the-board increases in duties later in the period. In 1962–63, for example, import duties were raised on some iron and steel items, silk yarn, copra, cars and machine tools. In 1963–64 the budget was used to raise import duties further on machinery, raw cotton, rubber, palm oil, iron and steel manufactures, mineral oils and dyes, among other commodities.

Beginning with the 1963–64 budget, however, the principle of across-the-board rate revisions was introduced. For 1963–64 a *surcharge* was levied on all dutiable articles at a flat rate of 10 percent of the existing import duty. In addition, a genuine across-the-board "regulatory duty" was levied at 10 percent *ad valorem* (unless the additional rate figured at 25 percent of the existing duty worked out higher, in which case this higher rate was applicable).[3]

While the later budgets continued to raise average tariffs, the only major change introduced was through the supplementary budget in 1965–66, when the principle of across-the-board tariffs was further underlined by a major revision in the tariff rates which aimed at reducing the wide range of selectivity and reducing the rates to a smaller number. The broad structure of the nominal tariffs that emerged from these changes is reproduced in Table 4–2. Thus, while import duties were being raised in lieu of the devaluation which was to come only in 1966, attempts were clearly made to introduce more uniformity in the tariff rates. This provided the backdrop to the move toward a formal rate change and greater unification of the exchange rates for different activities, which was to begin with the devaluation.

TABLE 4–2

Average Rates of Nominal Import Duty on Broad Classes of Commodities, after the Supplementary Budget, 1965–66

Item	Percentage Rate of Import Duty[a]
Plant and machinery	35
Agricultural machinery	15
Basic industrial raw materials	40
Processed industrial materials	60
Consumer goods	100

SOURCE: Government of India, Ministry of Finance, Department of Economic Affairs, New Delhi.

a. To these rates we must add the regulatory duty of 10 percent.

REMITTANCES SCHEME

The attempt to bring effective exchange rates to more realistic levels had also been extended to remittances with the National Defense Remittance (NDR) scheme in October 1965.

In principle, this scheme involved an extension of the import entitlement principle to remittances, so that invisibles were brought within the purview of subsidization for the first time. Under this scheme, Indian nationals resident abroad were given import licenses to the value of 60 percent of their remittances to India. Since these licenses were marketable at a premium, in effect the remittances were being subsidized by the full amount of the price at which the licenses could be sold. The remittances were to total approximately Rs. 700 million during the period of the operation of the NDR scheme.

We may note, however, that, in consonance with the bureaucratic restrictions on entitlements for exports, numerous restrictions were built into this scheme as well. The NDR import licenses could, in general, be sold only to producers ("actual users") for certain permissible imports or to general traders who, in turn, were permitted to import, for resale, only those commodities which were specified in Public Notices published from time to time. Again, the NDR licenses once issued to actual users could not be retransferred to other actual users. Furthermore, the list of commodities, once opted for by the actual user in getting his license issued to him against his NDR purchase, could not be changed even if this change was sought within the *overall* list of permissible imports. The bureaucratic nature of such inflexibility, and its economic irrationale, were strikingly highlighted when, with the introduction of liberal import licensing along with the June 1966 devaluation, many actual users who had got sulfur specified on their NDR licenses, in view of its high premium, found sulfur prices tumbling and wished to shift to other imports. The government eventually permitted this to be done, but again with considerable reluctance and restrictions: for example, the sulfur licenses could be converted only into mutton tallow licenses. Bureaucratic notions about "priority," without any demonstrable rationale, had carried over into the operation of the NDR scheme as well.

PARTIAL INDUSTRIAL DE-LICENSING

The reader will recall that, in addition to import licensing, the government also used industrial licensing to regulate the growth of industrial capacity. The end of our period of analysis in this chapter was to be characterized also by partial industrial de-licensing, essentially in the form of exemptions of certain industries from industrial licensing. Thus, in May 1966, eleven industries were formally de-controlled, including iron and steel castings and structurals and cement and pulp. At the same time, the government announced that it would continue to attempt such de-control in regard to industries which did not make substantial (direct) demands on the balance of payments through importation of components and raw materials and which did not encroach on areas sought to be reserved partially or wholly for the small-scale sector.[4]

While all the measures which we have reviewed thus far represented significant shifts toward liberalization of the unduly rigid economic regime, they fell short of restructuring the system on the basis of clear and hard analysis. Nonetheless they did represent significant attempts at loosening up the existing regime. The June 1966 announcement of the devaluation was, in a sense, therefore, the culmination of this entire process of reform in the economic regime of Phase I during Phase II (1962–66) and can be conceived of as the initiation of Phase III, aimed at more significant liberalization *and* rationalization of the trade and payments regime.

NOTES

1. The discussion in this chapter is based on Bhagwati and Desai, *India,* pp. 468–480.

2. Needless to say, we are aware of the well-known difficulties associated with our measure of the tariff level (as well as with alternative measures). We do think, however, that it is an adequate method of underlining the fact that the government increasingly resorted to tariff increases throughout the period.

3. This regulatory duty came into effect only on February 17, 1965.

4. The momentum toward industrial de-licensing was to be carried beyond June 1966 by further exemptions. At the same time, the government was to ease the scope and restrictiveness of industrial licensing for the licensed industries by raising the exemption limit for industrial licensing to units which sought to invest less than Rs. 2.5 million (with some exceptions). Furthermore, in regard to the licensing requirements for "substantial expansion" involving expansion by more than 10 percent of the registered capacity, the government raised this figure generally to 25 percent. Another relaxation, just after June 1966, related to the diversification of production by units licensed for specific products. Subject to qualifications (such as the exclusion of products mainly made in the small-scale sector), 1966 therefore witnessed the grant of permission to diversify production up to 25 percent of the existing capacity. Note that this measure of liberalization also represented a halting and ill-defined move toward a more efficient system. The decision to stop diversification at 25 percent of the originally licensed capacity was based on (1) choice of 25 percent without any clear rationale as to the relevant numbers; (2) a failure to think the problem through and ask why further diversification should not be permitted; and (3) the consequent inability to see that a system under which full diversification was automatically permitted except for a small list of priority outputs (whose production might be required on schedule) and with a small list of prohibited, nonpriority items of manufacture, would have made greater sense, both administratively and in terms of economic efficiency.

Part III

Liberalization Episode

Chapter 5

The Dimensions of the Liberalization Episode

By the time of the devaluation in June 1966, the government's efforts at liberalization had gathered some momentum. None of them, however, yet represented anything more than partial and halting measures. In particular, the exchange rate remained overvalued: import premia remained high and export subsidies had steadily been mounting to offset, however inefficiently, the adverse effects of the overvaluation on export performance. In fact, with the Indo-Pakistan War in late 1965 and the suspension of aid thereafter, the shortage of foreign exchange and the resulting rise in import premia had become serious.

The major motivating factors underlying the decision to devalue were twofold: (1) the adjustment of the parity in a situation of overvaluation seemed to fit in rather well with the government's earlier, slow attempts aimed rather at reducing the ill-effects of the overvaluation of the parity by offsetting measures such as export subsidization; and (2) more important, the Aid-India Consortium had virtually made a major devaluation a precondition for the resumption of aid, leaving the government little maneuverability because of the acute shortage of foreign exchange.

These two factors bear critically on both the policy package that went with the devaluation and on the outcome of the policy package. The fact that a major impulse behind the devaluation was the growing realization that the export subsidies and tariffs were only an inadequate and inefficient substitute for the formal parity change that was called for, meant that the government desired the devaluation primarily to substitute for the existing measures. Hence the degree of the devaluation was to reflect mainly the *existing* levels

83

of export subsidization and *only partially* to go beyond that. The formal parity change was therefore accompanied by a substantial elimination of the export subsidies and a significant reduction of the tariffs that had been increasingly used during Phase II in lieu of devaluation. The pressures applied by the aid donors to bring about the parity change, with the continuation of aid (at the normal levels prior to aid suspension in 1965) made presumably conditional on devaluation, also meant that another major aspect of the policy change was supposed to be a significant rise in the immediate availability of aid-financed imports, accompanied by an official commitment (in principle) to a policy of liberalized imports.

The full *policy package,* as we shall hereafter describe it, consisted of (1) the formal parity change resulting in a devaluation of the Indian rupee; (2) a substantial elimination of the export incentives on non-traditional exports, a simultaneous imposition of countervailing duties to offset the devaluation on traditional exports where oligopolistic competition from rival suppliers was expected (as on tea) and a significant reduction of the high import duties; and (3) a significant increase in the availability of aid-financed imports, accompanied by official declaration and implementation of a policy of liberalized import licensing.

In evaluating the outcome of the "liberalization episode" (in the Bhagwati-Krueger terminology) that this policy package constituted, we will also have to take into account the following factors:

1. an early revival, already in 1966, of subsidization on the export of major non-traditional exports;

2. a second, disastrous agricultural drought in 1966–67, which led to wage-good-scarcity-induced price increases;

3. a resulting deceleration in monetary expansion and in fiscal expenditures during 1966–67, which reflected fears of adding otherwise to the price increases;

4. a similarly motivated shift in the composition of fiscal expenditures temporarily away from capital to current expenditures; and

5. a massively adverse political reaction to the devaluation, largely in view of its having been widely regarded to be a result of pressures exercised by the Aid-India Consortium.

In the analysis that follows, we begin in Chapter 6 by quantifying the net devaluation when the parity change has been adjusted for the simultaneous removal of the export subsidies in the shape of the import entitlement schemes, the imposition of countervailing duties on traditional exports and the reduction of import duties. In Chapter 7, we then trace the different kinds of export subsidization that did carry over from the pre-devaluation period and the important new subsidies that were introduced in the post-devaluation period; and we attempt quantification of these subsidies, essentially to develop very broad orders of magnitude. Then it is possible for us to analyze carefully the different dimensions of the economy: price level and economic activity in Chapter 8 and export performance in Chapter 9. Since the role of the Western aid donors in bringing about the devaluation was critical, the political implications of their involvement as well as their interaction with the outcome of the liberalization episode are discussed in Chapter 10. Finally, several major lessons—for India, for developing countries and for donor-developed countries—are drawn together from this analysis in Chapter 11. The relapse of the economy into Phase II by 1968–70, rather than its transition to Phase IV, is also noted there.

Chapter 6

Net vs. Gross Devaluation in June 1966

On June 6, 1966, the rupee was devalued by 57.5 percent, computed as the increase from Rs. 4.76 to Rs. 7.50 in the official rate on the dollar.[1] The devaluation was accomplished by various other measures including, in particular, a removal of the major export subsidy device—the import entitlement schemes —and a significant reduction in import duties.

It is the purpose of this chapter to quantify the degree of effective devaluation, when the parity change is adjusted for these and other changes in trade subsidies and tariffs. We thus distinguish between the pure parity change, which may be described as the "de jure," "gross," devaluation, and the "de facto," "net" devaluation. Remember that we are adjusting *only* for the simultaneous changes in trade taxes and subsidies and *not* for the effects of other measures such as import liberalization in the shape of larger (maintenance) aid flows.

It is also necessary to note that the export subsidies were soon to be revised and steadily increased through 1966–70, a process which we describe and whose magnitude and effects we seek to quantify in later chapters. In the present chapter, we confine our statistical analysis to the net devaluation as of June 6, 1966, when the formal parity change and the changes in the export subsidization schemes and import duties were announced by the government of India.

Exports.

Among the changes in export subsidies and duties which accompanied the devaluation were:

86

1. the imposition of a number of countervailing export duties on "traditional" exports, aimed at partially or wholly neutralizing the effect of devaluation thereon on the assumption that India had monopoly power in trade in these items;

2. the elimination of the import entitlement schemes, described in Chapter 3, as well as the tax credits which had been granted in the 1963, 1964 and 1965 budgets; and

3. the elimination of a few cash subsidies which had been introduced in the year preceding the devaluation on selected engineering goods.

EXPORT DUTIES

We analyze initially the impact of the imposition of the export duties. Table 6–1 lists the exports on which the duties were levied at the time of the devaluation. It is interesting to note that duties were levied on exports amounting to as much as 62–63 percent of the overall export values. Thus an effort was made to offset devaluation on a *very* wide front.

Table 6–1 lists, in columns (4) and (5), export duties before and on the date of devaluation. Since the duties were, for the most part, specific, they had to be converted into effective *ad valorem* equivalents. The only way to do this, in practice, is to take appropriate export unit values, f.o.b., for each product and to relate the specific duty to them, converting the duty into an *ad valorem* figure. We did this, using the average export unit values in dollars for the relevant items for the two years 1964–65 and 1965–66, in column (3). This estimate of the export unit value was multiplied by the pre-devaluation rupee-dollar rate of 4.76, the pre-devaluation export duty (nil) then being deducted therefrom to arrive in column (6) at the net f.o.b. earning (in rupees) from the unit export of each item. The same procedure, for the post-devaluation situation, involved multiplying these unit export values by the post-devaluation parity rate of 7.5 and subtracting the new duties in column (5), to arrive in column (7) at the net realization (in rupees) from the unit export of each item after the devaluation. The proportionate increment in this net realization from unit export, in column (8), represents, then, the estimated *ad valorem* change in export incentives thanks to both the parity change and the export duty.[2]

Note that the net devaluation on these export items, constituting over 60 percent of the total, was still positive. The net export incentive effect amounted to a negative number only in the case of jute waste (which represents, however, 14–15 percent of jute exports in 1964–65 and 1965–66). We will shortly weight the incentive changes in different exports by their export shares. Prior to that, however, we proceed to analyze the effects of the change in the export subsidy schemes.

TABLE 6-1

Net Change in Export Realization from Devaluation and Export Duty Imposition

Items (1)	Unit (2)	Average (1964–66) Unit Value of Exports (value divided by quantity) U.S. $ (3)	Export Duty (Rs. per unit) just before 6/6/66 (4)	Export Duty (Rs. per unit) as of 6/6/66 (5)	Old Export EER (3) × 4.76 minus (4) (6)	New Export EER (3) × 7.5 minus (5) (7)	(7)−(6) (8)
1. Jute manufactures	m. ton	397.4			1891.6		
a. Carpet backing	m. ton	604.6	nil	900	2877.9	3634.5	26.3
b. Hessian	m. ton	440.2	nil	900	2095.4	2401.5	14.6
c. Sacking and other products	m. ton	309.4	nil	600	1472.7	1720.5	16.8
d. Cotton bagging	m. ton	226.4	nil	600	1077.7	1098.0	1.9
e. Jute waste	m. ton	98.6	nil	600	469.3	139.5	−70.3
2. Tea	Kg.	1.2	nil	2	5.7	7.0	22.8
3. Coffee	Kg.	1.0	nil	0.50	4.8	7.0	45.8
4. Black pepper	Kg.	0.8	nil	1.25	3.8	4.8	26.3
5. Oilcakes other than copra cakes	m. ton	87.2	nil	125	415.1	529.0	27.4
6. Raw cotton	m. ton	519.8	nil	1000	2474.2	2898.3	17.2
7. Cotton waste	Kg.	0.2	nil	0.30	1.0	1.2	20.0
8. Raw wool	Kg.	1.2	nil	1.00	5.7	8.0	40.4
9. Tobacco (unmanufactured)	Kg.	0.7	nil	0.75	3.3	4.5	36.4
10. Mica	Kg.	0.6	nil	0.50	2.9	4.0	37.9
11. Hides, skins and leather, tanned or untanned	Kg.	2.9	nil	10% a.v.	13.8	19.6	42.0
12. Coir and coir manufactures	Kg.	0.3	nil	10% a.v.	1.4	2.0	42.8
13. Manganese ore	m. ton	17.5	nil	7.00 to 20.00	83.3	124.2 111.2	49.1 33.5
14. Iron ore and concentrates	m. ton	7.3	nil	5.00 to 10.00	34.7	49.8 44.8	43.5 29.1

a.v. = ad valorem

SOURCE: *Economic Survey, 1967–68*, Government of India, Ministry of Finance, Department of Economic Affairs, New Delhi.

EXPORT SUBSIDIES

We have already seen that the major method of export subsidization prior to the devaluation was the import entitlement schemes. Under these schemes, the eligible exporters were entitled to retain a prespecified part of their f.o.b. value of export earnings. These entitlements, given the exchange control regime, had a market premium, so that they could be construed as export subsidies and reduced to equivalent *ad valorem* rates by calculating the proportionate increment in net realization from unit f.o.b. export earnings that they provided.[3]

The diversity of the entitlement rates, as well as their variability and plasticity in manipulation, make it nearly impossible to measure their net impact on export subsidization during 1966 with any reliability. It is clear, however, that by June 1966 the import premium had risen dramatically on a number of entitlements; and premia of the order of 100 percent do not appear to have been exceptional if we base our judgment on interviews. Indeed, in certain markets such as rayon piece goods, the premium on the entitlements was as high as 400 percent and thereabouts by mid-1965 and until the devaluation.

In the absence of reliable data on the premium on entitlements in each of the entitlement schemes, as of the months preceding the devaluation, we have calculated the effective export subsidy arising from the different import entitlement schemes, on the assumption of a premium on entitlements of 100 percent except in the case of engineering goods, rayon (where we reliably know it to have been around 400 percent) and cotton textiles.[4]

Table 6–2 presents the calculations of the resulting export subsidy for each scheme, stating explicitly the assumptions made regarding the entitlement rates and the premia for the period immediately prior to the devaluation. They also represent therefore the extent to which the elimination of these schemes offset the devaluation. The "net" effect of the devaluation, allowing for the removal of the entitlements, is thus given as the difference between these estimates in column (4) and 57.5 percent, which was the formal devaluation. This is recorded in column (5). It is thus clear that the devaluation was more than offset (as of June 6, 1966) by the elimination of the entitlement schemes on a sizable fraction of the exports in this area.

TAX CREDITS

We next make adjustment for the removal of the tax credits. Introduced in the Finance Act, 1963, and amended through the 1964 and 1965 Finance Acts, the pre-devaluation tax credits applied at differential rates (2–15 percent) to a number of eligible industries.[5] Since these were rebates on income tax, related to f.o.b. export value, and since the tax amounted to 50 percent of the profits, the equivalent *ad valorem* export subsidy implied by these re-

TABLE 6–2

Net Devaluation on Exports Previously under Import Entitlement Schemes, June 6, 1966

(percent)

Groups (1)	Average Entitlement Rate[a] (2)	Estimated Premium[b] (3)	Effective Devaluation before June 6, 1966 (4)	Net Change after June 6, 1966 (5)
1. Engineering goods	60	125	75	−17.5
2. Chemicals and allied products	75	100	75	−17.5
3. Plastics and linoleum goods	50	100	50	7.5
4. Certain natural essential oils	30	100	30	27.5
5. Handicrafts	50	100	50	7.5
6. Finished leather and leather products	35	100	35	22.5
7. Woolen carpets, rugs and druggets	35	100	35	22.5
8. Silk fabrics and ready-made garments from silk fabrics	45	100	45	12.5
9. Cotton textiles[c]	—	—	50	7.5
10. Books, journals, paper and paper products	75	100	75	−17.5
11. Fish and fish products	15	100	15	42.5
12. Processed foods	15	100	15	42.5
13. Coir yarn and coir products	6	100	6	61.5
14. Tanned hide and skins	19	100	19	38.5
15. Cashew kernels				

16. Pearls, precious stones, diamonds, imitation jewelry, etc.	80	100	−22.5
17. Gold jewelry and gold articles	50	100	7.5
18. Wooden manufactures and timber	75	100	−17.5
19. Fabrics of synthetic fiber and spun glass (including art silk fabrics)		400	
20. Vanaspati—hydrogenated oils and refined vegetable oils; refined castor oil, groundnut oil, cottonseed oil, etc.	70	100	−12.5
21. Cinematographic films and other films	75	100	−17.5
22. Agarbattis and chandon dhoop	25	100	32.5

a. The entitlement rate within each group varies, as indicated in Table 6–3. We have put down here an average figure, based on interviews. This has to be treated as only an "approximation," especially because the rates were "adjustable" upward on executive discretion in many instances.

b. The premium estimate is also "approximate," based on market interviews for some major groups (1, 2, 3, 6, 7, 9, 19) at the time prior to the devaluation and generalized to other groups. Cotton textiles had a complicated premium structure: see Bhagwati and Desai, *India*, p. 420; we have taken the simple average of the net incentive in row (8) in Table 19.5 in Bhagwati and Desai, which works out to 49.3 percent and put it down as 50 percent above in row (9), column (4).

c. See Note b.

bates was *twice* the stated rates. Note also that the tax credits were to be abolished on both the exports which lost the entitlements and the exports on which duties were levied with the devaluation. The net effect of the elimination of tax credits on these industries can thus be estimated as in Table 6–3 (which lists all the items in the import entitlement schemes and a few other minor items as well).

CASH SUBSIDIES ON ENGINEERING GOODS

In the year preceding the devaluation, a few cash subsidies on engineering goods had been introduced at different rates. Steel carried 5 percent, steel pipes and tubes 20 percent, iron castings 4 percent, bicycles 39 percent, bicycle parts 30 percent and wire nails and screws 4 percent. Between them, the 1965–66 exports of these items were only $20.2 million. The export-share weighted average cash subsidy on engineering goods amounted to about 3.3 percent.[6] In Table 6–3, we therefore adjust the entry for this item in column (5) downward by 3.3 percent to allow for the withdrawal of these subsidies on June 6, 1966.   .

OVERALL ESTIMATE OF "NET" DEVALUATION ON EXPORTS

For the items which overlap those affected by the import entitlement schemes and the export duty changes of June 6, 1966, therefore, we can *subtract* the estimated reduction in export subsidy due to tax-credit elimination in Table 6–3 from the "net" devaluation estimates in Table 6–1, column (8) and Table 6–2, column (5), respectively, to arrive at our *final* estimate of the net devaluation on all these items when the export duties and removal of the entitlements, tax credits and cash subsidies are *all* taken into account. These estimates are presented in Table 6–3, column (5). The net devaluation on exports can then be estimated as the weighted average of these net devaluation rates on each of the listed items. We have weighted these rates by the share of the exports of these items in total exports during 1964–66, to arrive at the total figure of 21.6 percent in row (52), column (5) of Table 6–3.[7]

Invisible Earnings.

The formal devaluation changed the effective rate on all invisible earnings by an identical amount with one significant exception, namely, the National Defense Remittance (NDR) scheme which had been instituted in October 1965 and which was formally abolished with the devaluation.

The devaluation was thus offset on remittances by the removal of the subsidy implicit in the NDR scheme. If we take the effective subsidy *via* the NDR scheme as the *average* of all the quotations during May, June and July 1966, this comes to 110 percent.[8] Subtracting 57.5 percent as the parity

TABLE 6-3

Net Devaluation in June 1966 after Adjusting for All Changes in Export Subsidies and Duties

Product or Product Group (1)	F.o.b. Value of Exports in 1964-65 plus 1965-66 (Rs. millions) (2)	Net Devaluation Based on Parity Change, Imposition of Export Duties and Elimination of Entitlement Schemes (3)	Effect of Tax Credit Elimination (4)	Full Net Devaluation Adjusted for All Changes (5)
1. Jute manufactures				
a. Carpet backing	306	26.3%	-13%	13.3%
b. Hessian	1,979	14.6	-7	7.6
c. Sacking and other products	1,023	16.8	-7	9.8
d. Cotton backing	132	1.9	-7	-5.1
e. Jute waste	3	-70.3	-7	-77.3
2. Tea	2,395	22.8	-5	17.8
3. Coffee	266	45.8	-1	44.8
4. Black pepper	178	26.3	-1	25.3
5. Oil cakes other than copra cakes	730	27.5	-1	26.5
6. Raw cotton	203	17.2	-1	16.2
7. Cotton waste	61	20.0	-1	19.0
8. Raw wool	141	40.4	-1	39.4
9. Tobacco (manufactured)	445	36.4	-1	35.4
10. Mica	210	37.9	-1	36.9
11. Hides, skins (raw)	186	42.0	-5	37.0
12. Coir and coir manufactures	222	36.8	-7	29.8
13. Manganese ore	242	33.5 to 49.2	-31	2.5 to 18.2
14. Iron ore and concentrates	799	29.1 to 43.5	-21	8.1 to 22.5
15. Engineering goods	312	-17.5	-7	-27.8ᵃ
16. Chemicals and allied products	153	-17.5	-7	-24.5
17. Plastic and linoleum goods	8	7.5	-3	4.5
18. Certain natural essential oils	56	27.5	-3	24.5

TABLE 6–3 (concluded)

Product or Product Group (1)	F.o.b. Value of Exports in 1964–65 plus 1965–66 (Rs. millions) (2)	Net Devaluation Based on Parity Change, Imposition of Export Duties and Elimination of Entitlement Schemes (3)	Effect of Tax Credit Elimination (4)	Full Net Devaluation Adjusted for All Changes (5)
19. Handicrafts	201	7.5	−1	6.5
20. Finished leather and leather products	4	22.5	−7	15.5
21. Woolen carpets, rugs and druggets	99	22.5	−3	19.5
22. Silk fabrics and ready-made garments made of silk fabrics	52	12.5	−7	5.5
23. Cotton textiles	1,128	7.5	−7	0.5
24. Books, journals, paper and paperboard	23	−17.5	−1	−18.5
25. Fish and fish products	136	42.5	−3	39.5
26. Processed food	25	42.5	−7	35.5
27. Coir yarn and coir products				
28. Tanned hides and skins	554	23.0	−7	16.0
29. Cashew kernels	564	57.5	−5	52.5
30. Pearls, precious stones, diamonds, imitation jewelry, etc.	279	−22.5	−1	−23.5
31. Gold jewelry and gold articles	31	7.5	−1	6.5
32. Wooden manufactures and timber	45	−17.5	−7	−24.5
33. Fabrics of synthetic fiber and spun glass (including art silk fabrics)	144	57.5	−7	50.5
34. Vanaspati—hydrogenated oils and refined vegetable oils, refined castor oils, groundnut oil, cottonseed oil, etc.	167	−12.5	−7	−19.5
35. Agarbattis and chandon dhoop	6	32.5	−3	29.5
36. Fresh fruits and vegetables	152	57.5	−21	36.5
37. Coal	71	57.5	−21	36.5
38. Crushed bones	54	57.5	−21	36.5

39. Tiles and earthen wares[b]	7	57.5	−21	36.5
40. All mineral ores other than iron and manganese ores	40	57.5	−31	26.5
41. Ferro manganese	102	57.5	−31	26.5
42. Alcoholic beverages	0.1	57.5	−31	26.5
43. Processed mica powder[c]	1	57.5	−31	26.5
44. Sugar	333	57.5	−7	50.5
45. Rubber goods[d]	39	57.5	−7	50.5
46. Glass	10	57.5	−7	50.5
47. Cement and gypsum products[e]	7	57.5	−7	50.5
48. Cigarettes	21	57.5	−7	50.5
49. Deoiled rice bran[f]	18	57.5	−5	52.5
50. Calcium magnite	16	57.5	−11	46.5
51. Other products[g]	1,910	57.5	−1	56.5
52. All commodities	16,258	—	—	21.6[h]

NOTE: Just before the devaluation, export industries were being accorded incentives in the form of relief from direct taxation. A number of export industries, mainly the traditional ones, were given tax credit certificates at varying rates subject to a maximum of 15 percent of the f.o.b. value of exports. Besides the relief in the form of tax credit certificates, 10 percent of profits attributable to exports could be deducted by exporters of *all* products from their taxable income. In the case of certain specified industries (those figuring in the First Schedule of the Industries (Development and Regulation Act 1951) a further deduction—to the extent of 2 percent of f.o.b. value of exports—from taxable income was permitted. All these forms of tax incentives were abolished when the rupee was devalued. The effect of the elimination of tax incentives thus equals $(2t_c + 2 + .10\pi)$, where t_c is the rate of tax credit certificates and π is the rate of profit as a proportion of f.o.b. value. This formula assumes a 50 percent tax on profits and applies only to industries which were eligible for all the three tax incentives, with appropriate modifications being made for industries not eligible for all the three incentives. The figures in column (4) assume a value of 10 for π.

a. This figure includes −3.3 percent for cash-subsidy elimination as explained in the text.
b. Red earthen tiles.
c. Mica powder.
d. Rubber manufactures not elsewhere specified.
e. Cement.
f. Rice bran.
g. This includes refractories, guar splits, ceramics, timber products, arms and ammunitions, surgical cotton and dressings and cinematographic films and other films.
h. This figure is 16.9 percent when "Other products" are not included.

TABLE 6–4
Changes in Import Duties as of June 6, 1966

| (1) | Effective *Ad Valorem* Duty[a] (percent) | | Effective Devaluation (percent) (4) | Share in Total Imports (1964–66) (percent) |
	Pre-Devalu-ation (2)	Post-Devalu-ation (3)		
1. Iron and steel	63.6	49.6	44.0	9.99
2. Metals other than iron and steel and silver	22.7	19.3	53.1	6.26
3. Machinery	37.4	26.1	44.5	40.67
4. Motor cars, cycles, scooters, chassis, omnibuses, vans, lorries and parts thereof	78.9	63.2	43.7	3.52
5. Chemicals	37.6	25.1	43.2	6.48
6. Petroleum products	204.7	132.2	16.7	4.40
7. Raw cotton	12.9	3.2	43.9	5.14
8. Artificial silk yarn and thread	217.0	176.7	37.5	0.91
9. Wood pulp, paper and stationery	51.1	50.9	57.3	1.99
10. Cinematographic films	66.4	37.0	29.7	0.26
11. Spirits and liquors	537.8	929.6	154.3	0.04
12. Spices	68.3	—	−7.0	0.05
13. Tobacco	1330.0	600.0	−31.3	0.03
14. All others	67.0	57.1	48.3	20.26
15. Total	53.9	39.6	42.3[b]	100.00

SOURCES: Directorate General of Commercial Intelligence and Statistics, and Ministry of Petroleum and Chemicals, Government of India, New Delhi.

Explanatory Memorandum to the Central Government Budget, Government of India, New Delhi, for data on duty collections.

a. The effective duty rates reported in columns (2) and (3) are obtained by dividing duty collection by the value of imports. Though devaluation took place on June 6, 1966, the effective rate for the year 1965–66, ending on March 31, 1966, has been identified with the pre-devaluation rate and that for the year 1966–67, starting from April 1, 1966, with the post-devaluation rate. To the extent that the pre-devaluation rates were higher than post-devaluation rates, this procedure will overstate the pre-devaluation rates. Even though this procedure yields a weighted average rate for each group of items, the weights are not the same in the two years—each year's rates are weighted by that year's imports.

b. The figure in column (4) is obtained as follows: $\dfrac{157.5\,[1 + \text{col. (3)}]}{[1 + \text{col. (2)}]}$. If we compute it instead as: $57.5 - [\text{col. (2)} - \text{col. (3)}]$, the total figure changes only to 43.2 percent.

change, we then arrive at −52.5 percent as the *reduction* in the incentive to remit.

Since (inward) remittances during 1964–66 were 30.8 percent of the invisible earnings and since invisible earnings other than remitttances had not been subsidized in any way prior to the devaluation, we can arrive at a weighted, net devaluation figure of 25.6 percent for invisibles (earnings).

Imports.

We must now adjust the estimate of the devaluation on the side of imports by netting out the effect of the reduction in import duties.

A number of tariffs were reduced at the time of the devaluation. There were changes in standard as well as preferential tariff rates. However, data on imports are not readily available according to the duty rates applicable. We have therefore used the ratio of duty collected to the value of imports as an approximate measure of effective duty rates.

We then quantify the change in the degree of effective devaluation due to these tariff changes by weighting the duty reductions by the share of these items in total imports during 1964–66. We have done this in Table 6–4. The resulting weighted-net-devaluation is 42.3 percent for imports, adjusted for both the duty changes and the parity change.

If we bring in also the invisibles (payments), to which only the parity change was relevant, the net devaluation figure (for the *entire* current account payments) rises to 44.8 percent.

Total Net Devaluation.

The total net devaluation on the (visible) trade account therefore may be approximated as amounting to: 21.6 percent for exports and 42.3 percent for imports. For the entire current account (including invisibles), the estimates are: 22.3 percent for receipts and 44.8 percent for payments.[9]

NOTES

1. Conversely, computed as the decrease in the dollar value of the rupee, the devaluation was 36.5 percent.
2. Remember that we are *not* estimating the net change in the incentive *in toto*. To do so we would have to allow for the effects of changes in import costs of raw materials, for example, as well as for macro-effects on the price level.
3. For a detailed discussion of these schemes and the limitations of calculating *ad valorem* rates in the manner described above, see Chapter 3. See also Bhagwati and Desai, *India,* pp. 396–450.
4. We should warn the reader that owing to the suspension of aid, these premia

were exceptionally high. We adjust for this fact in assessing the impact of the devaluation on export performance, etc., in later chapters.

5. See Tables 19.7 and 19.8, Bhagwati and Desai, *India*, p. 433.

6. See Mark Frankena, "Export of Engineering Goods from India" (Ph.D. dissertation, MIT, 1971), Table III–8, for details of these subsidies.

7. Note that we have ignored the very small entitlements that were received prior to devaluation by some of the commodities in (1)–(14). For example, tea had an entitlement rate of 1 percent of f.o.b. value prior to devaluation. No significant error in our estimates would occur from these procedures. We should re-emphasize, however, that our estimates conceal much variation among *individual* exports *within* the 51 groups listed.

8. The basic data are in Bhagwati and Desai, *India*, pp. 469–470.

9. In Table 6–3 we have treated all items for which no explicit export promotion schemes were operating prior to devaluation as items for which full parity change (except for tax credit elimination) is applicable. If we exclude these items from total exports, the net devaluation on exports goes down to 16.9 percent and on total current account receipts to 18.7 percent.

Chapter 7

Revival and Expansion of Export Subsidies during 1966-70

Although the June 1966 devaluation was accompanied, as we have seen, by the elimination of the budgetary tax credits and the import entitlement schemes, the ensuing period was characterized by a steady growth of export subsidization, again largely of a selective and variable nature and embodying, in practice, many of the features of the schemes prior to devaluation.

We shall first trace the major developments, organizing our analysis by type of subsidization rather than by strict chronology. Next, these diverse subsidies will be quantified with a view to determining the degree of subsidization they provided at different points in time, so that both their importance and their effects on export performance can be assessed.

METHODS OF SUBSIDIZATION

Cash Subsidies.

The major change in methods of export subsidization in the post-devaluation period was the large-scale introduction of cash subsidies on an *explicit* basis. These were introduced in August 1966 for most engineering goods and chemicals and were successively extended to a number of items. By the end of 1967, they embraced the bulk of engineering goods, chemicals, processed foods, paper products, sports goods, woolen carpets, steel scrap, prime iron and steel, and cotton textiles, yarn and "made-up" goods amounting to over 15 percent of total exports in 1964–65 and 1965–66.

1. The subsidies were *selective*. They ranged from 10 to 25 percent *ad valorem*.[1] In contrast to the main thrust of the pre-devaluation subsidies, therefore, the selectivity was clearly narrower, confined to a very limited number of rates. As *between* the different groups, the range was again narrower than before, from 2 to 25 percent. However, the inter-group differences in rates were not altogether negligible. Cotton piece goods had subsidies ranging from 2 to 8.5 percent; made-up cotton goods generally carried 4.25 percent; steel scrap had 5 percent; biscuits had 3 percent; confectionery was 17 percent; and 25 percent applied to many engineering goods.

2. Furthermore, there is unmistakable evidence that the export subsidies were adjustable upward, not merely by explicit changes in the rates in periodic announcements, but also by special dispensation if the export order in question was "sizable." Frankena has shown, on the basis of interviews with leading exporters of engineering goods, that the government was willing to consider an *ad hoc* increase in cash subsidy when this was considered necessary to secure (i.e., to induce an exporter to quote a low enough price on) an export order worth $0.67 million or more, and there are several cases where additional cash subsidies of 2.5 to 5 percent of the f.o.b. value were given.

Import Replenishments.

Although the import entitlement schemes were abolished with devaluation, they were soon replaced in August 1966 by import replenishment schemes. Under the latter, exporters were again assigned import licenses of a value which was a pre-specified percentage of the f.o.b. export value. While the two schemes were virtually alike in their modes of operation, except for a few differences to be noted shortly, the major difference was supposed to be that the replenishment licenses merely replaced the supposed import content of the export whereas the entitlement licenses were alleged to have been generally at *twice* this import-content value (and hence embodying an element of "open" subsidy).

Of course, in a situation where imports carry a scarcity premium, a replenishment license will also amount to a subsidy on exports. And we must therefore take it into account in estimating total export subsidization in the Indian economy.[2] The "equivalent" *ad valorem* subsidy may further be approximated by multiplying the replenishment rate by the premium at which the replenishment license can be sold.[3]

It is significant that, despite the intention to differentiate the replenishment scheme from the earlier entitlement schemes, many features of the latter were quickly to emerge in the former:

1. The *transferability* of the licenses was subjected to control, as before. We have already noted the irrational nature of the restrictions on transfer-

ability of licenses as among the numerous entitlement schemes. Identical restrictions were to be carried over into the replenishment schemes, thereby lowering the subsidy-worth of the scheme and also making its operation cumbersome without any justifying rationale.

2. Furthermore, just as the rule that the entitlements should be twice the import-content was rarely observed in practice, and in fact was violated in favor of larger allotments, the available evidence points to identical tendencies of the replenishments to go well beyond the value of the (direct) import-content. Thus, Frankena has found that in many cases, including machine tools, stationary diesel engines, electric fans, sewing machines and certain chemicals, the face value of licenses was considerably greater than the average current import-content of the exported product.

3. The restrictions on transferability were accompanied by restrictions on *what could be imported,* in common with the entitlement schemes. Again, as with the latter, these restrictions were occasionally evaded by the authorities. Further, the early entitlement scheme restrictions on eligible imports had already been weakened over time—especially in that exporters were allowed to import items other than those identified as the direct import-content of the exported products, provided they were direct inputs into what the exporter produced *altogether* (e.g., he may have a multi-product operation) or into items produced by the entire export promotion *group* (e.g., plastics) within which the entitlements had eventually come to be transferable. The same pattern of (restricted) eligibility was to be carried over into the replenishment schemes; and no further "liberalization" was permitted in principle.

4. Aside from the fact that "banned" items were occasionally made available under the replenishment licenses, these licenses carried a premium in the market (despite the import liberalization during the post-devaluation period) in part due to the fact that they were not source-tied as against the AU licenses which frequently made imports possible only against (higher-cost) source-tied aid.[4]

The only respect in which the replenishment scheme appears to have been different from the entitlement scheme is in the relative stability of the rates (which, as before, were set as a percentage of f.o.b. export value). In addition, exports to the Soviet bloc were to become eligible for replenishment with free-foreign-exchange licenses.

Supply of Indigenous Materials at International Prices.

Although the idea of supplying domestic materials at international prices for export purposes had been conceived and implemented in respect to the supply of iron, steel and tinplate to the engineering industry, prior to the devaluation, it was adopted at a significant level in May 1967 for the supply of iron and steel with eligibility for all manufacturers using primary iron and steel.

These schemes eventually were to extend to winding wires, PVC resin and aluminum as well. However, as Frankena has noted, the latter schemes were not operated with the same efficacy as the steel scheme. Thus, the PVC resin scheme during 1969 and 1970, under which some raw materials for plastics and cable insulation were supplied at international prices, required an *offsetting* transfer by the exporter of part of his replenishment licenses to the supplier of these materials—thus reducing the subsidy on that front. Further, in some cases, as with aluminum supplies to user-exporters at international prices, this meant an effective subsidy to the users but, on the other hand, the sale of aluminum at these concessional prices was counted as an offset against export obligations of the aluminum producers. Furthermore, some of the concessions were not of durable value, since they were based on informal agreements with the government rather than legislation. For example, in 1967 the manufacturers of winding wires agreed to give a price concession to exporter-manufacturers of electrical equipment such as fans, motors and transformers; in 1969 several manufacturers of winding wires were withholding such a price concession to user-exporters.

The steel scheme did work more effectively, however, as it was based on the principle of direct subsidization of the steel price.[5] And the subsidy element in the scheme was indeed positive (as quantified in the next section) since the domestic steel prices exceeded the foreign prices—until the rise in international steel prices above the Indian control prices in late 1969.

Unfortunately, however, the scheme had drawbacks similar to those of the other subsidy schemes we have just reviewed. The subsidy was restricted (without any economic rationale that we can find) to steel of certain kinds, and again to steel produced by certain major producers; and there were administrative delays.

Other Subsidies.

In addition to the three forms of subsidization reviewed above, the post-1966 period was characterized by three other measures which amounted to direct subsidization of the export sector: (1) drawbacks and rebates on import and excise duties paid on direct inputs; (2) subsidization through the State Trading Corporation of a growing range of exports; and (3) subsidization of freight rates.

Furthermore, numerous *indirect* subsidies operated at different levels, in a variety of guises. Thus preferences were increasingly granted to exporting firms in respect of (1) AU and CG licenses on volume and source-tying, (2) facilities to invest abroad, (3) licenses to expand capacity domestically and (4) supply of rationed inputs.

Moreover, the government occasionally resorted to policies aimed at "taxing" the firms which did *not* export, by (1) requiring penalty-carrying export obligations prior to licensing, for example, and (2) actually penalizing firms (by denial of AU licenses, etc.) in certain industries when they did not export pre-specified shares of their estimated production.[6]

We review all these policies, in turn.

DRAWBACKS AND REBATES

The refund of excise and import duties on direct inputs into exports pre-dated the devaluation, as we already know from Chapter 3. These policies were continued into the post-devaluation period.

STATE TRADING CORPORATION

Effective export subsidization had also occurred in regard to products such as rice, sugar, art silk fabrics and jute goods. The State Trading Corporation (STC) sold these exports at losses which were financed by profits that arose from imports canalized through the STC. This policy was also carried into the post-devaluation period.

SUBSIDIZATION OF FREIGHT, MARKETING AND CREDIT

The pre-devaluation subsidies had extended to freight concessions to exporters in the hinterland, grants to promote participation in exhibitions abroad, and credit concessions. These policies were to continue into the post-devaluation period. Thus, in the engineering goods sector, transportation to a port more than 200 miles distant normally entitled the exporter to rail freight concessions up to 50 percent.

The marketing promotional subsidies extended not merely to participation in foreign exhibitions and overseas expenses, but also to visits of foreign delegations to India. There were also income tax concessions for all export marketing expenditures. In addition, the government continued to expand credit facilities to exporters. Thus, during 1967, the Reserve Bank of India began to charge a concessional rate of 4.5 percent to commercial banks for refinancing facilities relating to the pre-shipment and post-shipment advances made by banks to exporters. During 1969, export credits up to 10 years at 6 percent by exporters were subsidized provided certain conditions were fulfilled relating to low import-content and repayment in hard currency. Even these conditions were occasionally waived.

PREFERENTIAL SUPPLY OF RATIONED INPUTS

Since scarcity cannot always be meaningfully translated into dearness, it is useful to mention here government allotments of rationed materials to exporters on a preferential basis. In addition to the scheme for supplying indigenous steel at concessional, international prices, the supply of scarce and rationed iron and steel to exporters was accorded high priority in principle. This was also the case with aluminum, cycle tires and materials for tires and plastics. However, no quantitatively spelled-out policy in this regard can be discerned in the policy announcements during the post-devaluation period.

Preferential Licensing to Expand Capacity and to Utilize Existing Capacity

Preferential allocation of AU and CG licenses to firms that export was also to become an explicit and an important part of government export-promotion policy in the post-devaluation period. Thus, in 1968, engineering firms exporting more than 10 percent of their production were made eligible for such treatment by an announcement from the Ministry of Foreign Trade, and later in 1968 the Ministry announced that licenses of the value of $2.7 million had already been issued to 46 export-oriented industrial firms.[7] Moreover, in 1969, the government allowed firms exporting more than 10 percent of their output to import (under their AU allocations) from preferred sources. During 1970–71 firms which exported 25 percent of output in 1969 were given all AU licenses for import against free foreign exchange (source-untied), firms which exported 10 to 25 percent were given two-thirds of their AU licenses to import with untied funds and firms which exported less than 10 percent were given only half their AU licenses to import with untied funds.

Preferential Treatment for Foreign Collaboration

Among the important preferential treatments promised to exporting firms was the possibility of a more lenient attitude toward them when foreign collaboration was sought. The leniency was sought in the direction, not merely of expediting decisions, but also in the sense of permitting collaboration in "non-priority" industries and even in industries such as "trade" where collaboration was traditionally banned. In fact, in several such cases the government actually went so far as to make a formal export obligation a pre-condition for approving a foreign collaboration or investment, as with IBM and Coca-Cola prior to devaluation.

Preferential Treatment Regarding Foreign Investment by Exporters

The government also gave preference to exporters for investing abroad. This privilege was of value to firms (1) whose domestic investment outlets were being restricted—the case with the Large Industrial Houses under the revised industrial licensing policy aimed at stricter, effective control of their expansion; (2) who found foreign investments more profitable than domestic investments; and (3) who were seeking effective ways to export capital illegally, a process somewhat facilitated if the firm had foreign equity investments.

This preference took basically the form of permitting firms to purchase equity in a foreign enterprise when this resulted in the sale of machinery exports by the firm to this foreign enterprise. It was thus of value mainly to exporters of machinery and hence more restricted in scope than the other policies we have been reviewing. However, on occasion it could extend to firms not themselves exporting machinery (e.g., Oberoi Hotels) or to more complex deals.

PENALTIES FOR NON-EXPORTING FIRMS

As we have noted, government policy embraced contractual export obligations prior to permission to construct or expand capacity, with or without foreign collaboration, and in "priority" and "non-priority" industries. In addition, the government also resorted to an explicit policy of pressing producers in several of the (59) priority industries (to which import liberalization since June 1966 had been extended) to export at least 5 percent of total production or to face *de facto* penalties in the form of reduced AU allocations, restrictive source-tying of import licenses and refusal to expand output. This policy pre-dated the devaluation on an informal *ad hoc* basis; but it was formalized in 1968 and 1969.[8]

Clearly, therefore, the post-devaluation period was to witness an active resumption and expansion of export subsidization programs.[9] We now proceed to quantify their magnitude.

QUANTIFICATION OF SUBSIDIZATION

The analysis in the preceding section has already indicated the complex nature of export subsidization even subsequent to the devaluation of June 1966. Unfortunately, this complexity is so considerable, especially in view of the number of rates of cash subsidy and replenishment licenses and the vastly greater number of premia on import replenishment licenses, that we must warn the reader that the (partial) quantification of the export incentives which we now attempt must be regarded as indicative only of broad orders of magnitude and as enabling us to assess *broadly* the trends in export performance since the devaluation.[10] One should properly regard the great difficulty of developing reliable measures of effective subsidy rates in an economic regime of the type India possesses, and the consequent inability of the government to undertake any systematic analysis of export policy and results, as an important and particularly unfortunate consequence of such regimes.

Cash Assistance.

Broad orders of magnitude concerning subsidies in the form of cash assistance may be provided for engineering goods, chemicals and other groups.

Frankena's detailed study of the engineering industry in India gives (among other things) the major cash subsidy rates for 1969–70 for 80 percent of the engineering exports in 1969. By weighting the subsidy rates by the relative share in exports, we estimate the average cash subsidy rate for engineering goods (plus iron and steel) as 12.4 percent during 1969–70 and as 17.6 percent for engineering goods (excluding iron and steel).[11]

We have also put together the cash subsidy rates for the entire post-devaluation period by the detailed classification by-product that is actually used to operate the scheme and which distinguishes among nearly 300 product-types. Unfortunately, while we did have these subsidy rates, we could not obtain a comparable classification for exports and therefore the export-share-weighted average cash subsidy rates which we wished to calculate (by even a rough-and-ready regrouping of exports by the subsidy-classification) could not be computed despite our attempts at securing the necessary information.

Domestic Materials at International Prices.

The principal scheme for providing exporters with inputs at international prices related to the supply of steel to the engineering industry. Quantifying this incentive as an *ad valorem* equivalent subsidy on exports of engineering goods required that we obtain the international London Metal Exchange (LME) prices for different types of steel, the corresponding domestic Joint Plant Committee (JPC) prices, multiply the difference (when $LME < JPC$ prices) by the corresponding a_{ij} coefficients for the relevant steel inputs into engineering goods and then divide by the unit f.o.b. value of engineering goods exports.

The average (unweighted) subsidy implied by the difference between international and domestic prices of various categories of steel appears to have varied from zero during January–March 1970 to a high of 25 percent during October 1968–March 1969.[12] The cost of steel input as a proportion of total cost of production of engineering goods is estimated to be about 15 percent.[13] Thus, at its maximum value of 25 percent, the subsidy on steel input to the engineering sector amounted to about 4 percent of the domestic cost of production. If we assume that the f.o.b. price of exports of engineering goods was around 50 percent of the domestic cost—and this may not be too far out, as Frankena's estimated range is 50–75 percent—the steel input subsidy would then be of the order of 8 percent of f.o.b. prices.

This number compares reasonably well with Frankena's estimate of 14 percent subsidy for steel pipes, tubes, and fittings and 8 percent for transmission line towers and other fabricated steel structures for mid-1969.[14] Moreover, recent studies of selected exporting firms in 1968–69 indicate that, for railway wagon exports, the steel subsidy was more like 19 percent.[15]

Such schemes for providing materials at international prices apparently tended to increase during this period, and were of some importance for chemicals and plastics. Thus, in the plastics industry, raw materials such as low and high density polyethylene, PVC and polysterene were made available at international prices which were as much as 75 percent below the domestic price in some instances.[16]

Duty Drawbacks and Tax Rebates.

The import duty and indirect tax drawbacks and rebates had a vastly differential incidence among different products. Thus the different indirect tax rebates that were estimated for 1969 by Frankena in the engineering industry ranged from 2 percent of f.o.b. value to 49 percent. A more comprehensive sample survey during 1969–70, which noted the importance of such drawbacks and rebates for exporters of lamps and tubes, cables and wires, radio and auto accessories, tires and tubes and small tools, found this incentive to range from 2 to 60 percent during this period.[17]

We have found it impossible to arrive at a meaningful average figure for the export-subsidy equivalent of these benefits by different groups. We may note, however, that the export-share-weighted average rate for the engineering goods studied by Frankena for 1969 turns out to have been between 17.5 and 18 percent.[18] Thus, despite the continuing administrative difficulties attendant on getting this benefit, it would appear that it did provide a fairly sizable export incentive during the post-devaluation period.

State Trading Corporation Losses.

In terms of its announced policies, the STC was prepared during the post-devaluation period to absorb losses on exports of rice, sugar, copra extractions, coffee, fruit and vegetables, processed foods, art silk fabrics, jute goods, cement, plywood, figures and wired glass, sports goods and human hair. During 1969–70 to 1971–72, the major losses were absorbed in art silk fabrics and in jute goods. The export-share-weighted average subsidy on all STC exports assisted in this way, calculated as the ratio of losses to export value, was 14 percent in 1969–70 and 20 percent in 1970–71.[19] The subsidy rates, so calculated, on the two major items, art silk fabrics and jute goods, turn out to have been 23.5 percent and 10.5 percent, respectively, as an average for 1969–70 and 1970–71.

Overall Assessment.

Unfortunately it is nearly impossible to indicate even the orders of magnitude of the benefits implied by the other export incentives which we listed in the preceding section. Unpublished sample surveys and interviews during 1968 to 1970 strongly suggest that some of these other incentives may well have implied, for specific firms, incentives in the order of 10 to 20 percent on an *ad valorem* basis, particularly in the engineering industry.[20]

Thus, for example, the grant of "preferred-source" AU import licenses to exporting firms was important in machine tools, diesel engines, small tools, abrasives, tires and tubes, batteries and accessories and transformers, among other products, in 1969–70. The preference for expansion of capacities was claimed to be of importance by the interviewed firms in batteries, tires and tubes and electric lamps, where there was fuller capacity utilization. The occasional ability to procure banned and restricted items under AU imports against export performance also improved profitability in some instances.

The vast complexity of the total "package" of export assistance thus precludes any citing of a reliable number as *the* "effective" equivalent *ad valorem* export subsidy rate during the different years since the devaluation. It is clear, however, that in engineering goods in particular and to a large ex-

TABLE 7–1

**Approximate Range of Average Subsidy of Selected Exports
since the 1966 Devaluation**

Scheme	Range of Effective, Equivalent Export Subsidy (% of f.o.b.)
1. Cash subsidies	15–20
2. Import replenishment licenses	15–30
3. Domestic materials at international prices[a]	5–15
4. Drawbacks and rebates	10–20
5. Preferential licensing	10–20
6. Total range[b] (i)	50–90
(ii)	55–105

NOTE: These average rates apply mainly to the groups: engineering goods, chemicals and plastics, as mentioned in the text. They conceal considerable variation among individual products. Also note that there are products which are known to have had subsidies outside of the figures we have put down, so that we are indicating only what appear to us, on the basis of the foregoing analysis, to be the average orders of magnitude in subsidization on each account since 1966; and further, that in many of the categories the subsidization moved upwards toward the upper end of the range with the lapse of time.

a. Recall that these are important only for steel and some plastic inputs.

b. (i) excludes row (3) and (ii) includes it. STC losses are excluded from these totals but should be added for art silk fabrics: they amount to 10 to 20 percent of f.o.b. values.

tent in chemicals, plastics and other "new" industries (i.e., sports goods, paper products and processed foods, in the main), the export incentives since devaluation must have averaged around 50 to 90 percent on an effective, *ad valorem* basis (Table 7–1).

NOTES

1. See S. N. Krishnan, *Export Incentives and the Exchange Rates* (New Delhi: USAID, 1967), for detailed statements of the subsidy rates in the two major groups, engineering and chemicals.

2. The notion that this is *not* a subsidy, however, seems to be prevalent in certain bureaucratic circles. It is partly an erroneous result of the notion, which has some economic rationale, that exports must be exempted from import duties on inputs.

3. There *are* qualifications to this method. However, as an approximation, it seems to be the best that can be managed empirically.

4. An additional advantage claimed by importers was that bureaucratic delays were less of a problem than they were with AU licenses. Further, multi-product firms could always use their replenishment licenses to import inputs for "non-priority" production within the firm, even when AU licenses for such purposes were restricted.

5. However, see qualifications below.

6. For some evidence, see Frankena, "Export," pp. 344–346.

7. *Ibid.*, p. 190.

8. Frankena states that "according to press reports, maintenance import licenses were cut 5 percent in 1969–70 for 250 firms in engineering and non-engineering industries and were to be reduced by 20 percent in 1970–71." *Ibid.*, p. 194.

9. We have not been able to secure any systematic and reliable evidence on whether the government sought to effectively subsidize exports by buying preferentially from exporting firms or whether public sector enterprises were *de facto* subsidized in order to promote foreign sale of their production. We should also mention that barter-deal trade which permitted exports at rather better prices than if they had been undertaken in freer markets and correspondingly involved similarly higher import prices in turn, could also be regarded as a form of export-subsidization.

10. In our statistical analysis of export performance in Chapter 9, therefore, we do not use these calculated subsidy rates as inputs into our regressions although it would have been useful to take the subsidy-inclusive export prices as an explanatory variable. Instead of using these rates, we have tried to estimate the impact of the liberalization package through dummy-variable analysis and to assess the results of this analysis in light of the necessarily very rough and broad orders of export subsidization developed in this section.

11. Note that where we did not have detailed breakdowns of exports by relevant subcategories we have used simple average cash subsidy rates and multiplied them by the overall export figure for a category, as with iron and steel. See Frankena, "Export," Table III–7.

12. The details on the domestic and international prices of some major types of steel during this period were acquired by us from the Ministry of Steel and the Engineering Export Promotion Council, Bombay.

13. This figure is obtained from the inter-industry flow table for the year 1964–65 prepared by M. R. Saluja of the Indian Statistical Institute, by dividing the cost of steel

input (at 1960–61 producer's prices) by the value of output (at 1960–61 producer's prices) of electrical equipment, non-electrical equipment, transport equipment and metal products. It is clear that the composition of production will not necessarily correspond to the composition of exports; however, to add this extra sophistication to our exercise would involve tremendous work and still a lot of guesswork.

14. Frankena, "Export," Table III–7. His overall estimate is 3 percent, p. 344.

15. This information is based on unpublished studies conducted by the Administrative Staff College of India, Hyderabad.

16. Thus, in 1968, the international price of low-density polyethylene was Rs. 1,900 per metric ton whereas the domestic price was Rs. 7,480; for polysterene, these prices were Rs. 1,800 and Rs. 6,460, respectively; and for PVC, they were Rs. 1,675 and Rs. 3,944, respectively. The full list of materials available in 1971 at international prices included low-density and high-density polyethylene, PVC resin, polysterene, phenol and urea formaldehyde molding powder and PVC.

17. Administrative Staff College at Hyderabad Sample Survey: results communicated to us in official interviews.

18. In this case, it makes little difference whether one includes or excludes iron and steel.

19. These calculations leave out the items which did not attract losses in the relevant year.

20. Frankena, "Export," p. 191. The author calculates a figure of 25 percent on one license. This underlines the fact that the figures in Table 7–1 represent, as we clearly emphasize, only broad and necessarily rough orders of magnitude.

Chapter 8

Devaluation, the Price Level and Economic Activity[1]

One of the common arguments against devaluation in India has been that it would be inflationary. If indeed this were the case, any price advantage that devaluation might confer in export markets would be blunted and might even be completely neutralized.

There was price inflation in India, at any rate since 1962–63, and the pace of price rise indeed quickened in 1966–67. This led some uncritical observers to attribute this phenomenon to devaluation on a *post hoc ergo propter hoc* basis. Hence it is necessary to examine the issue of the endogenous impact of the devaluation package on the price level carefully and in depth. Indeed, as we show presently, meaningful analysis of this question must bring in the effect of the abnormal drought in two consecutive years on cereal and raw material prices and through these on the prices of other commodities; and when we have done this, and considered other pertinent factors, the judgment reached on the issue of the impact of the devaluation package changes drastically.

First, let us examine the few pertinent facts that we have collected in Table 8–1. The major features there are: (1) the impact of the two consecutive droughts as reflected in the fall in real income originating in agriculture in 1965–66 and 1966–67 as compared with 1964–65; (2) the continued rise in the wholesale price index, a process that began in a sustained fashion from 1962–63; (3) a rise in the relative price of food articles as compared with the prices of manufactures in general and prices of equipment in particular; (4) a shift away from investment toward consumption in public sector expenditure; (5) a drastic fall in non-food aid disbursements net of debt service payments

111

TABLE 8–1
Key Economic Indicators, 1964–68

	1964–65	1965–66	1966–67	1967–68
1. Index number of wholesale prices (1961–62 = 100)				
All commodities	122.3	131.6	149.9	167.3
Cereals	112.0	135.2	146.2	173.7
Food articles	135.4	144.6	171.1	207.8
Raw materials	115.9	132.8	158.4	156.4
Manufactures	109.0	118.1	127.5	131.1
Cotton manufactures	109.6	114.4	121.6	128.9
Equipment	108.3	111.8	117.7	126.5
2. Public sector[a] (Rs. billions)				
Tax receipts of central, state and local government	26.94	30.48	34.26	36.38
Subsidies	1.47	1.91	4.12	3.55
Public consumption	20.05	22.96	24.96	27.80
Gross public investment	20.10	21.22	21.86	20.01
Net defense expenditure	8.06	8.85	9.09	9.68
Overall deficit	1.52	3.31	2.26	2.57
3. Private sector (Rs. billions)				
Consumption	178.49	180.02	213.18	256.85
Gross investment	17.55	21.60	24.01	28.01
4. Foreign trade[b] (U.S. $ millions)				
Exports	1,714	1,692	1,542	1,598
Imports	2,833	2,958	2,771	2,677
Of which: food	592	676	868	691
maintenance	1,684	1,726	1,393	1,508
complete machinery	435	438	363	289
iron and steel	219	205	131	142
non-ferrous metals	123	144	114	119
5. External assistance (U.S. $ millions)				
Gross aid disbursements	1,519	1,623	1,494	1,575
Of which: food aid	446	476	538	447
project aid	701	684	497	380
non-project aid	352	421	424	672
non-food PL 480 aid	20	42	35	76
Debt service	255	315	365	444
Net aid other than food	818	832	591	684

TABLE 8–1 (concluded)

	1964–65	1965–66	1966–67	1967–68
6. National income[c] (Rs. billions)				
At current prices	200.61	206.21	239.03	283.74
At 1960–61 prices	159.17	150.21	152.43	166.60
Of which: agriculture	72.24	61.45	60.94	71.93
others	86.93	88.76	91.49	94.67
7. Changes in money supply with the public (Rs. billions)	3.35	4.43	3.80	4.51
Of which (a) Reserve Bank net credit to government	1.36	3.98	1.89	1.66
(b) Commercial Bank holdings of government securities	1.41	1.14	0.83	0.96
(c) Total net bank credit to government [=(a)+(b)]	2.77	5.12	2.73	2.61
8. Some percentages				
i) $\dfrac{\text{Gross public investment}}{\text{Gross public outlay}}$	50.0	48.0	46.7	41.9
ii) $\dfrac{\text{Tax receipts}}{\text{National income}}$	13.4	14.8	14.3	12.8
iii) $\dfrac{\text{Gross domestic savings}}{\text{Gross domestic product}}$	14.2	15.6	13.5	12.2

SOURCES: *Economic Survey, 1967–68* and *1968–69*, Government of India, Ministry of Finance, Department of Economic Affairs, New Delhi.

Estimates of National Product, 1960–61 to 1969–70 and *Index Numbers of Whole-sale Prices in India,* annual numbers from 1962 to 1970, Government of India, New Delhi.

a. The total expenditure exceeds tax receipts plus the overall deficit because of non-tax revenue and capital receipts consisting of domestic and external borrowing.

b. Maintenance imports consist of intermediates, raw materials, spares and components of machinery. Therefore, they also include iron and steel as well as non-ferrous metals.

c. Provisional estimates, except for 1964–65.

after 1965–66; (6) a fall in exports as well as imports, particularly imports of complete machinery; and (7) a fall in the ratio of tax receipts to national income and gross domestic savings to gross domestic product. In analyzing this picture we shall attempt, to the extent possible, to separate the effect of the drought.

EFFECT OF THE DROUGHT ON PRICES

It appears that the prices of manufactures are determined by cost considerations since they are very closely related to the prices of industrial raw materials. However, the element of the cost-push mechanism that operates through the presumed relationship between *wages* and prices of food articles appears to be weak. This is seen from the following relationship:

$$(M_f)_t = 56.6215 + 0.0267f_{t-1} + 0.5050R_t - 8.1552D_t \qquad (8-1)$$
$$\quad\;\; (24.2922)\; (0.6332)\qquad (10.2962)\quad (-4.5728)$$

$\bar{R}^2 = 0.9778$; D.W. $= 1.15$; period 1951–1952 to 1960–61 and 1962–63
   to 1970–71,

where $(M_f)_t$ is the index of wholesale prices of manufactures with base 1950–51 up to 1960–61 and with base 1961–62 beyond 1960–61, f_t is the index of wholesale prices of food articles with an identical shift in base, R_t is the index of wholesale prices of raw materials again with shift of base beyond 1960–61, and D_t is a dummy variable which takes the value zero up to and including 1960–61 and the value 1 beyond (the dummy having been introduced to reflect the change in the base of the price index in 1961–62). Only the coefficients of R_t and the dummy are significant. Replacing f_{t-1} by f_t in the above relationship yielded the same results—namely, that only the coefficients of prices of raw materials and the dummy were significant. This is not surprising, since the prices of raw materials are closely correlated with those of food articles, a relationship which is the consequence of the fact that a large proportion of the raw materials is agriculture-based and factors that affect agriculture in general affect both the availability of raw materials and food articles similarly. This relationship is as follows:

$$R_t = 11.9317 + 0.6422f_t + 0.1789f_{t-1} - 0.8396D_t \qquad (8-2)$$
$$\quad\;\; (1.22)\quad\;\; (2.56)\qquad (0.75)\qquad (-0.97)$$

$\bar{R}^2 = 0.9097$; D.W. $= 1.57$; period 1952–53 to 1960–61, 1962–63 to
   1970–71.

Thus an explanation of the behavior of prices in the Indian economy has to be sought in an explanation of the behavior of the prices of food articles. Since foodgrains in general, and cereals in particular, form an overwhelming proportion of the consumer budget, cereals have a large weight in the index of prices of food articles.

We now turn to a simple simultaneous equation model to explain the prices of cereals. In a poor peasant economy such as India's, the bulk of the output of food crops gets consumed on the farm and never gets to the market.

But for explaining the behavior of food prices, the marketed portion of the output is relevant. Unfortunately, there is no time series available on marketed surplus. Some data on market arrivals in selected markets are available but the number of markets on which these are based have varied over time. However, Pranab and Kalpana Bardhan have constructed a time series of marketed surplus of cereals based on the National Sample Survey data on consumption expenditure.[2] Their series runs only up to 1964–65. We have extended it to later years by assuming that the marketed surplus changed in the same proportion as market arrivals of major cereals (fortunately, the number of markets on which the arrivals data are based has remained the same since 1964–65).

The behavioral model we have estimated is the following:

$$y_t = \alpha_0 + \alpha_1 Y_{At} + \alpha_2 P_t + u_t \qquad (8\text{--}3)$$
$$y_t + z_t = \rho_0 + \rho_1 Y_{NAt} + \rho_2 P_t + v_t \qquad (8\text{--}4)$$

where the endogenous variables are y_t, the marketed surplus of cereals, and P_t the wholesale price of cereals relative to that of cotton manufactures.[3] The exogenous variables are Y_{At}, the real income originating in agriculture; Y_{NAt}, the real non-agricultural income (both incomes being measured in units of 1 billion rupees); and z_t, the imports of foodgrains (in million tons). In the first equation, which is the supply equation, we postulate that marketed surplus is related to real agricultural income and the relative price of cereals. In the second equation—the demand equation—demand is related to relative prices of cereals and real non-agricultural income. The reduced form equation for P_t was estimated as:

$$P_t = 0.9030 + 0.0135 Y_{NAt} - 0.0133 Y_{At} - 0.0193 z_t \qquad (8\text{--}5)$$
$$(3.26) \quad (4.18) \qquad\qquad (-1.99) \qquad (-1.31)$$

$$\bar{R}^2 = 0.6154; \text{ period 1952--53 to 1969--70.}$$

The two-stage least squares estimates of the two structural equations are:

$$y_t = 5.6380 + 0.3707 P_t + 0.1828 Y_{At}, \quad \bar{R}^2 = 0.2939 \qquad (8\text{--}6)$$
$$(1.40) \quad (0.10) \qquad (2.40) \qquad \text{D.W.} = 1.91$$

$$y_t + z_t = 16.8539 - 12.4023 P_t + 0.2341 Y_{NAt}, \quad \bar{R}^2 = 0.8383 \quad (8\text{--}7)$$
$$(7.01) \quad (-2.49) \qquad (5.84) \qquad\quad \text{D.W.} = 2.30$$

In the supply equation, the relative price variable is not significant while the income variable is. In the demand equation, both the relative price and income variables are significant.

The reduced form equation for P_t can be used to assess the effect of the drought on the prices of cereals. This we do as follows. First, we get an estimate of the expected value of P_t under the assumption that real income originating in agriculture *maintained* the level attained in 1964–65 both in

TABLE 8–2
Index of Cereal Prices, 1964–67

Year (1)	Observed Value (2)	With Actual Values of Y_{At} (3)	With 1964–65 Values of Y_{At} for 1965–66 and 1966–67 (4)	With Trend Values of Y_{At} (5)
1964–65	139.3	133.6	133.6	135.3
1965–66	148.0	153.4	133.1	131.3
1966–67	175.8	175.0	152.3	146.3

SOURCE: Equations 8–5, 8–6 and 8–7.

1966–67 and 1967–68 as contrasted with the fall of 14.9 and 15.7 percent, respectively, in these two years. We convert these expected values of P_t to an expected value of index of cereal prices by multiplying by the observed value of the index of prices of cotton manufactures in these two years. (As mentioned earlier, the prices of manufactures in general and prices of cotton manufactures in particular are mainly influenced by the prices of raw materials. In the case of cotton manufactures, the basic raw material is cotton and raw cotton prices did rise, particularly in 1966–67, in response to lower output due to the drought. Thus, by using the observed prices of cotton manufactures in obtaining the expected values of index of cereal prices, we *are* understating the effect of drought somewhat since we are not removing the influence of drought on the prices of cotton manufactures.)[4] The picture that emerges is highlighted in Table 8–2.

Thus the expected prices of cereals should have been lower by approximately 10 percent in 1965–66 and 1966–67 had the drought not lowered real agricultural income (and hence the marketed surplus) in these years as compared with 1964–65. The above analysis suggests, therefore, that in the behavior of prices immediately after devaluation the effect of the two consecutive droughts of unprecedented proportion was the dominant one.[5]

ROLE OF MONETARY AND FISCAL POLICY

Not merely was a significant part of the post-devaluation price rise due to the exogenous fact of the droughts; in addition, the government's monetary and fiscal policies appear to have been designed to decelerate rather than accelerate the trend rise in expenditures and in money supply (which, in turn, largely reflects government spending as in many other LDCs). As will be evident from our discussion below, India was to experience an industrial recession together with a wage-goods price inflation brought about by the drought. And monetary and fiscal policy decisions were largely motivated by the fear of adding to the price rises resulting from the drought, rather than by considerations of the 1966 trade-and-exchange-rate policy package. In fact, the contractionary fiscal and monetary policy, so motivated, contributed significantly to the onset of the industrial recession, along with the shift in the *composition* (as distinct from the level) of government outlays away from investment to current expenditures (which resulted in reduced demand for the output of the capital goods sector).

1. The overall budgetary deficit of the Central and State governments *fell* from a level of Rs. 3.34 billion in the pre-devaluation year 'of 1965–66 to Rs. 2.26 billion and Rs. 2.57 billion, respectively, in the subsequent two years (Table 8–1). Though these are *ex-post* magnitudes, the budgeted or *ex-ante* deficits for 1966–67 and 1967–68 were even lower at Rs. .52 billion and Rs. .89 billion, respectively.

2. Furthermore, the money supply with the public increased by Rs. 3.8 billion and Rs. 4.51 billion, respectively, in the two post-devaluation years as compared with a rise of Rs. 4.44 billion in the pre-devaluation year of 1965–66. Further, a major element in the expansion of money in India as in other less developed countries—namely, increase in net bank credit to government—*fell* from Rs. 5.12 billion in 1965–66 to Rs. 2.73 billion and Rs. 2.61 billion in the subsequent two years.

It is, of course, of interest to note also that the effect of the fiscal and monetary contraction was accentuated by an accompanying shift in the *composition* of government outlays. As is clear from Table 8–1, the pattern of outlays shifted in favor of current expenditure and among the significant reductions in government outlays was a cutback on railway expansion. This accentuated the deflationary impact of the fiscal policy because, on balance, it must have implied that expenditure was shifting from items such as capital goods where output fell in consequence (as we shall discuss in greater depth) to items such as food where output could not increase owing to short-run production constraints. Thus, investment in the industrial sector decelerated on an accelerator-type mechanism whereas there was no offsetting impact through incremental outlays in agriculture. On balance, therefore, the effect of the shift in the composition of outlays must have been to accentuate the deflationary effect of decelerating government total outlays on production and investment.

Both the deceleration in total outlays and the compositional shift which we have just discussed were to be traced to two causes: one exogenous and major, and the other endogenous and only *minor* and possibly contributory, to the June 1966 policy package. The exogenous and principal factor was again the agricultural drought. It is clear from policy pronouncements (e.g., in the annual *Economic Survey* following the devaluation) that the government was afraid that any sustenance of the trend expansion in outlays would accentuate the rise in food prices that followed from the drought; and the same fears clearly dictated that, while current outlays could not be reduced (e.g., wages in the bureaucracy could not be controlled in a situation of risen prices without serious unrest), capital outlays could be axed without serious difficulty.

But the deflationary policy *may,* to a very small degree, have been inspired by the devaluation decision itself. There is some (though not considerable) evidence, in the writings of both the relevant Ministries and of outside economists, that the devaluation was thought to be necessarily inflationary. This belief, of course, stems from thinking in terms of the standard model of devaluation analysis, beginning with Alexander, Tinbergen and Meade's work, that devaluation is likely to switch expenditure from foreign to domestic goods and that, for this policy to lead to improvement in the balance of payments, an offsetting deflationary policy is necessary. This view ignores one critical element in LDC devaluations—namely, that the inflow of aid implies that the immediate effect of the devaluation is likely to be significantly deflationary because imports often exceed exports by a factor of even two. Also, the fact that the net, as distinct from the gross, devaluation was not quite as great as was commonly believed, as our estimates in Chapter 6 have shown, implied that any need for such a compensatory deflationary policy was correspondingly less, *ceteris paribus.*

On balance, we conclude that government decisions with respect to monetary and fiscal policy were quite naturally motivated by fear of inflation, prompted almost exclusively by the effects of the (exogenous factor of the) drought.

RECESSION AND INFLATION

We thus had the curious combination of a recessionary situation, with production and investment at reduced levels in the two years following the June 1966 change, along with an accelerated price increase. The latter was, as we have argued, very much the result of the droughts. And the former, as we have briefly indicated above and argue more substantively below, was equally so. Indeed, if anything, we argue presently that the June 1966 policy package mildly improved the level of industrial production and, in the same fashion, may have had a favorable (even if negligible) impact on investment. To this analysis we now turn.

EFFECT ON PRODUCTION

The (short-run) effect of the devaluation-cum-liberalization package of June 1966 on overall production can be analyzed by distinguishing four areas of activity.

TABLE 8–3

Index of Production (1949–50 = 100):
Actual and Estimated Trend Values
for 1965–66 and 1966–67

	1965–66			1966–67		
Crop (1)	Trend Value (2)	Actual Value (3)	Shortfall (percent) (4)	Trend Value (5)	Actual Value (6)	Shortfall (percent) (7)
Foodgrains	153.0	120.9	21.0	157.6	123.3	21.4
Cotton	230.4	183.0	20.6	240.9	191.1	20.7
Jute	183.6	135.5	26.2	190.0	162.4	14.5
Oilseeds	157.7	125.4	20.5	163.0	125.7	22.9

SOURCES: *Area, Production and Yield of Principal Crops in India, 1949–50 to 1967–68* and *Indian Agriculture in Brief*, 11th ed., 1971, Government of India, Ministry of Food and Agriculture, Directorate of Economics and Statistics, New Delhi.

Effect on Agricultural Output.

The behavior of agricultural production in the period immediately following the devaluation in June 1966 must be regarded as exogenous to the devaluation-cum-liberalization package. Indeed, the second consecutive drought in 1966–67 dominated agricultural performance as well as the performance of other sectors closely related to agriculture. The two droughts in the years 1965–66 and 1966–67 were no ordinary droughts, as the foregoing comparison (Table 8–3) of expected production (on the basis of observed exponential trends during the period 1949–50 to 1964–65) and actual values shows. These shortfalls, except in the case of jute in 1966–67, were statistically significant.

Effect on Agriculture-Based Industrial Outputs.

The index (with 1960 as base) of output of agro-based industries in the organized sector fell from a peak of 121.2 in 1965 successively to 120.0 and 114.7 in 1966 and 1967 and recovered to 118.3 in 1968. The impact of the drought on two of the major agro-based industries—namely, cotton textiles and jute textiles—can be estimated from the following two regressions:

Cotton textiles:
$$Q_{Tt} = 3289.7946 + 4.573 I_{Ct} - 0.9692 M_{Ct} + 21.6809 Y_t \quad (8\text{–}8)$$
$$(11.22) \quad\quad (1.79) \quad\quad (-0.79) \quad\quad (8.01)$$

$\bar{R}^2 = 0.93$ Period 1952–53 to 1969–70
D.W. = 2.05

Jute textiles:

$$Q_{Jt} = 604.7262 + 1.5320I_{Jt} + 1.9524I_{Jt-1} - 0.2168M_{Jt} \quad (8\text{--}9)$$
$$(2.71) \qquad (1.68) \qquad (2.33) \qquad (-0.59)$$

$$\bar{R}^2 = 0.41 \quad \text{Period 1952--53 to 1969--70}$$
$$\text{D.W.} = 1.07$$

where Q_{Tt}: Output of cotton textiles (mill and decentralized sectors), million meters

Y_t: Real national income (1960–61 prices), Rs. billion
I_{Ct}: Index of output of raw cotton (1949–50 = 100)
M_{Ct}: Imports of raw cotton, thousand tons
Q_{Jt}: Output of jute textiles, thousand tons
I_{Jt}: Index of output of raw jute (1949–50 = 100)
M_{Jt}: Imports of raw jute, thousand tons

The domestic raw material availability variables have the expected sign and are statistically significant (at 10 percent level or less) in both regressions.[6] One can conclude from these regressions that, *ceteris paribus,* had the outputs of raw cotton and raw jute been at their trend values in 1965–66 and 1966–67, the expected output would have been higher by 3.0 and 3.1 percent in the case of cotton textiles and by 6.4 and 12.3 percent in the case of jute textiles in the two years. In addition to this downward pressure on the output of these two industries on the supply side, there was a downward pressure on the demand side, particularly in the case of cotton textiles because of the drought-induced fall in per capita income (at 1960–61 prices) by 7.6 and 9.2 percent, respectively, in 1965–66 and 1966–67 as compared with 1964–65. Had there been no fall in income compared with 1964–65, the output of cotton textiles would have been higher by 2.7 and 2.0 percent, respectively, in 1965–66 and 1966–67, respectively. Thus the effect of the drought was to reduce the expected output of cotton textiles by at least 5.7 and 5.1 percent in these two years. We should further note that the effect of the drought on the output of jute textiles was reflected significantly in the export performance of this major traditional item.[7]

Effect on the Output of "Import-Intensive" Industries, Other than Capital Goods.

These industries include mainly chemical-based industries, some metal-based industries, and art silk manufactures. Production in all these industries should have, in principle, profited from the 1966 policy package, both because of the liberalized maintenance imports as promised in the package and because export subsidization was resumed soon after 1966. However, it turned out that maintenance imports (other than metals, components and parts of machinery) *fell* from a level Rs. 3,699 million (pre-devaluation) in 1965–66 to Rs. 3,488 million in 1966–67 and rose to Rs. 4,052 million and Rs. 4,189 million in 1967–68 and 1968–69, respectively. Further, there was a downward pressure on the domestic demand side since real income did not attain the levels reached in 1964–65 until 1967–68. Thus the following picture emerges:

TABLE 8–4

**Percentage Change from Preceding Year
in Production in Selected Import-Intensive Industries, 1965–66 to 1969–70**

(including capital goods)

	Weight[a]	1965–66	1966–67	1967–68	1968–69	1969–70
1. Metal-based of which:	16.55	+22.11	−10.58	−2.82	+5.71	+5.78
i. electrical machinery	3.05	+17.30	+10.10	+8.10	+14.00	+16.20
ii. non-electrical machinery	3.38	+46.50	−7.90	+2.80	+9.10	+6.90
iii. others	10.12	+15.41	−17.71	−7.99	+2.08	+2.27
2. Chemical-based	8.94	+5.57	+11.41	+5.33	+14.22	+10.31
3. Art silk fabrics	0.08	n.a.	−1.8	+6.4	+10.2	−14.6

SOURCE: Government of India, Department of Statistics, Central Statistical Organization, New Delhi.

a. In industrial production index.

Table 8–4 shows that the chemical-based industries, constituting a weight of 8.94 (out of a total of 100 in the industrial production index) managed to experience an increase of 11.41 percent in production in the year following the devaluation. This strongly suggests that the improved imported-input supply position and export incentive resumption since June 1966 helped bring about this outcome.[8] The output of metal-based industries (other than machinery), on the other hand, fell by 17.71 percent and the liberalization package does not seem to have helped this group. This result, however, may well be explained by an "over-expansion" during 1965–66 at 15.41 percent and by the fact (to be discussed in the next section) that the near decline in the output of the capital goods industries may well have had an indirect impact on the production performance of this group. The performance of art silk fabrics, whose weight in the industrial production index is less than 1 percent, also was one of absolute decline during 1966. The downward shift in real income caused by the drought and the diminished export incentives of the 1966 policy package must have offset improvements in the supply position that resulted from import liberalization for inputs.

On balance, therefore, we may conclude that the effect of the June 1966 policy package itself on production was favorable for chemicals and for metal-based industries other than machinery and perhaps mildly adverse for (the relatively insignificant) art silk fabrics, but that an improvement in production performance was registered only for chemicals and was offset by exogenous factors for the metal-based industries other than machinery.

Effect on the Output of Capital Goods (i.e., Machinery) Industries.

The capital goods industries, essentially a subgroup of the engineering industries group, were also part of the import-intensive industry group we have just analyzed, and therefore subject to the same influences. But the favorable effect on their production was heavily swamped by the fact of decelerating real investment which (as we have argued earlier) was again a factor virtually exogenous to the June 1966 policy package. This is seen readily by noting that Q_{It}, the index of capital goods production, has a strong and expected relationship with I_t, gross real investment, and with M_t, imports of complete machinery:

$$Q_{It} = -141.5980 + 0.1277 I_t - 0.0592 M_{It} \qquad (8\text{--}10)$$
$$(-4.03) \qquad (10.94) \qquad (-2.79)$$

$$\bar{R}^2 = 0.91; \text{D.W.} = 2.20$$

for the period 1960–61 to 1970–71, where Q_{It} = index of production of capital goods (1960 61 − 100); I_t = gross real investment, in Rs. 10 million at 1960–61 prices; and M_{It} = imports of capital goods in million U.S. dollars. If we use gross *fixed* real investment rather than gross real investment (inclusive of inventory changes), rewriting the variable as FI_t we get:

$$Q_{It} = -81.6576 + 0.1150 FI_t - 0.0484 M_{It} \qquad (8\text{--}11)$$
$$(-3.17) \qquad (12.96) \qquad (-2.70)$$

$$\bar{R}^2 = 0.9392; \text{D.W.} = 2.89$$

and it is evident that both regressions, (8–10) and (8–11), lead to similar conclusions. Thus it is clear that had gross investment been maintained at the value reached in 1965–66 rather than been allowed to drop by over 10 percent from that level during 1966–67 and 1967–68, the expected value of the index of capital goods production should have been significantly higher in these two years. In fact, we have calculated it, using both the above regressions (8–10) and (8–11), and have tabulated the results in Table 8–5. We see there that, if the investment levels had been maintained during 1966–67 and 1967–68 at the 1965–66 level, we should have had substantially im-

TABLE 8–5

Capital Goods Production Index under
Alternative Investment Estimates, 1966–68

		Expected Value of Index of Capital Goods Production		
Regression (1)	Year (2)	With observed values of the investment variables (3)	With the 1965–66 values of the investment variable for 1966–67 and 1967–68 (4)	Percentage increase of (4) over (3) (5)
(8–10)	1966–67	205.09	250.86	22.36
	1967–68	211.80	256.89	21.29
(8–11)	1966–67	196.82	251.92	27.99
	1967–68	221.53	256.84	15.94

NOTE: The investment estimates for 1965–66, 1966–67 and 1967–68, which we used for the computations reported in Table 8–5, are as follows:

Year	Gross Real Total Investment (Rs. millions at 1960–61 Prices)	Gross Real Fixed Investment (Rs. millions at 1960–61 Prices)
1965–66	34,400	32,330
1966–67	30,810	27,540
1967–68	30,870	27,260

SOURCE: Equations 8–10 and 8–11.

proved production of capital goods in the order of an average of over 25 and 18 percent increment in the capital goods production index, respectively.[9]

While, therefore, the output of the capital goods industries registered a decline induced by factors exogenous to the June 1966 policy changes, these policy changes themselves must have exercised a favorable impact on production. It will be recalled that the parity change and the resumption of export incentives as well as the easing of imported supplies of inputs very likely had an impact on the export of engineering goods, of which capital goods are a part.

EFFECT ON INVESTMENT

While, therefore, the effect of the June 1966 policy package (relating, of course, to trade and payments policies as distinct from the government's expenditure policy, consistent with our definitions in Chapter 5) on production appears to have been mildly favorable, though not anywhere near enough to offset the adverse effect of the drought, the effect on *investment* behavior is far more difficult to disentangle. This is because of two major difficulties: (1) the data on investment are very tenuous, and are not available by inter-industrial sectoral breakdown; and (2) the overall estimates of real investment, both total and as a percentage of national as well as industrial income, show a decline from pre-1966 levels *right through* to 1969–70, suggesting that there might be underestimation of investment and/or a trend decline which has probably nothing to do with the 1966 policy package as such. We begin by examining the probable causes of this decline in total, as well as in industrial, investment.

1. The decline in government capital outlays, reflecting both the deceleration in government total outlays and the shift away from capital expenditures, led (as we have seen) to a decline in the output of capital goods industries; it is likely also to have led to a decline in the investments in these industries. But this mechanism was triggered by the exogenous factor of the droughts and cannot be charged to the June 1966 policy package.

2. Another factor discussed in India to explain the decline in total and industrial investment, has been the so-called "Eastern Region" problem. It appears to be clear from the data on private, organized sector investment that the relatively anarchic character of West Bengal's politics (where there was, for a long time, neither a stable left-wing nor a stable alternative government) has led to a decline in private sector investments without an offsetting increase in government investments. This problem, arising from "anarchy in one state" (and one which could arise also if there was a stable "socialism in one state") is admittedly an important issue; but it is doubtful whether it can explain a significant decline in *total* investments, for many investments could have gone to other states, if not profitable in the Eastern region.

3. Another explanation could be that total investment did not decline quite as much in non-industrial activities as is indicated by the present estimates. Rather, it may represent underestimation of rural construction plus rural investments by farmers on their own farms. There are reasons to believe that the methods by which the Central Statistical Organization constructs its investment index would lead it to underestimate these two types of investment which apparently have, according to other indications, been the principal types of investments in rural areas, especially in light of the investment opportunities arising from the Green Revolution since 1964–65.

4. It is also conceivable, though not probable, that an increasing part of the rural incomes has gone into gold hoarding, implying acceleration in gold smuggling. The differential between the external and internal gold prices has not widened particularly. On the other hand, it is possible that this has been the result of increased diversion of remittances and funds from faked invoices to this channel of illegal entry into India.

5. An important contributory role appears to have been played by the effect of import liberalization in the period immediately following devaluation. As we note later at some length in Chapter 13, an important consequence of the import licensing mechanism was the creation of an incentive to add capacity in the face of under-utilized capacity in an industry. This was because the only way to get more imports of inputs (legally) was to add to (licensed) capacity. This incentive was largely eliminated as imports of raw materials were increased for many industries with the policy of import liberalization after the June 1966 devaluation and remained so for over two years before tightening began and *de jure* import liberalization became overlaid by *de facto* import deliberalization. Hence it was to be expected that plans to add to capacity (i.e., to invest) would receive a setback during this period.

6. The effect of the increased availability of imported raw materials and intermediates is likely to have been to depress the inducement to invest in some industries in yet another way. Increased production from under-utilized capacity, now feasible, could well lead to reduced prices, increased competition and lower profits. Jean Baneth has pointed out an extreme illustration in the case of the copper wire industry. All firms in it had been operating well below desired capacity utilization levels, but all of them were quite profitable. The devaluation, along with a coincidental sharp rise in world copper prices, more than doubled the cost of their main input. The firms, which had initially been happy to find that they could get as much copper as they wished, soon found that, given the existing vast under-utilization of capacity, a major over-supply situation developed which prevented these firms from substantially raising copper wire prices and greatly depressed their profit margins. The result was that some firms folded up (and others were pushed into exporting, a favorable effect which we shall note in Chapter 9 and the Appendix thereto). The net effect was clearly to depress the incentive to invest in this and other industries in a similar situation.

7. We may finally note here an additional factor which, while not particularly significant in the years immediately following the June 1966 policy package, possibly explains the continuing slack in industrial investment in the private sector beyond 1968–69. This factor relates to the industrial licensing policy of the government. With perfectly good intentions, the government loosened up the industrial licensing system, as we have discussed earlier, for a number of industries around June 1966. However, there were two major qualifications to this change, one of which appears to have affected the expansion of industrial investment in the country in the post-1966 period. (1) Industrial de-licensing was partly negated by the continuation of import licensing; thus the import licensing authorities became, *de facto,* industrial licensing authorities through their allocation of the imports necessary to production. (2) At the same time, the government, feeling that increasing concentration of economic power in the Large Industrial Houses should finally

be checked, was to combine these moves toward industrial de-licensing with greater restriction on the ability of the Large Houses to invest since 1968–69. These firms, which had provided earlier the major thrust of private investment (thus naturally attracting the criticisms that led to the restrictions just mentioned), were to be restricted to the so-called "core sector" of heavy and complex industries and to investment in the backward areas. At the same time, the establishment of the Monopolies and Restrictive Practices Commission in 1969 provided a further check on their expansion. Thus, the net result appears to have been to inhibit the investment by the Large Industrial Houses either by preventing it or by confining it to less lucrative areas such as heavy industry (where, as we have discussed, profitability was declining due to a shift of government outlays toward current expenditures) and backward regions. The nationalization of the principal banks in 1969, and the active pursuit of policy since then to encourage smaller business, should have compensated for this inhibition of Large House investments; clearly, however, it did not. It appears that the absolutely desirable policy of attempting to curb the social effects of Large Industrial House control of economic power was wrongly premised on restricting their investments when they alone seemed to have the necessary organization and skill to carry through investment on a sufficiently large scale. Instead the government would have been better advised to permit their investment programs, treating their investing ability as a national asset at the present time, and curbing the adverse social effects of their expansion by instruments such as a capital levy, stiffer wealth and inheritance taxes, the appointment of public interest directors to their boards, by the steady build-up of institutions to promote truly small-scale entrepreneurship, and by strengthening of the ability of the public sector to invest, save and run efficiently as definite objectives of a socio-economic policy.[10]

8. The decline in government savings and hence investment, in itself, constitutes a major part of the estimated decline in post-1966 savings, in addition to the seven possible reasons discussed above for decline in the private investment figures. This phenomenon seems to be attributable to the decline in foreign aid inflow, as well as to the inability to decrease the growth in defense and current outlays and the continuing failure of the public sector enterprises to generate profits.[11]

In short, there are several factors, none of them connected with the June 1966 policy package, which appear to have accounted for the stagnation in investment since 1966–67; and the role of the 1966 reforms in this unfortunate development in the economy appears to be almost nil. If anything, we might again argue that the net expansion in the post-1966 exports of the new manufactures, which our analysis picks up in Chapter 9, and which can be attributed in large part to the policy changes which were initiated (inclusive of the new export subsidies discussed in Chapter 7), may have encouraged some investment in these industries. However, we have no evidence on investments by industry breakdown to check this hypothesis.

OVERALL CONCLUSIONS

It would appear, therefore, that the basic developments in the price level, production and investment that dominated the economic scene in the two years following the June 1966 liberalization package (and indeed over the four years since the devaluation, in investment), were the product of factors that were substantially exogenous to the policy changes. In the main, the price rises were caused by the drought; the recession in production was also induced by the drought (in the sense we have discussed) and was not, as has sometimes been the case with LDC devaluations, the result of a concomitant "stabilization" policy aimed at an excessive deflation; and the investment decline was largely the result of complex factors interacting on the Indian economic scene.

NOTES

1. This chapter and the next were completed in December 1971 with the data *then* available. This is particularly relevant to our discussion of investment behavior and our statistical analysis of it. The regression results presented as part of our analysis are based on data obtained from the following branches of the Government of India, New Delhi:
   Basic Statistics Relating to the Indian Economy, 1950–51 to 1966–67, 1950–51 to 1968–69, 1950–51 to 1970, Department of Statistics.
   Economic Survey, annual issues, 1963–64 and 1972–73, Ministry of Finance, Department of Economic Affairs.
   Estimates of National Product, 1948–49 to 1962–63, Department of Statistics, Central Statistical Organization.
   Index Number of Wholesale Prices, various issues, Office of the Economics Adviser.
2. P. K. and K. Bardhan, "Price Response of Marketed Surplus of Foodgrains," *Oxford Economic Papers,* N. S. 23, no. 2 (July 1971).
3. In defining the relative price P_t, the price of cotton manufactures was used because cotton manufactures are a major consumer item and their price is highly correlated with the price index of manufactures in general.
4. The reason for not incorporating the effect of drought on prices of cotton textile manufactures through its effect on raw cotton prices is only that, for doing it satisfactorily, we need a more elaborate simultaneous equation model. In such a model raw-cotton prices will influence cotton manufacture prices and the latter will enter *non-linearly* in the relative price P_t used by us since it is the denominator of P_t.
5. We may emphasize the fact that in evaluating the effect of drought, the relevant comparison is between column (3) and either of columns (4) and (5). Take the comparison of columns (3) and (4). From column (3) we see that, given the actual values of real agricultural and non-agricultural incomes as well as imports of foodgrains, the results

derived from our model imply an increase in cereal prices in 1965–66 over 1964–65 and a more substantial increase in 1966–67 over 1965–66. Had there been no drought (in the sense that agricultural incomes in 1965–66 and 1966–67 were at their 1964–65 values), column (4) based on our model suggests very little price change in 1965–66 and an increase in 1966–67 over 1965–66 of the same order in percentage terms as in column (3). The price stability in 1965–66 and the substantial rise in 1966–67 in column (4) are due to the fact that while the urban demand for foodgrains increased because of the increase in real non-agricultural income Y_{NAt} in both years compared to 1964–65 (more so in 1966–67 because of a larger increase in Y_{NAt}), the imports of foodgrains which *increased* by 2 million tons in 1965–66 as compared with the previous year, *fell* by 1.50 million tons in 1966–67. Note also that column (5) shows the impact of the drought to be larger than that shown by column (4). The reason is of course the fact that the trend values of real agricultural income Y_{At} in 1965–66 and 1966–67 were higher than the actual value of Y_{At} in 1964–65 (which was itself *higher* than the trend value for that year). The fall in cereal prices in 1965–66 as compared to 1964–65 in column (5) is due to larger imports of foodgrains in 1965–66 (mentioned earlier).

6. The coefficients of the import variables M_{Ct} and M_{Jt} have the wrong signs in regressions (8–8) and (8–9) but are statistically insignificant and hence can be ignored.

7. The reader should refer, in this instance, to our discussion of jute exports in the next chapter.

8. The favorable impact of the liberalization package on exports of chemicals is discussed at length in Chapter 9.

9. It may be pertinent also to note here that if, instead of using the capital goods production index, we use as our dependent variable the index of capital goods *plus* consumer durables, the broad results mentioned above for capital goods alone are still valid. However, we consider it more economically meaningful to consider capital goods alone.

10. For further discussion of these policy changes, see J. Bhagwati, *India in the International Economy: A Policy Framework for a Progressive Society,* Lal Bahadur Shastri Memorial Lectures, 1973 (Hyderabad: Osmania University Press, 1973).

11. The decline in foreign aid seems, at least for maintenance imports, to have been partly a reflection of the internal recession itself. As we have noted, it was expected that external assistance, particularly non-project assistance, would be stepped up substantially after devaluation. Instead, there was a steep fall in disbursement of project assistance from $684 million in 1965–66 to $497 million in 1966–67 and to $380 million in 1967–68. Disbursement of non-project assistance was on the order of $421 million, $424 million and $672 million, respectively, in the three years. At the same time, project and non-project aid, taken together, *fell* in the year after devaluation (see Table 8–1) and recovered, though not to the level attained in the pre-devaluation year of 1965–66, in 1967–68.

Chapter 9

Liberalization and Export Performance

The effect of the June 1966 liberalization package on export performance should have reflected the interaction of the following factors:

1. The offsetting of the devaluation by export duties for several traditional exports implied that there was negligible "net" devaluation for these exports; hence there was no reason to expect that their export performance should improve.

2. The devaluation was neutralized largely on the "new" exports where the export subsidies were removed; while there were differential effects as between different industries within this group, the net devaluation was far less than the gross devaluation. Thus, on balance, *ceteris paribus,* only a modest (and possibly negligible) increase in exports might have been expected (on the assumption that price elasticities of demand abroad were favorable).

3. However, export performance might have improved yet further because of the boost that the June 1966 policy package would give to still newer exports, hitherto escaping the net of the earlier export promotion schemes which the devaluation was replacing, just as the "new" exports had themselves responded to the price incentives afforded by the earlier export subsidies.

4. Since, however, the devaluation implied a net increase in import parity that outweighed the net increase in the export parity when the changes in duties and subsidies were also taken into account (as shown in Chapter 6), the net effect of this difference could have been to inhibit exports by industries using imported inputs. This effect was, however, moderated by the strong probability that the parity on imports of intermediates did not rise quite as much as indicated by the *average* import parity increase discussed in Chapter 6.[1]

5. The scrapping of the export subsidies should have reduced significantly the incentive to over-invoice exports and might therefore have been expected to result in a net decline in the *recorded* export performance.[2]

6. Finally, the increased availability of imports under the import-liberalization program, given the excess capacity in several of the new import-dependent industries, implied an outward shift in the export supply schedule favorable to improved export performance in this non-primary-goods sector. On the other hand, this impact should have been slowed owing to delay in announcing the new import policy. We should also note the possible delays imposed by donor countries such as the United States because of their administrative procedures under which, for example, a contract generally could not be made for aid-financed imports except after a six-week public notice in the interest of small American sellers.[3]

Thus, the net effects of the devaluation plus the attendant changes in trade taxes and subsidies and the intended import liberalization, constituting the total liberalization package, could be expected to consist of a negligible impact on the exports of traditional primary products and, on balance, a mild, net improvement in the non-primary, new exports.

In addition to these direct effects of the policy package, we may consider one additional, indirect impact which must have influenced the outcome:

7. The suspension of the major pre-devaluation export subsidies (the import entitlements) was very soon replaced by cash subsidies and import replenishment schemes, as we have seen in Chapter 7; this should have been a major additional factor, leading to improved export performance in the non-traditional export sector. Thus, this major new factor reinforced the expectation of an improvement in the export performance of the non-traditional sectors but itself implied no change in the performance of the traditional exports.[4]

These expectations were indeed to be fulfilled in the case of non-traditional exports, especially iron and steel, engineering goods and chemicals. Thus, as compared with $53.9 million in 1964–65 and $71.6 million in 1965–66, the exports in these three groups grew to $76.8 million in 1966–67 and $128.6 million in 1967–68.

On the other hand, the traditional exports actually declined. In fact, the juxtaposition in Table 9–1 of major traditional export earnings (from jute and cotton textiles, tea, coir, tobacco, raw cotton, oilcakes and vegetable oils) against the major non-traditional export earnings (from engineering goods, iron and steel and chemicals) shows clearly that the major reverses on the former front were significantly offset by gains on the latter front in the post-devaluation period. Thus, if we take the 1965–66 and the average 1966–69 export values, the increment in the earnings from the non-traditional exports in Table 9–1 was $67.2 million. On the other hand, the decline in earnings

TABLE 9–1
Selected Indian Exports, 1964–65 to 1971–72
(U.S. $ millions)

			Cotton Fabrics			Selected Traditional Goods				
Year	Jute Manu-factures	Tea	Mill-made	Hand-loom	Total	Coir Yarn and Manu-factures	Oil-cakes	Tobacco	Raw Cotton	Vegetable Oils—Nonessential and Essential
1964–65	353.3	261.8	100.9	20.2	121.1	23.7	83.5	51.0	22.2	21.7
1965–66	383.9	241.1	99.0	17.5	116.1	22.5	72.8	44.4	20.4	13.5
1966–67	332.6	211.1	75.0	9.9	84.9	19.9	56.7	30.0	15.7	8.8
1967–68	312.1	240.2	79.4	7.7	87.1	17.1	50.7	47.5	19.7	10.3
1968–69	290.8	208.6	87.3	6.7	94.0	18.5	56.0	45.1	14.8	21.5
1969–70	275.5	166.0	83.2	9.7	92.9	17.9	55.3	44.5	19.6	12.3
1970–71	253.9	197.7	90.0	10.4	100.4	17.3	73.9	43.5	18.7	14.4
1971–72	356.1	210.0	89.7	13.4	103.1	18.0	54.1	60.4	22.3	15.0

(continued)

TABLE 9–1 (concluded)

| | Selected Non-Traditional Goods | | | |
Year	Engineering Goods	Iron and Steel	Chemicals and Allied Products	Grand Total
1964–65	30.1	9.2	14.6	1714.2
1965–66	34.9	17.5	19.2	1691.8
1966–67	30.7	31.6	14.5	1541.6
1967–68	43.5	69.2	15.9	1598.0
1968–69	89.8	99.3	23.3	1810.0
1969–70	119.3	102.9	29.6	1884.4
1970–71	173.9	89.6	39.2	2046.9
1971–72	158.9	34.2	37.1	2160.7

SOURCE: *Economic Survey,* annual issues since 1967–68, Government of India, Ministry of Finance, Department of Economic Affairs, New Delhi.

from (1) jute manufactures, tea and cotton manufactures was $120.7 million, and (2) these plus coir, oil cakes, tobacco, raw cotton and vegetable oils was $136.7 million. Thus, the increase in non-traditional export earnings was practically half of the decline in the traditional export earnings in Table 9–1.

In the following analysis, we examine the performance of several of the major traditional and the non-traditional exports since the June 1966 policy changes.

NON-TRADITIONAL EXPORTS

Three of the major groups of non-traditional exports are engineering goods, iron and steel and chemicals. Ideally, one would have analyzed the quantitative significance of export subsidies, availability of imported inputs, domestic demand and foreign demand on the exports of these groups. However, this ideal, like most ideals, is unattainable.

As we saw in Chapter 7, there were several export subsidization schemes including cash subsidy, import replenishment, freedom to import inputs from preferred sources, tax credits, easier access to investment licensing, and so on. Further, the quantitative significance of each subsidy varied from commodity to commodity and, in some cases such as the premia on import replenishments, only a broad range rather than the precise rates of subsidy could be established. Thus, while we have shown that in the later post-devaluation period the non-traditional exports got the benefit of parity change as well as subsidies, we have not been able to quantify the net, total benefit beyond the broad range indicated in Table 7–3.

Given this situation, in our regression analysis we have contented ourselves with distinguishing the pre- and post-devaluation periods by a dummy variable, D_t, which takes the value 0 for the years prior to the devaluation and the value 1 for the years after. The coefficient of this dummy variable, if significant and positive, is construed to mean that the devaluation-cum-subsidy schemes were effective in increasing exports.[5] In our analysis, one of the explanatory variables in the regression relation for exports is the domestic output of the same group of commodities—our hope is that this variable reflects also the availability of imported inputs into production; more or less appropriate proxies have been used to reflect domestic demand.[6]

We now turn to the export performance of each of the three groups.

Engineering Goods.

We ran regressions with E_t, the exports of engineering goods in millions of U.S. dollars, as the dependent variable and tried to explain its behavior as a function of domestic production, domestic demand (for which we took as proxy the domestic gross real investment); and we also introduced the dummy variable D_t to capture the effect of the devaluation.

Our results have turned out to be somewhat sensitive to the data on gross investment that we use. Our best results turn up for the investment figures as of June 1972, which further extended only as far as 1969–70. Using these estimates for gross real investment, I_t, in units of rupees 10 million at 1960–61 prices, we had the estimated regression equation as:

$$E_t = 47.0178 + 0.3619Q_{1t} + 1.0339Q_{2t} - 0.0707I_t \qquad (9\text{–}1)$$
$$(2.79) \quad\ (3.48) \qquad\ (4.80) \qquad\ (-4.10)$$
$$+ 26.3309D_t$$
$$(2.62)$$

$$\bar{R}^2 = 0.83;\ \text{D.W.} = 1.41;\ \text{Period 1951–52 to 1969–70}$$

where we had two output variables since the base of the index of output changed in 1960–61, so that Q_{1t} equals the index of output of engineering goods (with base 1951–52 = 100) up to 1955–56 and zero thereafter whereas Q_{2t} is the index of output of engineering goods (with base 1960–61 = 100) with value zero up to 1955–56 in the regression. The results are just what we would expect.

The coefficients of all the explanatory variables are statistically significant and of the expected sign. In particular, the post-devaluation increase in exports of engineering goods is seen to result from both the increased incentives due to parity change and reintroduction of subsidies *and* the easing of domestic demand pressure owing to the fall in real investment.

However, if we use the latest and revised data, just made available as this analysis is completed in October 1973, and also extend our observations to include 1970–71, the regression changes to:

$$E_t = 45.2699 + 0.3600Q_{1t} + 1.0094Q_{2t} - 0.0631I_t \qquad (9\text{--}2)$$
$$(1.37) \quad (2.07) \qquad (2.77) \qquad (-2.19)$$
$$+ 20.0628Dt$$
$$(0.96)$$

$$\bar{R}^2 = 0.7076; \text{ D.W.} = 0.82; \text{ Period } 1951\text{--}52 \text{ to } 1970\text{--}71$$

and the dummy, while of the right sign, is not significant.[7] This is also the case if we use gross *fixed* real investment and if we use shorter periods for our analysis:

$$E_t = 73.3257 + 0.5487Q_{1t} + 1.5318Q_{2t} - 0.1129FI_t \qquad (9\text{--}3)$$
$$(6.77) \quad (3.04) \qquad (3.61) \qquad (-3.12)$$
$$+ 5.6000D_t$$
$$(0.28)$$

$$\bar{R}^2 = 0.7536; \text{ D.W.} = 1.01; \text{ Period } 1951\text{--}52 \text{ to } 1970\text{--}71$$

$$E_t = 63.2478 + 1.1866Q_{2t} - 0.0795I_t + 14.2443D_t \qquad (9\text{--}4)$$
$$(1.35) \quad (2.55) \qquad (-2.03) \qquad (0.58)$$

$$\bar{R}^2 = 0.6683; \text{ D.W.} = 0.88; \text{ Period } 1956\text{--}57 \text{ to } 1970\text{--}71$$

where FI_t is the gross *fixed* real investment.

Thus, while there is some evidence that the devaluation may have favorably affected the performance of engineering goods exports, it is relatively weak.[8]

Iron and Steel.

Here the dependent variable, E_t, namely, exports, is measured in millions of U.S. dollars. The domestic output, Q_t, is that of finished steel in units of thousand tons. The domestic demand proxy is the same as in the case of engineering goods: FI_t, the gross fixed real investment at 1960–61 prices. The estimated equation is:

$$E_t = 19.1990 + 0.0185Q_t - 0.0201FI_t + 71.2445D_t \qquad (9\text{--}5)$$
$$(1.46) \quad (2.27) \qquad (-2.02) \qquad (7.32)$$

$$\bar{R}^2 = 0.85; \text{ D.W.} = 1.65; \text{ Period } 1951\text{--}52 \text{ to } 1970\text{--}71$$

The domestic demand variable, FI_t, the dummy, and the domestic supply variable, Q_t, have significant coefficients with the expected sign.

We should note, however, that if we use the later, revised data on fixed real investment, we get the following regression:

$$E_t = 1.0810 + 0.0040Q_t - 0.0020FI_t + 70.2371D_t \qquad (9\text{--}6)$$
$$(0.0643) \quad (0.296) \quad (-0.102) \quad (6.296)$$

$$\bar{R}^2 = 0.82; \text{D.W.} = 1.44; \text{Period 1951--52 to 1970--71}$$

The only significant variable continues to be the dummy, fortunately with the right sign. Again, the results indicate that the devaluation was probably helpful to exports in this sector; but the results are sensitive to the precise estimates we choose for feeding into our programs so that the evidence, while encouraging, is not as firm as one would wish.

Chemicals.

The chemicals sector (whose export performance is not sought to be explained in terms of domestic investment) yields a regression that has variables with significant and right-signed coefficients. E_t, the exports of chemicals, are measured in millions of U.S. dollars. The output variable is an index relating to chemicals in the index of industrial production. As in the case of engineering goods, there are two such variables, Q_{1t} and Q_{2t}, reflecting the change of base in 1960. The domestic demand proxy is the index of industrial production itself, again in terms of two series, R_{1t} and R_{2t}, reflecting the change of base of the index in 1960. The estimated equation is:

$$E_t = 11.6537 - 0.1254Q_{1t} + 0.4443Q_{2t} + 0.1216R_{1t} \qquad (9\text{--}7)$$
$$(1.43) \quad (-0.56) \quad (2.68) \quad (0.46)$$
$$- 0.4605R_{2t} + 3.5488D_t$$
$$(-2.41) \quad (0.81)$$

$$\bar{R}^2 = 0.53; \text{D.W.} = 1.25; \text{Period 1951--52 to 1969--70}$$

Both the domestic supply, Q_{1t}, and the demand, R_{1t}, in the pre-1961 period have coefficients with the wrong sign, but fortunately these are not statistically significant. For the later period, all variables have significant coefficients with the expected signs, except for the devaluation dummy which has the right sign but an insignificant coefficient.

To sum up, we have some evidence that devaluation and export subsidies altered the export performance of engineering goods and of iron and steel for the better. But domestic supply and demand conditions, reflecting mainly the fact of the recession, were also of some importance here and for chemicals.

TRADITIONAL EXPORTS

India's major traditional exports are jute textiles, tea and cotton textiles. Together they accounted for nearly 44 percent of total export earnings in 1965–66 and only 27 percent in 1970–71, registering both an absolute and a relative decline.

As we showed in Chapter 6, export duties were imposed after devaluation on a number of traditional exports, including jute textiles and tea, thereby reducing net devaluation considerably. Net devaluation on jute varied from −77.3 percent in the case of jute waste to 13.3 percent on carpet backing. Net devaluation on tea was only 17.8 percent and on cotton textiles a negligible 0.5 percent. These export duties were to be reduced substantially in later budgets following devaluation (Table 9–2), but these reductions came too late to have any perceptible influence on the export performance of traditional exports during the period studied. Let us now turn to the export performance of each of these groups.

Jute Textiles.

The regression relation that satisfactorily explained the performance of jute exports was the following:

$$E_t = 191.73 + 0.7395Q_t - 0.8028R_{1t} - 1.7764R_{2t} \qquad (9\text{--}8)$$
$$(1.74) \quad\ \ (8.10) \quad\ \ (-1.59) \quad\ \ (-3.81)$$

$$\bar{R}^2 = 0.80; \text{D.W.} = 2.55; \text{Period } 1951\text{--}52 \text{ to } 1969\text{--}70$$

where E_t is exports (thousand tons), Q_t is domestic output of jute textiles (thousand tons), R_{1t} is the index of industrial production with base 1951 up to 1959 and zero thereafter; R_{2t}, zero up to 1960 and after 1960, is the index of industrial production with base 1960. (Time trend as a proxy for external market conditions, and a devaluation dummy to reflect progressive withdrawal of export duties, were added but their coefficients were not statistically significant. These variables were therefore omitted.) In the above relationship, the coefficients of the domestic supply variable, Q_t, and the domestic demand proxies, R_{1t} and R_{2t}, have the expected sign though only two of them are statistically significant. This implies also that, *ceteris paribus,* had the droughts of 1965–66 and 1966–67 not reduced the output of raw jute and hence that of jute textiles, exports would have been higher in those years.[9]

Tea.

The marketing of this commodity is done by international companies which act very often as exporters from India as well as importers into the

United Kingdom. Also, the very same company has a share in the production of tea in a number of producing countries. Further, exports to Eastern Europe under rupee trade have been of increasing importance in recent years. All these factors make it difficult to build a simple and meaningful model of the tea economy.

A number of models were estimated including some simultaneous equation models where the domestic and export markets were treated as parts of the same system. The results were not very encouraging. It appears that the proportion of output exported is influenced more by domestic demand pull than by relative realization from sales in export markets compared with domestic sales. This is seen from the following regression relating Log E_t (logarithm of export share in output) to Log Y_t (logarithm of real income Y_t) and Log P_t (logarithm of the ratio of price per unit realized at auctions for domestic consumption and that realized at auctions for exports):

$$\text{Log } E_t = 2.9541 - 0.5462 \text{ Log } Y_t + 0.0177 \text{ Log } P_t \qquad (9\text{--}9)$$
$$(10.05) \quad (-3.36) \qquad \qquad (0.06)$$

$$\bar{R}^2 = 0.54; \text{ D.W.} = 2.27; \text{ Period 1952--53 to 1969--70}$$

The income variable has a significant negative coefficient and the price variable has a coefficient with the right signs but it is not statistically significant.

Two further regression equations were estimated, both relating to the U.K. market. In the first, the ratio n_t of North Indian (and generally superior) tea exports to the United Kindom to the sum of North Indian and Ceylonese tea was related to the corresponding price ratio p_{nt} in London auctions and time, t. The estimated equation was:

$$n_t = 0.7522 - 0.0550 p_{nt} - 0.0074t \qquad (9\text{--}10)$$
$$(8.61) \quad (-0.60) \quad (-2.85)$$

$$\bar{R}^2 = 0.34; \text{ D.W.} = 1.59; \text{ Period 1951--69}$$

The fit is rather poor and the price variable has an insignificant coefficient with the right sign, but the time variable has a significant negative coefficient indicating a secular decline in the share of North Indian tea in the U.K. market. The second equation related the share, s_t, of South Indian (and generally inferior) tea exports to the U.K. in the sum of South Indian and African tea exports to the U.K. to the corresponding price ratio p_{st} and time. The estimated equation was:

$$s_t = 0.7411 - 0.0504 p_{st} - 0.0249t \qquad (9\text{--}11)$$
$$(2.72) \quad (-0.24) \quad (-4.86)$$

$$\bar{R}^2 = 0.67; \text{ D.W.} = 1.51; \text{ Period 1951--69}$$

The fit is much better than in the case of North Indian tea, but the price ratio variable has again an insignificant coefficient with the right sign. The

TABLE 9–2
Export Duties: Changes since June 1966

	As of June 6, 1966	As of Nov. 1, 1968	As of April 1, 1969	As of March 1, 1970
Jute Manufactures				
(a) Hessians other than carpet backing and jute specialties (per metric ton)	Rs. 900	Rs. 500	Rs. 200	Rs. 200
(b) Carpet backing (per metric ton)	900	600	600	300
(c) Jute canvas, jute webbings, jute tarpaulin cloth and manufactures thereof (per metric ton)	900	500	500	200
(d) Jute specialties	900	nil	nil	nil
(e) Sacking (cloth, bags, twist yarn, rope and twine) (per metric ton)	600	250	150	150
(f) Cotton bagging (per metric ton)	600	200	nil	nil
(g) All other descriptions of jute manufactures falling under sub-item (iii) to item 2 to the Second Schedule to the Indian Tariff Act, 1934 (per metric ton)	600	250	150	150
Tea				
(a) Tea other than package tea covered by (b) and (c) below	Rs. 2 per kg.	20% reduced by 35 paise per kg, or Rs. 2.65 per kg, whichever is less	15% reduced by 55 paise per kg, or Rs. 1.70 per kg, whichever is less	nil
(b) Tea in consumer pack, packed in metal container, the aggregate weight not exceeding 1 kilo	Rs. 2 per kilo.	10% or Rs. 2.76 per kilo, whichever is less	nil	nil

(c) Tea in consumer pack, packed in container other than of metal, the aggregate weight not exceeding 1 kilo	Rs. 2 per kg.	15% or Rs. 2.76 per kg., whichever is less	5% or Rs. 1.70 per kg., whichever is less	nil
Coffee	50 paise per kg.	50 paise[a] per kg.	50 paise per kg.	50 paise per kg.
Black pepper				
(a) Light black pepper	Rs. 1.25 per kg.	90 paise per kg.	nil	nil
(b) Pinhead black pepper	Rs. 1.25 per kg.	50 paise per kg.	nil	nil
(c) Others	Rs. 1.25 per kg.	Rs. 1.25 per kg.	Rs. 1.25 per kg.	Rs. 1.25 per kg.
Tobacco (unmanufactured)	75 paise per kg. 20% per kg.[b]	20% per kg.	20% per kg.	20% per kg.
Raw wool	Rs. 1 per kg.	10%	nil	nil
Raw cotton				
(a) Bengal Deshi (per metric ton)	Rs. 1,000	Rs. 700	Rs. 700	Rs. 700
(b) Linters	Rs. 1,000	25%	25%	25%
(c) Assam Comilla/yellow pickings/ zoda cotton pickings and sweepings (per metric ton)	Rs. 1,000 Rs. 750[b]	Rs. 550	Rs. 550	Rs. 550
Cotton waste				
(a) Cotton waste other than soft cotton waste	30 paise per kg. 40%[b]	40%	40%	40%
(b) Soft cotton waste	30 paise per kg. 40%[b]	25%	25%	25%
Mica (except micanite)	50 paise per kg. 40%[b]	40%	40%	40%
Mica, loose splittings	50 paise per kg.	20%	20%	20%

(continued)

TABLE 9–2 (concluded)

	As of June 6, 1966	As of Nov. 1, 1968	As of April 1, 1969	As of March 1, 1970
Processed mica	50 paise per kg.	20%	20%	20%
Hides, skins and leather, tanned and untanned, all sorts, but not including snake skins and manufactures of leather	10%	10%	10%	10%
Snake skins	10%	25%	25%	25%
Coirs and coir manufactures				
(a) Coir yarn	10%	15%	15%	15%[c]
(b) Coir manufactures	10%	nil	nil	nil
Groundnut oil cake and groundnut meal (both deoiled) (per metric ton)	Rs. 125	Rs. 125	Rs. 125	Rs. 125
Manganese ore				
(a) More than 48% of manganese (per metric ton)	Rs. 20[d]	Rs. 20	Rs. 20	Rs. 20
(b) 10% or more and up to 48% of manganese (per metric ton)	Rs. 20[d]	Rs. 12.50	Rs. 12.50	Rs. 12.50
(c) Less than 10% of manganese (per metric ton)	Rs. 10[d]	Rs. 7	Rs. 7	Rs. 7
Manganese dioxide	20%[d]	20%	20%	20%
Lumpy iron ore				
(a) 63% iron content and above (per metric ton)	Rs. 10[d]	Rs. 10.50	Rs. 10.50	Rs. 10.50
(b) 60–63% iron content (per metric ton)	Rs. 10[d]	Rs. 6	Rs. 6	Rs. 6
(c) 58–60% iron content (per metric ton)	Rs. 10[d]	Rs. 5	Rs. 5	Rs. 5
(d) Less than 58% iron content (per metric ton)	Rs. 10[d]	Rs. 4	Rs. 4	Rs. 4
Iron ore (fines)				
(a) More than 62% iron content (per metric ton)	Rs. 5[d]	Rs. 4	Rs. 4	Rs. 4
(b) Other (per metric ton)	Rs. 5[d]	Rs. 3	Rs. 3	Rs. 3
Sillimanite	20%[d]	20%	20%	20%
Steatite (talc)	20%[d]	20%	20%	20%
Kyanite (per metric ton)	Rs. 40[d]	Rs. 40	Rs. 40	Rs. 40
Chrome concentrates (per metric ton)	Rs. 15[d]	Rs. 15	Rs. 15	Rs. 15

NOTE: Some of the duties were quite frequently readjusted between June 1966 and the present. The rates prevailing in November 1968 are given here because the government has calculated the rough *ad valorem* incidence of the schedule effective on that date. These are as follows:

Hessians other than carpet backing and jute specialties (per metric ton)	22.2%
Carpet backing (per metric ton)	15.5%
Sacking (cloth, bags, twist yarn, rope and twine) (per metric ton)	14.2%
Cotton bagging (per metric ton)	16.0%
Tea, other than package tea	15.8%
Coffee	7.9%
Black pepper: Light black pepper/Pinhead black pepper/Others	31.9%
Raw cotton: Bengal Deshi (per metric ton)	22.2%
Assam Comilla/yellow pickings/zoda cotton pickings and sweepings	11.9%
Manganese ore: More than 48% of manganese	11.0%
27% or more and up to 48% of manganese	8–20%
Lumpy iron ore: 63–65% iron content	14.6%
66–67% iron content	13.7%

SOURCE: Government of India, Ministry of Finance, Department of Economic Affairs, New Delhi.

a. 100 paise = 1 rupee
b. Subsequently revised rate effective retroactively from June 6, 1966.
c. Abolished since July 30, 1970.
d. Effective from August 2, 1966.

141

time variable has again a significant negative coefficient indicating a secular decline in India's share in the market for inferior tea as well.

It would appear, therefore, that the Indian share in the world tea market has been declining secularly over time; and this may well be due to the British policy of pulling out from India to other producing centers (such as East Africa) which the oligopolistic tea firms have been widely considered to be doing. The price effect *is* of the right sign, but not significant: it appears unlikely, therefore, that the neutralization of the devaluation by means of increased export duty could have had an adverse effect. The effect of the drought on tea output does not appear to have been serious either; on the other hand, if equation (9–5) is taken seriously, there might have been a mildly improving effect on the share of production exported owing to reduced incomes which should have neutralized the adverse effect, if any, of the reduced output on export performance. On balance, therefore, the reduction in tea exports through the post-devaluation period seems to have been a product of trend factors that were not seriously connected with the June 1966 policies.

Cotton Textiles.

India's exports of cotton textiles have been declining through most of 1960–70. Indeed, as Table 9–1 shows, the decline in cotton fabrics exports was particularly steep during the years after the devaluation and the average 1970 72 level of exports had not recovered to the average 1964–66 level, being below it by nearly 20 percent. But this decline merely continued a trend in the decline of mill-made cloth which had been evident at least since 1960–61.

While we have not been able to fit any regressions successfully to explain this decline, it is widely considered to be a result of increasing uncompetitiveness of Indian textiles in world markets, resulting even in the lack of fulfillment of the assigned quotas by India in the export markets as evidenced by the statistics on quota utilization in the United Kingdom market since 1965 and in the United States market since 1969 in particular (Table 9–3). Qualitative analysis seems to support this conclusion.

Thus, in a detailed analysis of the Indian cotton textiles exports, where he has examined the growth of world exports, regional exports, Indian labor, capital and raw material costs, and domestic demand pressure as well as the exchange rate policy, Nayyar concludes that the slow growth in world demand for textiles during the 1960s is probably not a factor in the stagnation (and even decline) in Indian cotton textile export earnings.[10] In fact, several rivals such as Taiwan, Pakistan and Hong Kong managed to increase their exports and shares quite dramatically during this period. The domestic rises

TABLE 9-3
Indian Utilization of United Kingdom and United States
Textile Quotas, 1963 to 1973

Licensing Period (1)	Quota Level (2)	Quota Utilization (3)	Shortfall (−) Excess (+) (4)	Percent Utilization (5)
UK: Cloth (million square yds.)				
12/1/62 to 11/30/63	195.00	212.17	+17.17	108.81
12/1/63 to 11/30/64	199.15	242.64	+43.49	121.84
12/1/64 to 11/30/65	206.08	172.05	−34.03	83.49
12/1/65 to 11/30/66	195.00	172.05	−34.03	88.23
12/1/66 to 11/30/67	196.95	182.18	−14.77	92.50
12/1/67 to 11/30/68	198.19	204.12	+4.93	102.99
12/1/68 to 11/30/69	195.71	101.92[a]	n.a.	n.a.
12/1/69 to 11/30/70	202.92	81.95	−120.97	40.39
12/1/70 to 12/31/71	222.03	145.62	−76.41	65.59
1/1/71 to 12/21/72	207.00	139.99	−67.31	67.63
UK: Yarn (million lbs.)				
12/1/62 to 11/30/63	11.5	9.04	−2.46	78.61
12/1/63 to 11/30/64	13.96[b]	13.00	−0.96	93.12
12/1/64 to 11/30/65	11.5	7.28	−4.22	63.30
12/1/65 to 11/30/66	11.5	7.91	−3.59	68.78
12/1/66 to 11/30/67	11.62	9.21	−2.41	79.26
12/1/67 to 11/30/68	11.73	8.92	−2.81	76.04
12/1/68 to 11/30/69	11.85	11.13[a]	n.a.	n.a.
12/1/69 to 11/30/70	11.97	10.27	−1.70	85.7
12/1/70 to 12/31/71	13.09	7.40	−5.69	56.5
1/1/71 to 12/31/72	12.21	8.80	−3.41	72.1
US: Cloth (million square yds.)				
1/17/63 to 4/16/64	37.50	38.94	+1.44	103.84
4/1/64 to 3/31/65	37.69	38.20	+0.51	101.35
4/1/65 to 3/31/66	38.87	41.18	+2.31	105.94
4/1/66 to 9/30/66	19.91	27.11	+7.20	136.16
10/1/66 to 9/30/67	79.00	69.70	−9.30	88.23
10/1/67 to 9/30/68	88.20	65.06	−23.14	73.76
10/1/68 to 9/30/69	92.61	97.49	+4.88	105.27
10/1/69 to 9/30/70	97.25	86.04	−11.21	88.47
10/1/70 to 9/30/71	110.00	88.39	−21.61	80.35
10/1/71 to 9/30/72	115.50	119.58	+4.08	103.53
10/1/72 to 9/30/73	121.28	73.72	−47.56	60.78

SOURCE: Compiled by K. M. Raipuria, Perspective Planning Division, Planning Commission, New Delhi, 1972.

a. The data cover 12/1/68 to 8/31/69.

b. Including the previous year's shortfall of 2.46 million lbs. allowed to be carried forward.

in costs plus lack of modernization plus domestic absorption seem to have been the major factors, according to Nayyar's analysis (though his conclusions are not supported by econometric analysis, in this instance). In particular, he notes that the 1966 devaluation almost certainly left the cotton textile industry with its *net* EER (effective exchange rate) more or less where it was prior to the devaluation (because of offsetting declines in export subsidization) and the domestic inflation is certain to have meant thereafter a decline in the PLDEER and also PPPEER to this industry. Thus the continuing decline in the export performance of the cotton textile exports is likely to have been a result, not of the devaluation as such, but rather of the further decline in export profitability as the PLDEER moved down in this sector.

The statistical evidence would thus seem to indicate that the drought did indeed cut significantly into jute textile exports and that the decline in tea earnings was largely the reflection of a secular adverse trend explained by growing domestic demand resulting from income expansion. The continuing sorry performance of cotton textiles exports since 1966 is probably also to be explained in terms of the relative unprofitability of export sales at the export price realization that existed *prior to* June 1966 and was accentuated by subsequent increases in the domestic price level. It is thus extremely probable that the June 1966 policy package, which left the EER on these traditional exports largely untouched, did little to affect their export performance in the post-1966 years, and that this export performance is largely to be accounted for in terms of the trend income and production factors (for jute and tea) and competitive factors (in the case of cotton textiles). On the other hand, one *can* make the rather different criticism of the policy package: that it should have permitted rather greater net increment in the EERs on these exports by leaving more subsidy element intact for cotton textiles and by not fully offsetting the devaluation of 1966 on tea and jute by countervailing export duties. Of course, we have seen that the export duties were later reduced (though perhaps this should have been done more quickly); and it is arguable that this was a policy more likely to meet with acceptance from rival suppliers in these oligopolistic markets than an outright increase in competitiveness resulting from what looked like a large devaluation. In any case, recall that we have not been able to detect any significant direct response of exports to price competitiveness in our regression analysis for tea and jute textiles; and the only possible response perhaps would have been through the longer-run effect on improving production if overall profitability of production increased through higher EERs. In the case of cotton textiles, the argument seems to be more directly in support of the contentions that the policy package should have left more improvement in the EER for textiles exports. We base this assertion on Nayyar's qualitative analysis, on the undoubted success that a number of other countries have had in improving their export sales through competitive pricing of their textiles, and on the fact that India is in much less of an oligopolistic position in this world market than is the case in tea and jute textiles.

CONCLUSIONS

It would thus appear that the effect of the "liberalization package" on export performance was a complex one. And this affected the assessments of the success of the devaluation as well.

To the superficial critic, the policy changes initiated in June 1966 were a failure. The most naive critics looked at the few months *immediately* following the devaluation, and this inattention to time-lags, combined with the industrial, aid and trade policy chaos in the six months prior to the devaluation, meant that devaluation was blamed for the stagnation of exports. The less naive critics looked at the lagged picture but saw only that the *overall* exports were relatively stagnant in the eighteen months subsequent to the devaluation and hastened to condemn the policy changes without adjusting for the exogenous impact of the agricultural drought on traditional-export performance as well as for exogenous secular trends.

When we take a more careful view of the impact of the June 1966 policy package on export performance, it looks significantly better. Allowing for the effects of the revived export subsidies, the performance is even more attractive. Clearly, the fear that export supplies would be inelastic was vastly exaggerated. The presence of excess capacity, admittedly aided by the jolt from the domestic recession, led to increased export sales as the relative profitability of the foreign market improved.

The Indian devaluation experience, therefore, underlines the fact that the view generally held by large LDCs that the price inelasticity of export supply and/or demand will make devaluations a necessarily harmful policy is not empirically sustainable. It also underlines the view that LDCs which rely on agricultural and agricultural-based exports should try to avoid devaluations *prior to a harvest:* naive criticism (and, as with Gresham's Law, invalid criticisms seem to drive out considered analysis in public debate) proceeds on the basis of *post hoc ergo propter hoc* and devaluation-cum-liberalization tends to be blamed for bad export performance whereas a smart policy-maker could use the improvement in export performance thanks to a good harvest to advantage by crediting the devaluation with this success!

Other lessons of significance relate to the fact that the distinctions between gross and net devaluation and between "rationalization" and change in the weighted average parity for export and/or import transactions are little understood. The fact that the improvement in non-traditional export performance should *not* be expected to have been *dramatic* because the net change in their parity was significantly below that implied by the devaluation itself was often lost sight of in the assessments of the failure of the change in policy in June 1966.

Furthermore, it must be remembered that the devaluation, insofar as it replaced the earlier, *ad hoc* and selective subsidies on exports, was aimed at rationalizing the indiscriminate and uneconomic way of subsidizing exports. Hence, it was to be expected that some of the *uneconomic* exports would *decline*. However, such declines were treated as evidence of "failure" rather than of success of the policy package, thus underlining the difficulty attendant on making a transition from policies of *de facto* to *de jure* devaluation.

Appendix:

Excess Capacity
and Export Performance

We have shown in the text that the recession (through its impact on demand), as well as the improved export incentives, had a favorable impact on export performance of the non-traditionals. It is also possible, in principle, to argue that this impact should have been stronger for firms with excess capacity, for the simple reason that the marginal cost of exportation for them would be the variable cost of production and not the (higher) opportunity cost of domestic sale—particularly, given the increased availability of raw material imports.

Unfortunately, the DGTD data on excess capacity, as we have seen earlier, are unreliable and hence unsuited to a direct test of this proposition. However, Frankena has shown persuasively, for the engineering industry, that excess capacity did help in improved export performance.[11]

His procedure was to use "information from interviews, company and trade association reports, and industry studies" to classify his twenty-six engineering industries into three groups: "Group I, those with substantial excess capacity due to inadequate domestic demand (industries 1 through 15); Group II, those without excess capacity (industries 16 through 20, and 26); and Group III, those for which capacity utilization could not be determined or for which it varied significantly between products in the industry (industries 21 through 25).[12]

Frankena's analysis, based on Groups I and II, is of interest because the export share of these industries was as high as 82 percent of the total engineering, iron and steel and tire exports in 1968–69.

Table 9A–1 contains Frankena's principal results on these two groups. It

TABLE 9A–1

**Exports by Industries with and without Excess Capacity due to
Insufficient Domestic Demand after 1966: 1964–65 to 1969–70**

Industries	1964–65	1965–66	1966–67	1967–68	1968–69	1969–70
Group I: Excess capacity						
Industries (1)—(15)						
Value (U.S. $ millions)	12.98	23.40	42.46	96.11	157.74	181.83
Percent of total[a]	29	41	59	74	75	73
Industries (2)—(15)[b]						
Value (U.S. $ millions)	7.06	11.77	16.45	24.80	65.34	80.88
Percent of total	16	21	23	19	31	32
Group II: No excess capacity						
Industries (16)—(20),						
Industries (26)						
Value (U.S. $ millions)	8.21	10.99	9.75	10.69	14.46	17.50
Percent of total	18	20	14	8	7	7

SOURCE: Frankena, *"Export,"* p. 135.
a. Total exports of iron and steel, engineering goods and tires.
b. Industry (1) is iron and steel.

is interesting to note that Group I has an export performance since 1966–67 which clearly dominates that of Group II, indicating that excess capacity was linked strongly to export performance, as one would expect. Frankena has concluded: "In interviews and in their annual reports the firms involved confirmed that excess capacity played an important role in the decision to export and in determining export prices . . . even after allowing for export promotion schemes a significant share of exports of engineering goods appears to have taken place at realizations which did not cover long-run average costs (and probably did not cover long-run marginal costs) or match realizations in the domestic market, particularly (i) before preferential maintenance import licensing for exporters began in 1968–69, (ii) in the case of firms which did not export enough to qualify for these preferences, and (iii) on the margin for firms which exported beyond the level necessary to qualify for these preferences. It can be concluded that excess capacity was critical for export by a number of industries in cases (i)–(iii), given the implicit exchange rate on export."[13]

While, as Frankena himself has noted, the non-exporting industries were excluded so that some major industries such as metallurgical, mining equipment and heavy electricals with severe excess capacity and which did not export at all were counted out, the evidence presented above on Groups I and II *is* extremely suggestive and consistent with the view that excess-capacity industries generally were the better exporters during this period.

NOTES

1. We use the words "strong probability," rather than "fact," because our information is based on the judgments of officials and traders rather than on a scientific sample survey.

2. This is an *a priori* statement, partially corroborated by interviews with art silk producers. We have not been able to use meaningfully any of the statistical techniques available for detecting faked invoicing: those techniques are generally "weak" and are not up to the task of detecting first differences in such faking. For a discussion of these techniques, see Bhagwati, ed., *Illegal Transactions.*

3. As noted in the preceding chapter, the recession took hold by the time these delays had worked out, reducing the demand for imports.

4. In addition, the recession was to ease the domestic demand situation sufficiently in the new industries to improve their export performance still further. This improvement, like the recession, was exogenous of the June 1966 policies, however. An additional exogenous factor which affected the non-traditional exports as well was the closure of the Suez Canal after the Six Day War.

5. The PLDEER for exports declined in the post-1966 period relative to EER for exports, owing to (exogenously caused) inflation, as per our estimates in Chapter 2. Hence we do not expect the coefficient of this dummy variable to be as large as would be the case if this inflation were explicitly taken into account.

6. Foreign demand was introduced through a time-trend variable, but in all cases this variable did not have a statistically significant coefficient and has been omitted.

7. Given the relative weakness of the investment data in India, we feel that it is useful to report on regressions using alternative investment estimates.

8. In this connection, recall that the PLDEER for exports after the devaluation was less favorable than the EER for exports. The net improvement in the real incentive for exports of engineering goods after devaluation is thus likely to have been significantly reduced owing to domestic inflation.

9. Although we could not incorporate successfully any price terms into our regressions, it is probably worth noting that the invention of propylene to substitute for jute in carpet backing is an important new development that should make India's (and Pakistan's) export performance in jute rather more dependent on maintenance of competitive prices. This may, in fact, have been an important argument for quickly dismantling the export duties levied with the devaluation.

10. Deepak Nayyar, "An Analysis of the Stagnation in India's Cotton Textile Exports During the Sixties," *Bulletin of the Oxford University Institute of Economics and Statistics* (February 1973).

11. Frankena, "Export," pp. 131–138.

12. *Ibid.,* p. 132.

13. *Ibid.,* p. 136–137.

Chapter 10

The Political Response
to the Devaluation

Despite the overvaluation of the rupee and the chaotic and inefficient pattern of subsidization that had developed in that situation, the 1966 devaluation was to run up against intense political reaction. This was to make it nearly impossible for the government to gain either real political support for the measure *ex-ante* or a rational appraisal of its success *ex-post*. An analysis of the factors underlying this outcome is necessary in order to learn lessons, not merely for Indian policy-making, so that some of the pitfalls can be avoided the next time around; there are more general lessons for the policy-makers elsewhere too.[1]

The political impact of a devaluation, and hence the alignment of pressure groups, is usually conceived of in terms of the following factors: (1) opposition parties can be expected to play upon issues of national prestige as well as on the theme that government policies have led to this "debacle"; and (2) a devaluation that improves the payments imbalance may be expected to draw support from the export sector and to be resented by importing interests.

The Indian devaluation, both economically and politically, was a more complex phenomenon, but it was not entirely an unusual phenomenon for a developing country attempting to liberalize its payments regime. Among its important features were:

1. The government was energetically pushed into devaluation by the aid consortium which made large-scale significant resumption of aid practically conditional on India's changing the parity.[2]

2. The government was in a pre-election year and also relatively weak

in having a new Prime Minister (Mrs. Indira Gandhi) whose leadership of her party was not yet consolidated.

3. The government's long-standing refusal to devalue, which was overcome in part by a consortium offer to increase the (pre-suspension) level of annual commodity aid from about $400 million to $900 million, had led for a number of years, and in particular during the preceding year 1965–66, to strenuous propaganda that stressed the alleged demerits of devaluation. On the other hand, with the exception of a few economists, there had been no convincing and sustained argumentation in support of a devaluation; hence the public stage had been occupied almost exclusively by the opponents of devaluation, largely official.

4. Finally, the devaluation, as we have noted in Chapter 6, was accompanied by simultaneous changes in export subsidies and import duties. This implied that the objectives of the measure were, for the most part, those of merely "rationalizing" the existing system rather than of seeking a large "net" devaluation; this was little understood and was a major source of confusion and misdirected criticism. It also implied that the *objections* to the devaluation were likely to come from those hurt by these accompanying changes. At the same time, the substantial increase in commodity aid promised by the consortium meant that the *supporters* would include those benefiting from increased, liberalized imports.

The remarkably unfavorable political reception accorded the 1966 devaluation in the period immediately after its announcement is readily explained once the following factors are taken into account.

1. The government failed to elicit significant support from its own (Congress) party, either in Parliament or from the party's Executive Committee members; in fact, several senior Congress party members openly expressed criticism or skepticism. Some of the flak came from members who were clearly worried about the oncoming election and found the measure risky, as all governments seem to do, in that the government might lose prestige or be blamed for unpopular price increases. Others were offended at the secrecy and at not having been consulted on such an important decision, forgetting that secrecy is inherent in such a decision. This group included senior members of the Congress party who had maneuvered successfully to make Mrs. Gandhi the Prime Minister and feared that she was becoming independent, and also others (such as a former Finance Minister) who had long opposed devaluation. Yet others, essentially on the left in the Congress party, who had welcomed the succession of Mrs. Gandhi to premiership against a right-wing contender as promising a turn to the left in Indian economic policy, thought that the devaluation that they characterized as a "surrender" to the consortium's demands, signified that they had been wrong and wanted to serve notice of their displeasure rather than support the government of their

own party. In short, the relative weakness of Mrs. Gandhi's position in her own party, the failure of her new government to project a clear political image and the impending election made the prospect of getting broad-based support from her own party very dim indeed. As it turned out, only a handful of Cabinet Ministers who had been consulted on the final decision were to be articulate in their support of the devaluation, the contributions of other prominent members of the Congress party being one of lukewarm defense or, more generally, that of mild skepticism ranging up to outright criticism.

2. Three circumstances combined to convert the customary tendency of most opposition parties to denounce devaluation as a "defeat" of the government and an "admission" of its failures into a concerted denunciation in stronger tones: (a) For some years preceding the devaluation, in response to frequent rumors based on alleged World Bank and IMF recommendations to that effect and in response to the writings of some domestic economists, the government had indulged in strenuous propaganda against devaluation; this was particularly the case with the annual reports of the Ministry of Commerce and of International Trade. (b) Supporters of a more realistic exchange rate policy had opted out of the debate on the question since the early 1960s. This meant that the largely spurious arguments put out by official agencies against an adjustment in the exchange rates were left unanswered. (c) Finally, these two facts, in conjunction with the financial inducement and pressures by the consortium, led to a situation where public opinion was generally receptive to the notion that the devaluation was *economically unsound* and was imposed on the country for "non-economic" reasons.[3]

Two factors therefore became critical in determining the overall response to the devaluation: (a) resentment at foreign influence itself, accentuated in turn by the notion that India could no longer control her own policies in her own interest; and (b) the widespread feeling that the devaluation had to be judged ultimately by what it signified beyond itself in broader political and economic terms.

3. Thus, the minority that supported (or did not oppose) the devaluation was confined to (a) economists who chose to assess the measure within its own terms, (b) several industrial groups which saw the measure as signifying an impending move toward a larger role for private enterprise and less "socialism," (c) a few isolated exporting groups whose benefit from the devaluation outweighed their loss from the simultaneous elimination of the earlier export subsidies and (d) producer groups that saw sufficient profits resulting from the raw-material-import liberalization that would follow from the grant of significant aid after devaluation.

4. These were, however, outweighed in political terms and in articulation by the critics. The alleged economic demerits of the decision and the perceived economic need of having succumbed to foreign pressure were the major focal

points of criticism from political parties on the left as well as the right, in Parliament and in the press. (Only the laissez-faire and industry-oriented right-wing Swatantra Party was schizophrenically positioned for reasons spelled out in the preceding paragraph.) In addition, the parties of the left were particularly articulate about their fear that the devaluation represented the turning point for progressive sacrifice of socialist policies regarding private foreign investment and private domestic enterprise. The critics also included the overwhelming majority of exporters who saw that the major thrust of the devaluation was aimed at reducing reliance on the *ad hoc* and selective export subsidies which had indeed proved very lucrative to the influential exporters.

All in all, therefore, the devaluation ran into an unusually hostile reception. The political lessons seem particularly pointed with regard to the use of aid as a means of influencing recipient policy, even if, in some objective sense, the pressure is in the "right" direction. The Indian experience is also instructive for the political timing of a devaluation: foreign pressure to change policies, if brought to bear when a government is weak (both for internal-structural reasons and because of an impending election, which invariably prompts cautious behavior), can be fatal. Mason and Asher, in their study of the World Bank, characterize the Indian case as "perhaps the most striking example of attempts by the Bank to use 'leverage' to bring about changes in a borrowing government's 'performance' " and one which "did not leave the Bank's relations with India unscathed."[4]

To say that there should be no "performance conditioning" in providing aid is not to suggest that there should be no evaluation of aid utilization. We think, however, that such evaluation and subsequent pressure for policy change, if any, must also recognize that economic analysis is rarely so compelling as to command universal approbation—even if one does not quite take the cynical attitude that where you have six economists, you get seven opinions. Indeed, there is much to be said, if the aid relationship is to be mature and relatively free from the frictions of the preceding decade, for the donors' influence to take the form of advice rather than prescription. In this regard, it is well worth noting that the Soviet practice of confining scrutiny to the performance of aid-financed projects, and not attempting to evaluate and influence the whole plan or set of economic policies of the recipient country, has helped to avoid the kind of adverse reaction the Western donors have provoked, however well intentioned their pressures may have been.[5] Here we again have that paradox of political economy: that a program approach, which makes much sense from an *economic* point of view (given substitution possibilities), makes little sense from a *political* point of view.

We also do not share the view that pressure to change major policies by foreign donors, especially of the type applied to India in 1966, is helpful because it "strengthens the hands" of those who, within the recipient country, want the "right" policies adopted. It is the opinion of nearly all of those few who had argued for a devaluation in the Indian context during the period preceding June 1966 that the external role at the time of devaluation compromised their political viability.[6]

NOTES

1. The following analysis and conclusions are based on an extensive examination of the relevant documents such as newspapers, journals, Lok Sabha proceedings and Rajya Sabha proceedings. The reactions and pronouncements of politicians (in and out of office), political parties, newspaper editorials, influential magazines and journals, industrial and business groups, and economists were examined. The analysis is thus confined to the so-called "elite groups"; besides it is primarily a medium-run response analysis, though there is little reason to think that anyone really changed his position on the policy option exercised by the government in June 1966, in light of longer-run developments. The only exception is the Prime Minister herself (who is reported to have been less than enthusiastic about the policy changes in light of the tremendous opposition that they elicited). Our full-length analysis (with K. Sundaram) has been published in three parts in *Economic and Political Weekly,* September 2, 9 and 16, 1972.

2. Note, however, that PL 480 food aid was continued throughout this period and that aid already in the pipeline was not halted either; only fresh commitments were held up by the U.S., though even here two new loan agreements were signed by the U.S. with India between October 1965 and June 1966. Note that aid to both India and Pakistan had originally been suspended during the war of October 1965.

3. This widely accepted view failed, of course, to recognize that the economic aspects of the problem had been discussed at length for several months prior to the decision to devalue. The Finance Ministry had before it an extensive report on the current export subsidies and the merits of a devaluation, which it had commissioned from J. Bhagwati, then at Delhi University, during mid-1965. Besides, other economists had also written in support of a new parity. Most of the major contributions on the subject have been reprinted in *Devaluation of the Rupee and its Implications* (New Delhi: Institute of Constitutional and Parliamentary Studies, 1966). In addition, see K. N. Raj, "Food, Fertiliser and Foreign Aid," *Mainstream,* April 30, 1966; C. N. Vakil, *The Devaluation of the Rupee* (Bombay: Lalvani Publishing House, 1966); and B. N. Ganguli, *Devaluation of the Rupee* (Delhi: Ranjit Printers and Publishers, 1966).

4. Edward S. Mason and Robert E. Asher, *The World Bank Since Bretton Woods* (Washington, D.C.: The Brookings Institution, 1973), p. 197. This study also stresses what the authors consider to be the disappointing features of India's economic performance that led the Bank, with the strong support of the United States, to press for reform of India's balance of payments and agricultural policies in particular.

5. Note, however, that we do not mean to imply that Soviet aid has been entirely without friction. For an interesting account and analysis of difficulties in the case of Soviet financing of the Indian steel plant at Bokaro, see Desai, *Bokaro,* especially Chapters 5–7.

6. In particular, the adverse political consequences of the 1966 experience may well have had a lasting impact on the ability of the official economists to argue for exchange rate flexibility in the future without being condemned as unwitting, if not willing, tools of

capitalist donors. In a country such as India, where the word "socialism" wins elections rather than loses them, as in the United States, an official's (as well as a Congress politician's) efficacy and possibly even his ability to get ahead in life depend significantly on whether he can operate within the broad framework of mild-to-strong left-wing politics. And one has only to examine the Indian response at the time of the Smithsonian parity changes (discussed in Chapter 11) to see the force of the point that, even in the long run, the ability of officials to press successfully for exchange rate flexibility was compromised by the 1966 experience.

The Liberalization Episode: Evaluation and Lessons

In light of the analysis in chapters 6 through 10, what can we conclude about the success of this liberalization episode, and what lessons can we draw from it regarding the prerequisites of a successful liberalization package?

WAS THE LIBERALIZATION EPISODE SUCCESSFUL?

In deciding whether the liberalization episode was successful, we need to distinguish sharply between the way it was regarded by public opinion, including elite opinion, and an objective appraisal of the results in relation to the aims of the liberalization effort. These two different ways of judging the outcome are important to distinguish because the undertaking was a *complex* of policies. In consequence, it was difficult to assess and its objectives were not clearly understood. We now examine (1) the objectives of the package, (2) how far they were achieved in practice, and (3) what the general assessments are.

The Objectives.

The June 1966 policy reforms appear to have had the following objectives, in the main:

1. the replacement of the inefficient *de facto* devaluation by a *de jure* devaluation; and

2. the reduction, through the net additional devaluation plus import liberalization, of the adverse impact of the QR-regime on export performance.

Of these two objectives, the emphasis in the official pronouncements seems to have been on the former. The theme that the export subsidization programs were inefficient and needed to be replaced by a formal devaluation was repeatedly stressed. On the other hand, official pronouncements also promised an improved export performance, clearly basing this on the net devaluation which had been built into the June 1966 package, as well as on the improved availability of aid for raw material imports *and* on the theme that even the replacement of the subsidies by a formal devaluation would, in the longer run, give more stable incentives for export promotion.

3. It is not equally clear whether the government also intended to usher in import and industrial licensing policies that would have provided a more efficient set of incentives for the *pattern* of import substitution. In the beginning the "import liberalization" apparently *was* conceived to imply not just additional availability of raw material imports (on AU licenses); there are some indications that the principle of automatic protection by means of the indigenous availability system was also expected to be steadily dislodged. Industrial licensing policy, as we saw in Chapter 5, was also being amended in favor of more extensive de-licensing of industries. It seemed, therefore, as if the June 1966 policy changes were intended, in themselves and in the overall context of ongoing changes in industrial licensing, also to (a) reduce the reliance on QRs through improved export performance and (temporarily) increased availability of aid, (b) reduce simultaneously the element of automatic and indiscriminate protection that had resulted in a chaotic pattern of import substitution, (c) increase the element of competition by permitting freer domestic entry in the de-licensed industries and greater role for imports, and finally to (d) improve export performance also by making investment and production responses to export incentives more readily possible than under the cumbersome licensing procedures.

Were They Achieved?

We can therefore judge the outcome in terms of these three sets of objectives. In these terms, the liberalization episode must be described as less than successful, at best, and as bordering on failure when the credits and debits are totaled up.

1. The replacement of the *de facto* by the *de jure* devaluation was clearly accomplished in the very act of the June 6, 1966, policy announcement. As we have noted, the import duties were reduced and export subsidies were removed on that date. But, in the long haul, the intended reform of the trade and payments regime was not achieved, resulting in a lapse into

Phase II, as the cumbersome complex of multi-sided and selective export subsidization was revived (as noted in Chapter 7). The rationalization of the export subsidy situation was extremely short-lived indeed! It would appear that, with the overvaluation of the exchange rate still continuing after June 1966—the import premia still continuing to obtain on the overwhelming bulk of imports, at sizable levels, and the exchange control mechanism, therefore, still occupying its central role in the regime—the logic in favor of export subsidization was indeed strong: in principle, to offset the discrimination against exports in an overvalued system, export subsidization makes sense. On the other hand, the indiscriminate, administrative selectivity and other inefficiencies of subsidization do *not* make sense; and these were indeed, as we saw in Chapter 7, to reappear, implying that the government had more or less failed in its objective of rationalizing the export subsidization schemes on a continuing basis.

2. The objective of improved export performance was indeed achieved, if one has suitably adjusted for exogenous factors such as the second agricultural drought (as in Chapter 9). This (post-adjustment) improvement was nonetheless *not* dramatic because the size of the net devaluation was significantly lower than that of the gross devaluation.[1] At the same time, the revival of subsidization of the "new" exports clearly helped: our dummy-variable analysis picks up an *overall* effect which *includes* the effect of these subsidies as well. Thus we can conclude that the *total* policy package (inclusive of export subsidization) as of, and since, June 1966 did improve export performance. However, we must stress again that this improved export performance was based, insofar as it reflected the impact of revived export subsidization, on a set of subsidy policies that were conceived purely as export-augmenting policies rather than as *efficient* export-augmenting policies. Thus, the gain in export performance was, as before June 1966, bought at the cost of inefficiency in export promotion.

3. The explicit surrender of the objective of a rationalized export subsidy system was also to be matched by the frustration of similar objectives in the fields of import and industrial policies.

(a) The improvement in export performance did help, *ceteris paribus,* to ease the restrictiveness of the QR-regime. And the increased availability of aid after June 1966 also initially helped in this direction. However, as we have already shown, the utilization of this aid was hampered by the recipient's and donors' dilatory administrative procedures and was then partly frustrated by the onset of the industrial recession.[2] In fact, the aid *authorizations* after 1966–67, whatever the reasons, were never to reach the level presumably promised as an inducement for the June 1966 reforms, thus leading to the widespread charge that the government had been tricked into these policy changes with promises of accelerated aid flows that had failed to materialize—

an outcome of great significance in determining the political success, and hence the repeatability, of such a liberalization package. Thanks mainly to the recession, however, which was largely exogenous to the June 1966 policy package, the demand for imports appears to have been effectively low enough to lead to premia levels on imports that were somewhat lower than in the period prior to devaluation.

This is apparently true for both EI (traders') imports, as illustrated by premia on selected items in Table 11–1, as well as for the more substantial AU imports which went directly to the producers.[3] This effective reduction in the restrictiveness of the QR-regime, however, followed in large part from the recession which, according to our analysis, was a result of drought-induced fiscal and monetary policies which must be construed as exogenous to the 1966 package of trade and exchange rate policy changes.

And indeed, by 1967–68, as the industrial recession was giving way to a more buoyant industrial economy, the premia on several AU imports had already begun to reach higher levels. While it is not possible, in the nature of the case, to develop systematic time series on these premia because of the quasi-illegal aura surrounding the sale of imports or import licenses in the Indian context (as we saw earlier in Part II), we have been able to put together from different sources premia estimates for certain items, underlining our assertion that the premia on AU imports had begun reaching substantial levels by 1967–68 and continued to be at high levels through 1970–71 (when our study was being undertaken). Thus, copper, bronze, zinc, lead, nickel and other metal products, several steel products (such as steel wire and sheets), most chemicals, paper and paper products, glass and machinery (including ball-bearings and precision tools) had import premia ranging between 70 to 100 percent from 1967–68 to 1970–71.[4]

Thus, by 1967–68, the import liberalization did not quite match the original intentions of the government. After the devaluation and associated measures were announced, they were followed on June 21, 1966, by a press note on import policy which marked the major steps toward liberalization of maintenance imports. A list of 59 "priority" industries was soon set up, extending to about 80 percent of total organized-sector industrial production. Liberal licensing for these industries, which included several exporting industries as well, was announced so that the units in these industries would be able to meet their full requirements by merely going back to the DGTD and seeking additional import licenses. In addition, the policy was to be liberalized (in respect of IDA credits) in easing restrictions on the value of the license that could be expended on specific imports, thereby ostensibly releasing the firms from obligation to seek detailed specific permissions each time they wished to change the composition of the imports they sought. Imports in the nonpriority sectors were to continue being regulated as before. Toward the end

TABLE 11-1

Premium Rates for Import Licenses during the Pre-Devaluation and Post-Devaluation Months of 1966

(percent of c.i.f. value of imports)

		Jan.	Feb.	March	April	May	June	July	Aug.	Sept.	Oct.	Nov.	Dec.
Chemical products													
1. Drugs and medicines[a]	i)	230	205	186	245	125		62	38	45	37	40	43
	ii)				195	135		38	58	50	42		
2. Colors[a]	i)	158			189	175							58
	ii)					118							75
3. Perfumery				230					35	45		75	
Food products													
4. Dates		52			72	85		24	25	18			
5. Cloves[a]	i)	540	102	105	111	138	85		75	55	40	52	65
	ii)	550					138		70		44		
Surgical goods													
6. Surgical goods E&D[b]			325					95					138
Engineering and metal products[a]													
7. Motor parts: thin walled bearing	i)	275	275		190	200	140		150	175			
	ii)				200		145		65				
8. Stainless steel	i)	275	300			330	325	250	250	160	150		
	ii)	300				350			260		160		
9. Ball bearing	i)					180				55			
	ii)									60			

10. Motor parts consolidated quota	i)	220		145	200	150	65	58	200
	ii)			150			70	60	
Miscellaneous									
11. Polished silver		135							50
12. Foreign tallow		175	190		155	160	145	140	140	60
13. Gum		158				138	150	150	

NOTE: Blanks indicate that premium information is not available.
SOURCE: The information is based on interviews with traders by Dr. V. R. Panchamukhi. The items included are essentially those going through EI licenses in the hands of traders. The quotations are *not* based on a sample survey but represent scant pieces of information.

a. Items (i) and (ii) refer to two alternative quotations under the same, broad category.

b. 'Surgical Goods E&D' refers to quotation of premium by an identical category in *Vyapar*, a commercial daily, published in Bombay and carrying such quotations with some regularity.

of 1968–69, these relaxations had begun to be tightened; and by 1970–71, the system was substantially back where it had begun, indicating a relapse into Phase II-type import controls.[5]

(b) Therefore, while the liberalization of maintenance imports did not remain on a continuing basis beyond 1968–69, the extension of the liberalization to imports that were in competition with domestic production was even shorter-lived. Those who held the notion that the policy changes of June 1966 would also effectively dislodge the principle of indigenous availability and the consequent automatic protection of domestic production were to be disabused during 1966–67 itself. It quickly turned out that there was stiff opposition from domestic producers to such import relaxation; there were active and successful representations to the Ministers of Finance and Industry to halt such imports and to restore the sheltered market. Apparently, it was easy to seduce Ministers into such action because they had long been taught to believe that *any* import substitution was good. The corollary that domestic production in any activity should not be allowed to be replaced by "scarce" imports was therefore equally difficult to purge from the policy-makers' thinking. Thus, import liberalization came to mean *merely* that the imports of non-competing goods, in the main, would be increased.

(c) The increase in industrial efficiency that was expected to result from increased competition (de-licensing of industries eased domestic restrictions on entry), was also to be frustrated. Given the continuing operation of import licensing, the fact that a firm could establish new capacity in a de-licensed industry merely meant that the detailed scrutiny and possibility of rejection that characterized all licensing procedures now applied to requests for import licenses. Access to imports, since it continued to be administratively controlled rather than through the market, was then the point at which licensing was effectively being implemented! Little of substance, in relation to effective entry, was therefore to change in the system. Hence, increased efficiency from greater competition was *not* a gain to be had, in practice, from the June 1966 and related policy measures.

(d) Finally, the expected improvement in the ability of exporters to respond to enhanced export incentives, following on the liberalized licensing structure, was stymied for similar reasons. While, as we have seen in Chapter 9, the government undertook a number of measures intended to help exporters get around the difficulties and obstacles that the licensing machinery created for them in the first place, there is plenty of evidence from interviews that, in matters such as product design changes and expansion of capacity, the bureaucratic procedures and delays were continuing, contributory factors in reducing the responsiveness of exports to improved prices.[6] Thus gains on this account, while probably positive, appear to have been relatively small.

On balance, therefore, the basic objectives of the policies which peaked in the June 1966 set of measures do not appear to have been achieved to a significant degree.

Public Perceptions.

Curiously enough, the public evaluation, including that among financial commentators and not merely among the political and bureaucratic elite groups, appears to have been dominated by quite the opposite criteria! The "rationalization" of the trade and payments regime was hardly considered and was implicitly either disregarded or not understood. On the other hand, the success (or rather the failure) was judged essentially by reference to the presumed effect of the policy package on export performance and on the price level. In addition, the political circumstances surrounding the policy announcements were critical, and the policy of increasing aid flows on condition that the policy changes be implemented seems to have created expectations that were not to be fulfilled. Furthermore, some concern about the impact on the terms of trade was expressed. Surprisingly, while economists would naturally worry about the possibly deflationary (immediate) impact of an LDC-type devaluation,[7] public evaluation of the industrial recession that followed June 1966 does not seem to have *attributed* the recession to the liberalization policies. We take up each of these strands for more detailed comment now.

EXPORT PERFORMANCE

The public view of export performance, we must conclude, was deeply affected by the fact that total earnings failed to rise and even fell marginally in the two years after the devaluation. Two major aspects of the June 1966 package and subsequent developments were ignored: (1) the fact that the net devaluation was significantly smaller than the gross devaluation, and (2) the exogenous impact (largely from the drought) on the export performance of traditional exports. We have noted already that the *objective* situation was different, and indeed more favorable, than the superficial view of the situation would lead one to believe. But the superficial views did dominate the general reaction.

PRICE LEVEL

Similarly, the *post hoc ergo propter hoc* illogic applied to the phenomenon of rising prices that dominated public consciousness in the year following the devaluation. As we have noted in Chapter 8, the objective situation again was very different, with the effect of the exogenous drought responsible for the major price rise in the system.

POLITICAL REACTION

The political response to the liberalization package was, as we have seen in Chapter 10, extremely critical. The essential weakness of the package was the fact that it was widely considered, and with much justification, to have been forced upon India by Western aid donors.

In particular, since the Soviet Union, which is also a major aid donor of India, was not associated with this change of policies in June 1966, the charge has continued to stick in the popular mind that devaluation is an "imperialist," "neo-colonial" policy. The charge has also been made in the left-wing press, from time to time, against the civil servants and Ministers who had supported the devaluation decision, that they are the saboteurs of "socialism."[8] These charges were revived in December 1971 when the realignment of exchange rates around the world forced India to take a position on her own exchange rate. The Indian decision was a compromise solution: the rupee was partially devalued so that its parity vis-à-vis the dollar actually went up. The left-wing press took the opportunity to attack those who, though overruled, had sensibly proposed that India should at least devalue to the same extent as the dollar.[9]

The 1971 decision on the rupee also underlined the fact that the senior Ministers were unwilling to be caught supporting any devaluation of the rupee. The majority of them, including the Minister of Foreign Trade, felt that the devaluation was a politically unpopular policy, that it might have caused the Congress party its reverses in the 1967 elections, and that it was, in any case, politically risky to be vulnerable to left-wing charges of being "soft on the Americans" at a time when American hostility toward India in the Indo-Pakistan War had made any sympathy for policies popularly associated with the United States a serious liability.[10]

In fact, even the partial degree of parity change that was achieved was a triumph of skill and ingenuity on the part of the top-level advisers. By claiming that India should link itself with sterling, and by taking advantage of the fact that the United Kingdom's decision was to reduce its revaluation subsequent to the dollar devaluation, while leaving the sterling appreciated vis-à-vis the dollar, they managed to reduce the parity vis-à-vis the dollar by the same amount as the reduction in the percentage revaluation of the sterling. Thus, in effect, the rupee was devalued vis-à-vis the *old* dollar; but, given the larger devaluation of the dollar itself, the rupee parity with the dollar actually moved up from Rs.7.50 to Rs.7.28 per U.S. dollar.[11]

The political failure of the 1966 liberalization package can thus be regarded as overwhelming: not merely did the government face a political storm over it but the political capacity to repeat such a package was damaged.[12]

AID-INFLOW AND POLITICS

One interesting aspect of the decision by the donor countries virtually to impose liberalization on the Indian government by making continuation of large-scale aid virtually conditional on this and other changes in policies was that the policies were often to be judged in terms of how much aid actually did come in, subsequent to the devaluation. This was to work politically against the June 1966 reforms for the simple reason that, along with the general decline in aid flows during this period, the Indian aid receipts were to decline steadily.[13]

This was to lead to widespread criticism of the government by the influential press and politicians on the left, including the charge within the ruling Congress party that those politicians and economists who had accepted the imposition of these "market-oriented" and laissez-faire-type policies from the Western powers, and had hoped to be rewarded by large inflows of aid, had found that this "bribe" had not materialized and that the country had been unwittingly duped with the aid of these Indians.

It should be emphasized that (i) substantial aid did materialize after the devaluation and (ii) these Indian economists and politicians genuinely believed, and some of them had publicly argued to that effect even prior to the aid suspension and foreign pressures thereafter, that these policy changes were long overdue. These facts, however, are irrelevant to the fact that the unwise pressure on India in the general direction of measures such as those in the liberalization package had made the charges we have just described credible to vast numbers of people, and made them believe that here was one more powerful reason why the "devaluation had failed."

TERMS OF TRADE

Among the less frequent indications of success, though one not used outside financial circles, was the effect of devaluation on the terms of trade. Devaluation is traditionally regarded as a dangerous policy because it may lead to an adverse impact on the terms of trade. In a real sense, this is a fear based on confusion. If there is no reason, such as residual monopoly power in trade, to use tariffs (or tariff equivalents such as an overvalued exchange rate), then devaluation is indeed the optimal policy for regulating external accounts. And, if there is monopoly power in trade which is not yet exercised, then the optimum tariff argument itself requires that tariffs be used to improve the terms of trade and to restrict trade, in the first place, and then devaluation be used *beyond* that for regulating the external accounts. Concern with what happens to the terms of trade, as such, is therefore quite misplaced.

Since, however, in some assessments of the devaluation, the effect on the terms of trade was regarded as important, we may examine the behavior of the Indian terms of trade subsequent to the June 1966 devaluation. Note, of course, that the actual behavior of the terms of trade would reflect exogenous movements in the prices of traded goods abroad; also, insofar as the composition of exports and imports is likely to shift in response to a devaluation (e.g., new exports are likely to become more competitive and therefore to materialize), the movement in the terms of trade (as customarily measured) is not unambiguously interpretable.

The terms of trade index (defined as the unit export value index divided by the unit import value index) during 1966–67, taking only the ten months following the devaluation into account, actually improved from 109 in 1965–66 to 113; it rose yet further to 124 during 1967–68 (Table 11–2). Indeed, the terms of trade for 1963–64 to 1965–66 averaged 108 whereas for 1966–67 to 1969–70 the average improved to 119. Thus, by this fallacious but nonetheless influential index of failure, the devaluation in 1966 was not a failure; instead of worsening, the terms of trade actually improved.

THE RECESSION

It is interesting that there is little evidence of the June 1966 policy changes being blamed for the industrial recession. Objectively speaking, as we have shown in Chapter 8, the fiscal and monetary policies which were, at

TABLE 11–2
Terms of Trade, 1960–61 to 1969–70
(base: 1958 = 100)

	Exports		Imports		
	Volume Index	Unit Value Index	Volume Index	Unit Value Index	Terms of Trade[a]
1960–61	100	110	128	96	115
1961–62	105	109	121	98	111
1962–63	112	106	131	94	113
1963–64	126	105	135	97	108
1964–65	132	107	146	99	108
1965–66	124	113	154	104	109
1966–67[b]	119	169	149	150	113
1967–68	122	169	166	136	124
1968–69	142	166	151	141	118
1969–70	143	171	128	140	122

SOURCE: Government of India, Directorate General of Commercial Intelligence and Statistics, New Delhi.
a. Export unit value index divided by import unit value index.
b. Covers only the 10 months following devaluation, June through April.

least in large part, responsible for the recession were exogenous to the devaluation decision and were largely the result of the fear that otherwise the drought-induced increase in the price level would be accentuated. In fact, the influence of the June 1966 policy package (plus the revived export subsidies) is likely to have been mildly expansionary in having made exportation more profitable than earlier for the non-traditional exports. Thus, in this instance, the objective reality (of, at best, a mildly favorable impact on economic activity) was fairly close to the subjective evaluation (which did not link up the policy package with the recession, in any case).

LESSONS

What principal lessons can we draw from this analysis?

1. For the *donor* countries, it seems clear that the dominant lesson is *not* to force changes in policy, particularly ones with an ideological slant in the public view, by using withdrawal of aid as the lever. This may work with countries that do not have a free press and a democratic framework; it can be nothing short of disastrous in other contexts. Above all, it can ruin the political credibility of the local groups who support these policies and thereby compromise their ability to press for a repeated application of such measures in the future.

2. For the liberalizing country itself, the implication equally is that the appearance (and, even more so, the reality) of surrender to "aid blackmail" would compromise the political success, and hence the repeatability, of a liberalization package.

3. On the *timing* of devaluation-cum-liberalization, it is clearly important, in view of the tendency to judge major policy changes in terms of *post hoc ergo propter hoc* illogic, that LDCs (which typically have their price level and exports geared to their agricultural situation) should choose a time just after a good harvest.

4. It is also clearly important not to delay the adoption of a liberalization package to a point where a large *de facto* devaluation has to be replaced by a still larger parity change. The distinction between gross and net devaluations is too subtle to be grasped except by a few sophisticated economists and it seems not to arouse excessive expectations about improvements in export performance when the devaluation looks large. At the same time, the replacement of the *ad hoc* and selective export subsidization (which must invariably flourish under a large *de facto* devaluation) becomes both difficult and liable to contradict the assessed success of any net devaluation insofar as some exports, which are uneconomical but were promoted under indiscriminate export subsidization, are eliminated by the shift to a *de jure* devaluation.

5. The impossibility of dislodging the principle of indigenous availability and the consequent survival of sheltered markets underline the plausible conclusion that it is not easy to implement a "true" liberalization designed to improve the competitiveness and efficiency of domestic import substitution when exchange control over a long period has corrupted domestic industry, bureaucrats and politicians into considering any production that competes with imports as necessarily desirable and therefore automatically superior to rival imports. It does suggest, however, that the more feasible, *and* less disruptive, approach to the dismantling of such automatic protection would be to convert the implicit into explicit tariffs and then to set a gradualistic time schedule for bringing them to uniformity around a modest rate.

6. The *resumption* of the suspended aid flow was clearly helpful; but it tells us nothing about the issue of augmenting foreign credits as part of a liberalization package. There *is,* however, one point of substance that needs to be made here. As we saw, it took time for the resumed aid flow to actually reach importers: the delays were caused at both recipient and donor ends. These delays, which could have been reduced under better administrative arrangements, were to be followed by the recession which was largely brought on by the decelerating investments and outlays by the government which dreaded the possibility that otherwise the drought-induced price rises would be accentuated further. It is clear that if aid, which was largely available for "maintenance" imports (i.e., imports of raw materials and spares), had been partly available for increased imports of (the right) food grains, aid utilization would have been more rapid *in toto* and for maintenance, as the need for a deflationary policy would have been eliminated. The net effect thus should have been greater utilization of aid, greater production and investment levels in industry, and (at worst) only a moderate, adverse impact on non-traditional exports (because the reduced depression in domestic demand would have affected, *ceteris paribus,* the improved performance of the non-traditional industries, as indicated by our analysis in Chapter 9). The net result would have been, therefore, favorable, particularly if we take into account the fact that higher levels of activity would have permitted the import liberalization to be perhaps more genuine—in a recession, it is doubly difficult to attack the principle of indigenous availability. The lessons, therefore, are that the red tape in aid-disbursement and aid-tying-by-commodity-specification are both factors that can critically affect the performance of a liberalization package; and concentration merely on the total level of aid authorization or foreign credits can be counter-productive.

7. Finally, we may well ask whether the Indian policy package could have been improved, in any fundamental regard, so as to yield better results. This is a somewhat difficult question to answer as our analysis has indicated that there were several different factors interacting on the situation and the

outcome, some exogenous and beyond control and others within the set of available policy instruments. We must therefore work at several levels of approximation. If we assume that the Aid Consortium would necessarily have made aid flow conditional on the Indian government's undertaking a devaluation, and that the composition of the aid flow was also to be suboptimal (in the sense we have already discussed in this chapter), then the only meaningful questions relate to whether (1) the government could have done better by changing the policy package (e.g., choosing a different degree of devaluation) and by choosing also a different set of fiscal and monetary policies, and (2) the government could have done better by not succumbing to the pressure for devaluation. Taking the latter question first, it seems that the economic situation had deteriorated in the aftermath of the Indo-Pakistan War of 1965 and the interruptions in aid had led to shortages of imports that were hurting the economy badly. It seems, therefore, as if the effectiveness of aid diplomacy in forcing the government to devalue was very great; and it does not seem to us that, unless the government could reasonably count on resumption of significant aid, there was any real choice in the matter at that time. If we then suppose that the devaluation had to be undertaken anyway, was it the right amount? It is possible, in retrospect, to argue that it was either too much or too little. If we assume, as we must, that the drought was to follow the devaluation, it may have been quite sensible perhaps to make the devaluation, on a *net* basis, as low as possible and to claim unambiguously that the objective of the devaluation was *wholly* to replace the existing tariffs and export subsidies, which had been levied in lieu of the devaluation, and that short-term export performance improvement was therefore not an objective of the exercise at all. This might have eased the situation politically, however slightly. On the other hand, we might argue that the decision was going to be unpopular anyway, and that therefore the objective should have been to devalue as much as possible this time itself as it would not be possible to use the instrument again in the near future! In fact, since our analysis also has indicated that the devaluation (net) did help promote exports, it is arguable that an increased degree of (net) devaluation would have led to more exports and also to greater economic activity. Against this, however, we must balance the fact that, in an inflationary situation resulting from the drought, a greater degree of devaluation would have led to price changes that might well have been politically unsettling at a difficult time. Our own conclusion is that, given the external constraint of the demand for a devaluation by the aid donors as a precondition for the resumption of large-scale aid and in view of the severe drought to follow later, the government was probably wise in having acted in a reasonably cautious fashion by keeping the net devaluation within reasonable bounds. We probably need to stress again, however, that the optimal course of action, in light of later developments, would have been rather for the Aid Consortium merely to press for a substantial unification of the tariffs and subsidies (this was beginning to happen, as we noted in Chapter 5) and strongly urge that at a reasonable future point (after the new harvest had been reliably forecast as good) the *de facto* devaluation be replaced by a *de jure* change of parity, and resume the aid flow. This would have taken the sting out of the charges of political pressure for a change in the rate of the Indian rupee and made the transition to a better and more efficient foreign exchange regime more attractive to the policy-makers and the politicians and therefore also feasible. On the other hand, given the strong dissatisfaction that the Western aid donors felt with India's economic policies and performance, it would have been asking too much to expect them to forgo the opportunity provided by the suspension of aid during the Indo-Pakistan hostilities of October 1965 to make the resumption of large-scale aid conditional on prompt changes in Indian economic policy.

RELAPSE INTO PHASE II

In conclusion, we may note that the ultimate outcome of the attempted liberalization in 1966, which inaugurated Phase III, was a relapse into Phase II. Differential export subsidies emerged at significant levels; the QR-regime continued with high premia on several items; the principle of automatic protection was not abandoned; and industrial licensing continued in substance. The emergence from the recession around 1969–70 appears to have combined with severely declining aid levels to produce a "structural deficit" that increased import premia and the consequent stringency of QRs, a phenomenon which was to be accentuated as the economy recovered to more "normal" levels of activity in the industrial sector.

The hope that India would have moved into a liberal regime with judicious use of exchange rate flexibility (either *de facto* or *de jure*), and moderate tariffs to grant protection to industry, thereby achieving greater economic efficiency and growth, appears to have been belied although the situation in 1970–71 was somewhat better in this regard than in 1965–66.

The events on the Indian subcontinent, beginning with the crackdown by Pakistan's army in East Pakistan on March 25, 1971, the eventual influx of over ten million refugees into India's troubled Eastern state of Bengal, the staggering burden of this refugee relief and its economic and political consequences, the resulting war between Pakistan and India culminating in the creation of Bangladesh, have made it impossible for the economy to return to anything like a "normal" situation, or for the economist to analyze the recent behavior of the economy in a plausible manner.

But it is abundantly clear that, particularly with the virtual disappearance of U.S. aid since the dramatic political events on the Indian subcontinent during 1971, the importance of an improved and efficient production and export performance—contingent on a successful transition to Phase III—has become even more manifest. Whether this will be understood, and whether the tools of exchange rate policy and a more efficient and less wasteful form of domestic protection will be deployed in the coming years, remains to be seen.

NOTES

1. The effect on some of the major, "new" exports was, in fact, almost negligible and even negative for some sectors, as Table 6-3 in Chapter 6 has shown. Thus, the revival of the export subsidies on these items was critical to their improved export performance

2. The latter argument is compatible with the existence of finite, and even sizable, import premia in general because the QR-licensing regime continued to imply non-transferability of licenses as well as delays in licensing renewals.

3. In interpreting Table 11-1, however, we must allow for the fact that the period immediately preceding the devaluation in June 1966 was "abnormal" because of the suspension of U.S. aid, and several import premia were at exceptionally high levels.

4. For lack of space, we have not been able to reproduce here the import premia. However, they are available from Dr. V. R. Panchamukhi at Bombay University, on request.

5. Practically none of the cosmetics was to change; but effectively the restrictions were to be *de facto* back in operation, implying the relapse into Phase II.

6. Frankena, "Export." His chapter on design problems offers a useful discussion of such difficulties in the engineering industry during the post-1966 period.

7. See J. Bhagwati, "The Case for Devaluation," *Economic Weekly,* August 1962, pp. 1263–1266; and Richard Cooper, "Currency Devaluation in Developing Countries" (Paper No. 166, Economic Growth Center, Yale University).

8. The Prime Minister herself is exempted from this charge on the convenient assumption that she was wrongly advised; this represents nothing more than coming to terms with the reality of her lately acquired immense hold on Indian politics and amnesia regarding earlier attacks on her *bona fides* as well in the wake of the devaluation.

9. Thus, *Link* (a popular, left-wing weekly) carried the following story on December 8, 1971: "Fortunately, the suggestion that the rupee should also be revalued with the devaluation of the dollar was rejected by the Union Cabinet though some senior bureaucrats, including chief economic advisor I. G. Patel, who pleaded for it were reportedly supported by Planning Minister Subramaniam. A different viewpoint is understood to have been put forth by a section of the Finance Ministry's experts, including economic adviser Ashok Mitra. It must be said to the Finance Minister's credit that when he was called upon to give his personal opinion he opted against devaluation of the rupee. A repetition of 1965 [1966, *Sic*] was thus averted. . . ."

10. It is therefore really remarkable that the Minister for Planning, Mr. C. Subramaniam, who had been a member of the three-Minister group which advised the Prime Minister in 1966 on the devaluation, had reportedly the political courage to propose that the rupee rate be adjusted fully to maintain parity with the dollar.

11. If India had not changed its parity, the new rate would have been Rs.6.90 per U.S. dollar. This ingenious method of partially following the dollar devaluation could be put across and implemented only because few if any of the anti-devaluation Ministers could have followed the complex nature of the changes in parity rates at the time. The Prime Minister is reported to have remarked that she was out of her depth, with some claiming that the rupee had been revalued and others that it had been devalued!

12. We may note that in "Currency Devaluation" Cooper's criterion of political failure—whether the finance minister or the government falls shortly after a devaluation —is not helpful (as he himself admits). Though in this instance S. Chadhuri, the Finance Minister, did fall, he was a marginal minister anyway. The Planning Minister, Asoka Mehta, was eventually eased out, but for a whole complex of reasons. The Food Minister, C. Subramaniam, has survived, has continued to enjoy the prime minister's confidence and even advocates further devaluation. And ironically, the Prime Minister herself found that by sharpening her differences with the senior Congress bosses who had criticized her openly for her decision to devalue, she helped to bring on a struggle from which she has emerged as the undisputed leader of her party and country. In retrospect, not only did Mrs. Gandhi recover extremely well from this controversy, but she may well owe her political triumph to it.

13. See J. Bhagwati, *Amount and Sharing of Aid* (Washington D.C.: Overseas Development Council, 1970).

Part IV

Growth Effects

Chapter 12

Issues Relating to the Growth Effects of India's Foreign Trade Regime

In Part III we examined the issues raised by India's attempt at liberalizing the foreign trade regime (in its widest sense) since the mid-1960s. And earlier in Part II we examined the workings of the exchange control regime within the framework of domestic policies (such as industrial licensing), and highlighted certain of the inefficiencies and adverse economic consequences resulting therefrom. Our analysis in Part II, however, was mainly confined to the kinds of effects that are handled under the rubric of static efficiency effects. We now propose to extend our analysis to several issues that are raised more routinely in the context of the growth effects of foreign trade regimes.

1. The static efficiency effects are, in our view, a major aspect of the growth effects of any policy framework, insofar as efficiency must affect the productivity of given investments. We can therefore hardly emphasize more pointedly the importance of these effects than by drawing together in Chapter 13 the principal conclusions of our analysis in Part II. At the same time, we extend our analysis by developing in Chapter 13 statistical measures of the adverse resource-allocational effects of the Indian foreign trade regime and by examining more intensively the question of excess capacity in Indian industry in relation to this regime.

2. Since we have shown that India's export performance could have been improved by the pursuit of different trade and exchange rate policies, it is pertinent to ask whether the impact of this improvement would have been to better India's economic performance in general and, if so, to a significant extent. There are two broad ways in which this question may be approached: (a) If we take the techniques and efficiency of production within activities

175

as given, and also consider savings and foreign resource inflow to be deter-mined by overall policy exogenous to the export performance, then the gain from improved export performance really must come through its impact on the overall allocation decisions in the five year plans. To investigate this issue, therefore, we should really put the question into the planning context (which, for India, needs to be taken as institutionally given if our exercise is to be meaningful); and we also need to have a macro-planning model within which to assess this question. This is precisely what we attempt, in Chapter 14, by using the well-known Eckaus-Parikh multi-sector planning model in one of its versions. (b) On the other hand, it is quite possible to argue that the tech-niques and resources need not be taken as given and that an export-growth-oriented strategy would have led to improved technology by increasing re-search and development and faster growth of savings. We examine these issues in Chapters 15 and 16 respectively.

3. The impact of India's foreign trade regime on productivity change in her industries, through the encouragement or discouragement of research and development, is an important issue and one to which we address ourselves in Chapter 15 at some length. In this connection, we will distinguish the research and development issue from the rather different issue of cost-consciousness and so-called X-efficiency: could a regime less reliant on auto-matic protection, of the kind described in this study as characteristic of Indian policy, have led to increased efficiency and cost reduction by promoting inter-national competition, even if the *degree* of protection had not been reduced?

4. We also briefly address ourselves (in Chapter 15) to the relatively intractable problem of whether the foreign trade regime, in conjunction with the domestic policies, encouraged the growth of domestic entrepreneurship, and what effect it had on the quality thereof.

5. Finally, we treat at some length in Chapter 16 the question whether the foreign trade regime had any impact on the savings effort. Here, we can approach the issues at different levels. (a) Assuming that the policy of auto-matic protection by means of licensing and exchange controls, administered in the manner studied earlier in this volume, did encourage successfully the growth of modern import-substituting industries, we may ask if these exhibit different savings rates from the traditional and export-oriented industries. (b) Assuming that industry as a whole benefited from the import-substituting strategy, as against agriculture, we may ask whether the relative rates of saving are different between the two sectors. (c) Since the liberalization package of 1966 was linked directly to significant aid resumption, though at substantially lower levels than in the early 1960s, it is also worth asking what the impact of foreign aid is on domestic savings efforts in India.

Chapter 13

Static Allocational and Efficiency Impact on Growth

In principle, India's QR-regime, coupled with industrial licensing, could have diverse effects on the resource allocational system and on the efficiency of any given activity (e.g., the extent of capacity utilization). We have already noted many of these in Chapter 2. In this chapter, we supplement that analysis in two important respects. First, we analyze the impact on the *pattern* of resource utilization among different industries.[1] Next, we analyze the impact on capacity utilization *within* industries.

INEFFICIENCY IN THE PATTERN OF RESOURCE UTILIZATION

One would expect that an economic regime (as in India) that depends so critically on direct and detailed regulation of imports and the creation of industrial capacity would exhibit strikingly different social returns on different activities because the framework of economic policies governing industrialization does not induce or permit systematic attention to costs, as we have argued at some length in Chapter 2.

The index we have used to indicate the inter-industrial *disparities* that one would expect from our analysis of the economic policies governing trade and industrialization is the domestic resource cost (DRC) per unit of foreign exchange. This index is broadly indicative of the differences in the returns to deployment of domestic resources, using the approximation that observed unit export values measure true opportunity costs to society. Aside from the well-known limitations of this measure, we should note two things:

1. Wide differentials in DRCs among alternative activities do not *necessarily* mean commensurate losses to society because reallocation of resources intended to reduce these differentials may run into sharply increasing costs and diminishing returns (e.g., international prices would not be the same at increased levels of exportation). On the other hand, the potential for such "substitution" in production and trade should not be underestimated in an economy such as India's.[2] And even if one adds up the orders of magnitude involved in making pairwise, notional reallocations among activities, they often emerge high enough to indicate that the gains in sizable sectors of industry may be even 30 to 50 percent of the social returns earned from the resources utilized in these sectors.[3]

2. While we believe that the DRC measure is, in principle, superior to the effective rate of protection (ERP) measure, particularly insofar as the analyst is able to take into account *shadow* prices of domestic inputs and also *marginal* rather than average international prices, the DRC estimates we present for nearly the entire economy for 1963–65 and 1968 are *not* adjusted in this way and therefore are rigidly related to the ERP estimates (which we also present) by the fact that:

$$DRC = \frac{V_j}{V_j^*} \cdot r$$

$$ERP = \frac{V_j}{V_j^*} - 1$$

$$DRC = (ERP + 1)r$$

where V_j^* is value-added in Indian rupees in the process at international prices, V_j is value-added in Indian rupees in the process at domestic prices and r is the number of Indian rupees per unit dollar.

Table 13–1 presents the estimates of DRC for 1963–65 for 69 activities, based on the 77-sector input-output table for 1965.[4] The sectors which show negative value-added at international prices and hence negative numbers in their DRC estimates indicate that (on current techniques) these activities cause losses to the economy. The remaining activities show again a wide variation in their DRC estimates.[5]

Table 13–1 also presents DRC estimates for the same sixty-nine sectors for 1968–69, thus defining a comparable set of DRCs before and after the 1966 policy changes. Presumably because of the short-run period since 1966, the differentials in DRCs among the different activities continue in 1968 to be as large [if one takes the comparison of values in row (i) in Table 13–4 as one should, because the heavy impact of extreme values reflected in row (ii) is really misleading].[6] There is nonetheless a slight fall in the standard deviation and a more perceptible fall in the coefficient of variation. Also, the

TABLE 13–1

Estimates of Domestic Resource Cost and Protection in Indian Industries, 1963–65 and 1968–69

Sector Number and Description[a] (1)	Domestic Resource Cost[b] (rupees per dollar)		Implicit Tariff Rate (percent)		Effective Rate of Protection (percent)
	1963–65 (2)	1968–69 (3)	1963–65 (4)	1968–69 (5)	1968–69 (6)
2. Electrical equipment	14.3	16.5	175	90	119.6
3. Non-electrical equipment	14.1	14.1	182	90	87.8
4. Transport equipment	11.4	12.1	137	70	61.2
5. Metal products	9.5	17.5	120	110	133.5
6. Iron and steel	18.2	18.9	206	127	151.9
8. Cement	10.6	10.8	83	50	43.8
9. Non-ferrous metals	17.4	10.3	144	40	37.9
10. Other minerals	6.1	10.4	30	40	38.7
11. Rubber	183.0	negative	29	67	250.7
12. Leather	4.7	17.1	15	120	127.6
13. Leather products	28.7	16.5	231	120	120.0
14. Leather footwear	9.7	16.9	50	120	124.0
15. Animal husbandry	7.3	negative	30	125	103.1
17. Sugar	11.9	25.1	40	75	235.1
18. Plantations	4.7	7.2	0	0	–4.0
19. Gur and khandsari	negative	259.2	40	50	3,354.0
20. Vegetable oils	13.7	18.0	55	80	139.5
21. Vanaspati	6.8	12.4	55	80	65.2
23. Starch	negative	negative	243	75	146.7

(continued)

TABLE 13–1 (concluded)

Sector Number and Description[a] (1)	Domestic Resource Cost[b] (rupees per dollar) 1963–65 (2)	1968–69 (3)	Implicit Tariff Rate (percent) 1963–65 (4)	1968–69 (5)	Effective Rate of Protection (percent) 1968–69 (6)
24. Milk products	negative	46.6	277	225	521.8
25. Breweries and soft drinks	15.0	13.6	160	100	81.6
26. Biscuits, confectionery	29.6	55.8	176	200	644.1
27. Cigarettes and cigars	61.1	16.0	393	110	113.5
28. Bidi	4.1	6.6	0	0	–12.4
29. Other tobacco products	4.7	16.0	393	110	113.0
30. Fruits and vegetable products	30.6	21.0	150	150	179.8
31. Cashew nut processing	negative	14.0	145	150	86.2
32. Food grains	4.8	7.5	0	0	–1.0
33. Cotton	6.2	11.5	30	50	53.2
34. Cotton yarn	4.4	15.6	10	70	107.8
35. Cotton textiles	53.5	24.3	61	100	223.7
36. Jute	5.2	11.6	10	50	54.9
37. Jute textiles	22.6	41.8	66	110	457.3
38. Woolen yarn	7.2	9.5	40	70	26.6
39. Woolen textiles	17.0	24.8	100	110	230.2
40. Raw silk	negative	15.2	609	40	102.1
41. Silk textiles	33.7	65.8	609	100	776.8
42. Man-made fibers	1,048.7	negative	609	590	105.2
43. Artificial silk fibers	41.4	11.7	609	110	55.5
44. Other textiles	14.1	16.1	136	110	114.4
45. Oil seeds	6.8	13.4	40	70	78.3
46. Sugar cane	4.6	7.5	0	0	–0.25
47. Tobacco	10.0	16.6	100	110	120.7

48. Fruits and vegetables	7.2	23.9	50	201	218.7
49. Other crops	4.8	7.5	0	0	0.0
50. Fertilizers	4.2	42.1	0	201	461.8
51. Ceramics and bricks	32.3	12.2	308	60	62.5
52. Glass and glasswares	31.8	11.1	83	60	47.7
53. Wood products	6.6	14.2	40	80	89.3
54. Timber	6.7	10.7	40	60	43.1
55. Chinaware, pottery	9.5	17.5	83	110	125.9
56. Wood (others)	6.2	13.5	30	80	80.0
57. Other forest products	5.7	13.5	20	80	80.0
59. Petroleum products	negative	47.6	65	75	535.1
61. Rubber footwear	6.8	18.4	50	110	144.9
62. Tires and tubes	5.3	12.7	35	75	59.7
63. Other rubber products	6.0	17.7	40	110	135.6
64. Paper and paper products	22.2	20.4	198	125	171.3
65. Plastics	12.8	20.0	161	150	166.2
66. Dyestuffs	13.2	17.0	170	113	126.1
67. Paints and varnishes	29.0	18.1	190	113	141.0
68. Insecticides and pesticides	12.0	12.4	150	70	65.0
69. Drugs and pharmaceuticals	11.8	12.7	140	70	68.8
70. Soap and glycerine	2.7	19.9	20	110	165.8
71. Perfumes and cosmetics	19.5	10.8	155	100	44.3
72. Miscellaneous chemicals	20.3	15.3	180	89	104.1
75. Coal and coke	4.7	10.9	0	50	44.9
76. Matches	10.1	16.9	100	110	124.8
77. Printing and publishing	3.6	5.9	0	0	−21.0

SOURCES and METHODS: See Appendix to this chapter.
a. As given in 1964–65 inter-industry table for India, *Sankhya*, 1968.
b. Per unit of foreign exchange earned or saved.

level and variations in import premia did fall significantly during the period between mid-1966 and 1968–69 owing to import liberalization and the recession (as indicated earlier in this volume), so that the extremes in the DRC results of 1963–65 are not so evident in the DRC results of 1968–69.[7] Note also that (as is evident from Table 13–4), the average DRC (when we compare rows (ii) again) rose only slightly between 1963–65 and 1968–69 despite the shift in the exchange rate from Rs. 4.75 to Rs. 7.50 per dollar. This is, however, attributable to the fact that value-added, while going up in domestic prices, increased significantly at international prices: implicit tariffs had fallen, in general, more sharply for outputs than for inputs in 1968–69 compared with 1963–65, the fall in import premia thus exhibiting a negative escalation with respect to processing. The latter phenomenon may well have to be explained by reference to the recession which led to serious pressures on domestic output prices and on continuing import controls, despite import liberalization, which implied not so serious pressure on domestic input prices.

We also include for 1968–69 an estimate of ERPs in Column (6) of Table 13–1.[8] As is to be expected, these also show great differentials among the different activities.[9] It is also interesting to note that, for most of the activities, the implicit (nominal) tariffs in Column (5) are below the effective tariffs.

Table 13–2 gives the simple and weighted average estimates of ERPs and DRCs for 1968–69, grouped by the following major categories: (1) consumer goods, (2) intermediate goods (primary), (3) intermediate goods (semi-finished and finished) and (4) capital goods. Within each of these major groups, we have further distinguished among different subgroups with different interactions with international trade, essentially separating the agro-based industries from the others in each group. The weighted average rates have been derived by using the value-added at international prices as the weights.[10]

The ERPs for primary consumer goods are the lowest, and those for the non-food consumer goods are the highest. Agro-based intermediate goods of semi-finished/finished type receive much higher effective protection than the other intermediate goods. Capital goods receive lower effective protection than intermediate goods (except the agro-based primary type) and consumer goods (except the primary type). The domestic resource cost is 8.38 for primary goods; 19.93 for non-food, semi-finished and finished consumer goods; 18.21 for agro-based, semi-finished and finished intermediate goods; and 13.36 for capital goods. The rather steep protection of the (non-primary) consumer goods and (to a lesser extent) of certain intermediates and many capital goods, which appear to have been among the major beneficiaries of the industrialization process, and their attendant high domestic resource cost, would appear to conform to the notions one has from more casual knowledge of the economy and the planning strategy.

The DRC estimates given above are necessarily approximate, particularly in relying on market premium rates which can be very unreliable and which had to be applied to a large range of industries, and in having to cope with literally thousands of items at a highly aggregated level in such calculations. They are nonetheless adequate for pointing out the high coefficient of variation in the returns on different activities.

It is useful, however, to know that even detailed estimates for the automobile ancillary industry, based on personal interviews and data collection, corroborate these conclusions in "microcosm." Thus, in Table 13–3, we have Anne Krueger's estimated thirty-four DRCs for products/firms. Taking only the positive DRCs into account, they range from 7.87 to 184.27.[11]

It seems reasonable, therefore, to conclude that in ignoring costs—an indifference amply documented by an analysis of the actual allocational policies toward import and industrial licensing—the economic policies of the government have not merely made it likely that the resulting allocations would be inefficient but have, in actuality, led to such an outcome. We should point out that we would be rather more skeptical in reaching this conclusion if we merely had available to us the statistical results on the variance in the DRCs among activities, for it is arguable that the data base of these estimates is not so firm as one would wish. Thus, even in an economy in which the government paid attention to costs and refrained from massive intervention in resource allocation, one could well find, on taking a cross-section measurement of DRCs, a fairly wide spread and variance among them because the economy would be in a perpetual state of disequilibrium and flux resulting from factors such as changing international prices, technologies, availability of information, and so on. But our inference that the wide variance observed does indicate that the system is sub-optimally organized is considerably reinforced by our detailed observation (see Chapter 2) that the system is indeed designed to ignore opportunity costs in making allocational decisions. It is therefore the *conjunction* of this rather institutional but extremely vital evidence on the method of allocation of imports and licensed capacities, with the observed pattern of DRC spread among different activities, that makes our inference of an inefficient allocation mechanism that much more plausible than it would otherwise be.

INDUSTRIAL CAPACITY UTILIZATION AND THE QR-REGIME

Indian manufacturing has been characterized by great excess capacity in a number of industries. The official data on capacity utilization are quite hopeless in that they compound inevitable conceptual difficulties with several statistical drawbacks.[12] Principal among these drawbacks is the fact that the

TABLE 13–2

Sectoral Average Tariff Rates, Effective Rates of Protection and Domestic Resource Cost Estimates, 1968–69

Sector Description (1)	Sector Numbers (2)	Implicit Tariff (3)	Simple Average		Weighted Average	
			Effective Rate of Protection (4)	Domestic Resource Cost per Unit of Foreign Exchange Earned or Saved (5)	Effective Rate of Protection (6)	Domestic Resource Cost per Unit of Foreign Exchange Earned or Saved (7)
A. *Consumer goods*						
A.1 Primary	15,32,48,49	81.5	80.2	13.0	11.75	8.4
A.2 Semi-finished and finished						
A.2.1 Food and beverages	17,19,21,23,24,25, 26,27,28,29,30,31	110.4	201.7	21.6	90.8	14.1
A.2.2 Non-food	14,61,35,39,41,44, 52,55,65,71,70,76	107.5	190.8	21.9	165.1	19.9
B. *Intermediate goods (primary)*						
B.1 Agro-based	11,18,33,36,40,45, 46,47	48.4	77.2	11.9	33.1	10.1
B.2 Others	7,10,12,54,56,57, 60,75	71.7	62.8	12.7	47.1	11.4

C. *Intermediate goods* (semi-finished and finished)

C.1 Agro-based	20,34,37,38	82.5	182.8	21.2	142.5	18.2
C.2 Others	5,6,8,9,13,42,43, 50,51,53,59,62,63, 64,66,67,68,69,72	122.5	140.4	18.2	106.0	15.5
D. Capital goods	2,3,4	83.3	89.5	14.2	77.9	13.4

NOTES: 1. Negative DRCs have been omitted in making the calculations presented in the table.

2. The weighted averages have been derived by using the value-added at international prices as weights. Where value-added at international prices was negative, value-added at domestic prices was used. In these cases the ERP index was also calculated with value-added at domestic prices in the denominator of the formula for ERP, which puts the increment in value-added (due to protection) in the numerator.

SOURCE: Calculated from Table 13–1.

185

TABLE 13-3
**Price Ratios and Domestic Resource Costs
in the Auto Ancillary Industry, 1970**

(1)	$\dfrac{\text{Indian Price}}{\text{Foreign Price}} \times 100$ (2)	Domestic Resource Cost (rupees per dollar) (3)
Assembler 1	137	8.25
Assembler 2	139	8.62
Assembler 3	125	7.87
Assembler 4	197	34.95
Assembler 5	140	10.91*
Assembler 6	118	8.85
Metal fabricator 1	128	19.95
Metal fabricator 2	236	27.80
Metal fabricator 3a	161	83.92
Metal fabricator 3b	149	17.85
Metal fabricator 4	260	negative
Metal fabricator 5	175	14.62
Metal fabricator 6	137	9.45
Metal fabricator 7	180	26.47
Metal fabricator 8a	180	11.17*
Metal fabricator 8b	181	20.41*
Metal fabricator 9a	167	20.10*
Metal fabricator 9b	167	8.67*
Metal fabricator 9c	167	21.45*
Chemical 1a	227	17.47
Chemical 1b	202	11.55*
Chemical 2	133	10.95*
Chemical 3	173	33.75
Chemical 4a	244	33.15*
Chemical 4b	309	negative
Chemical 4c	278	184.27
Chemical 5	175	12.07
Chemical 6	286	180.60**
Miscellaneous product 1a	192	44.47*
Miscellaneous product 1b	158	12.81
Miscellaneous product 2	183	17.53*
Miscellaneous product 3	156	18.15
Miscellaneous product 4	167	17.25
Miscellaneous product 5	262	49.05*

NOTE: All price data are based on ex-factory domestic price and Indian f.o.b. export price except where denoted by an asterisk. One asterisk indicates that the relevant foreign price is the United Kingdom ex-factory price; two asterisks indicate that the foreign price employed is a c.i.f. Bombay price.

SOURCE: Krueger, *Import Substitution.*

TABLE 13–4

Means, Standard Deviations and Coefficients of Variation among Alternative Estimates of DRCs and Implicit Tariffs in Tables 13–1 through 13–3; 1963–65, 1968–69 and 1970

Item (1)	Number of Observations (2)	Mean (unweighted) (3)	Standard Deviation (4)	Coefficient of Variation (5)
1963–1965				
DRC	(i) 63 (excluding all negative DRCs: 6 items)	33.21	131.22	3.95
	(ii) 61 (excluding *also* Nos. 11 and 42)	14.11	12.08	0.86
Implicit tariffs	(i) 69 (including items with zero values)	128.93	149.68	1.16
	(ii) 61 (excluding 8 items with zero values)	145.84	151.25	1.04
1968–1969				
DRC	(i) 65 (excluding negative DRCs: 4 items)	21.67	31.79	1.47
	(ii) 64 (excluding *also* No.19)	17.96	11.46	0.64
Implicit tariffs	(i) 69 (including zero values)	96.61	75.86	0.79
	(ii) 63 (excluding zero values)	105.81	73.00	0.69
1970				
DRC	(i) 32 (excluding 2 negative values)	31.39	41.87	1.33
	(ii) 30 (excluding *also* 2 extremely large values for *Chemicals* 4c and 6)	21.32	15.47	0.74

NOTE: For DRCs, the figures in the second row do not include certain extreme values, whereas for implicit tariffs they exclude zero values. All DRCs are calculated, excluding negative values.
SOURCE: Tables 13–1 through 13–3.

187

DGTD, which compiles the data, also regulates AU allocations and therefore the capacity estimates have tended to lie anywhere within the range defined by entrepreneurs who wish to exaggerate capacity in order to get more AU licenses, and by DGTD officials who will refuse to "recognize" capacity augmentation because this would increase their apparent obligation to provide AU licenses.[13]

We have therefore refrained from including here any analysis based on the statistical tables containing these unreliable, and almost meaningless, estimates of excess capacity in India. On the other hand, we note that interviews, chairmen's annual reports to their companies and studies of individual firms and industries uniformly indicate that the incidence of under-utilization of capacity has been particularly severe in the "new" industries, i.e., in engineering goods and chemicals, both of which have depended significantly on imports of materials for their production.[14] And we also include one set of recent estimates of under-utilized industrial capacity for 1961 to 1964 for selected industries, in Table 13–5.[15]

Under-utilization of capacity, even in the import-intensive industries, cannot be charged entirely to the QR-regime and to licensing policies although, as we argue below, they do have important effects in that direction. Labor problems resulting in strikes and lockouts, electricity breakdowns and interruptions in transportation are generally held to have accounted for considerable under-utilization.

In addition, the ready availability of project as against maintenance aid in the pre-1966 period of India's industrialization is generally believed to have resulted in the creation of more capacity (to use up project aid) in the face of existing excess capacity. However, this hardly seems plausible. One finds it difficult to understand why firms should want to add to capacity, or why new firms should seek to enter an industry already troubled by excess capacity, just because they can import the necessary capital goods. It is rather the QR-(and industrial licensing) regime that appears to have led to the utilization of available project aid in areas where capacity utilization was already inadequate. Let us turn now to the arguments linking the QR-regime to excess capacity.

1. The tendency to relate equity in the allocation of AU licenses to installed capacity led to an incentive to create capacity by linking the availability of premia-fetching imports with creation of more capacity. Thus, as Bhagwati and Desai have argued, an entrepreneur, with a given capacity that was under-utilized for lack of imported inputs, could not (under the Indian QR-regime) expand output through additional utilization of capacity.[16] The only way he could increase production was by getting more capacity installed and having some import quota allotted to him on the basis of it. But even if the entrepreneur were allowed access to more imports at market prices[17] so that he could

TABLE 13–5

Estimates of Underutilization of Capacity for Selected Groups of Industries, 1961–64

Industry group	Underutilization (percent)				
	1961	1962	1963	1964	Average (1961–64)
Food products	9.9	9.3	24.4	16.9	15.1
	(7.5)	(6.5)	(21.6)	(15.2)	(12.7)
Tobacco products[a]	10.6	4.4	5.2	12.7	8.2
Textile products	7.0	7.9	9.1	6.3	7.6
	(6.3)	(7.3)	(8.2)	(5.8)	(6.9)
Wood and cork products[a]	35.1	27.1	16.9	16.0	23.8
Paper and paper products[b]	11.2	10.5	7.8	11.7	10.3
Leather and leather products	59.9	57.8	54.4	56.0	57.0
	(27.6)	(24.4)	(17.9)	(21.5)	(22.8)
Rubber and rubber products	16.1	23.1	25.6	26.7	22.9
	(5.7)	(7.1)	(11.2)	(10.6)	(8.7)
Chemicals and chemical products	53.5	56.8	59.3	55.3	56.2
	(29.0)	(23.9)	(21.2)	(30.0)	(26.0)
Non-metallic— mineral products	36.2	34.7	33.0	35.3	34.8
	(22.1)	(20.7)	(19.0)	(21.4)	(20.8)
Basic metals	21.1	11.3	8.8	11.1	13.1
	(13.3)	(4.5)	(5.3)	(7.9)	(7.8)
Metal products	53.9	56.2	54.8	54.2	54.8
	(23.0)	(22.2)	(17.4)	(17.3)	(20.0)
Machinery except electrical machines	26.1	32.1	26.6	37.2	30.5
	(12.7)	(11.4)	(7.3)	(21.1)	(13.1)
Electrical machinery and appliances	39.7	43.6	45.4	41.8	42.6
	(8.3)	(11.7)	(11.7)	(10.6)	(8.1)
Transport equipment	49.3	42.2	41.8	35.7	42.4
	(22.5)	(18.2)	(16.3)	(10.7)	(16.9)

NOTE: This table is based on both present and desirable working conditions. Figures in parentheses are for present working conditions.

SOURCE: *Underutilisation of Industrial Capacity* (New Delhi: National Council of Applied Economic Research, 1966), Table 2.

a. For present working conditions, these industries show overutilization.

b. The number of shifts working at present and the number considered desirable are the same for industries of this group.

expand utilization of existing capacity, he would have to purchase inputs at import-premia-inclusive market prices, whereas expansion of capacity would enable him to expand output by access to premia-exclusive import allocations. This would then certainly bias, *ceteris paribus,* his choice between these two courses of action toward creating more capacity.

Furthermore, the artificial cheapening of CG imports under an overvalued exchange rate system based on direct allocations could lead to suboptimally increased capital intensity in relation to the primary factor, labor.

Even more important in practice than these two arguments is the fact that (for most industries, until 1966 at least) licensing constrained the creation of capacity and QR policy guaranteed domestic sales at high enough prices to let licensed firms make large profits even at low levels of capacity utilization. Thus, even when there was excess capacity, it would pay a new firm to enter an industry, provided it could get the license to do so, then get its pro-rata-to-capacity share of scarce AU imports, and still earn a large profit. On the other hand, with free entry and competition for imported materials in the market, such a venture would have been untenable.

2. In addition to the consequences of licensing intermediates and capital goods in this fashion, there was another mechanism that accentuated excess capacity in the system *via* import licensing. In an economic regime where efficient firms can bid intermediates away from the inefficient, the former will achieve greater utilization of their capacity whereas the latter will be forced out. This process, which is also efficient because not all capacity is desirable and the undesirable must be scrapped to avoid larger losses, necessarily leads to higher overall rates of capacity utilization than in the current, Indian-type regime where inefficient firms automatically get "squatters' rights" to AU allocations.[18]

3. Another way in which the QR-regime must have affected capacity utilization was the bottlenecks it created. Undoubtedly, bottlenecks would arise in *any* regime, but the ability to correct them was severely constrained, for a number of firms, by the difficulty of effecting remedial imports. There is substantial evidence of this phenomenon in the *Redbooks* on Import Policy where occasional notices of special dispensation can be found in cases where action was finally taken to ease a particularly glaring bottleneck. Interviews with industrialists have confirmed this picture.[19] These bottlenecks add to excess capacity in two ways: (1) by preventing speedy availability of inputs into a process, and (2) by holding up the importation of critical spares and balancing equipment which would enable the existing capacity to be exploited more effectively. The former set of bottlenecks came from the restrictions built into the AU licensing system; the latter related to both CG and industrial licensing procedures.

4. Yet another way in which the import-control regime in India affected capacity utilization was by inhibiting the utilization of excess capacity for export markets. While, as we have argued in Chapters 8 and 9, there is evidence that firms with substantial excess capacity did manage to improve capacity utilization through exports after the June 1966 liberalization policy changes, we also note there that the export effort was badly compromised by the inabil-

ity of the firms to exploit the intended liberalization of imports meaningfully. The liberalization permitted the firms to renew their "normal" AU quotas only *after* evidence of substantial utilization of the initial AU license. This resulted in a substantial lag in the utilization of the augmented foreign credits for maintenance imports and prevented quicker export sales. The severe restrictions on transfers of licenses and on permissible imports also continued, preventing quick adjustments in production and capacity to respond to international orders. In effect, the substantial inflexibility of the import control regime has made it difficult for firms, when presented with export opportunities to reduce capacity under-utilization at low marginal costs, to exploit these opportunities. If we are to reckon on the full impact on capacity utilization from this cause, we should take the primary effect just discussed and add to it the secondary effect which is implied by the fact that additional export earnings would ease the import situation and make more maintenance imports available for further capacity utilization.

It is not possible to quantify meaningfully and accurately the extent of production and value-added lost to society by the effects of the (trade and industrial) direct-allocational regime, arising from the kinds of mechanisms that we have analyzed. Since, however, there is little reason otherwise to expect serious under-utilization to have emerged and persisted (except for reasons such as strikes, electricity breakdowns and the post-1966 recession) in sectors such as engineering goods where the phenomenon has been acute for a long time, it would not be unreasonable to conclude that their production would have increased significantly under a different economic regime.[20]

OVERALL EFFECTS

It would thus seem reasonable to conclude that the foreign trade regime led to a wasteful misallocation of investible resources among alternative industries and also accentuated the under-utilization of investments within these industries. If we also recall from Chapter 2 that the regime greatly reduced the degree of competition to which the firms in these industries were subject, and thus practically eliminated the incentives that such competition normally provides for reducing costs, the regime can be regarded as being wasteful in a threefold fashion. Needless to say, when we also add to these inefficiencies the several other adverse effects which we discussed in Chapter 2, there is little doubt that returns on Indian investments must have been substantially reduced by the regime. Hence, we would be justified in saying that the analysis in this Chapter and in Chapter 2 shows rather persuasively that, by reducing the productivity of investment, India's foreign trade regime adversely influenced the economy's growth performance as well.

Appendix:

Sources and Methods

1. For the DRC and ERP estimates in Tables 13–1 and 13–2, for 1963–65 and 1968–69, we have used the 1964–65 input-output table (at 1960–61 prices) prepared by M. R. Saluja and published in *Sankhya,* 1968. For the 1968–69 estimates, the sectoral price indices for 1968–69 (with 1965 as the base) are derived from the volumes of "Wholesale Prices in India" and these are used to convert the input and output values in 1965 prices into those in 1968–69 prices. The implicit tariffs for 1968–69 are derived from various sources: for some sectors, the method of direct price comparison is adopted, whereas for some others the data on premium rates on import licenses and the nominal tariff rates are used to derive the implicit tariffs. The ratio of domestic price to international price is given by (1 + implicit tariff rate). These ratios are used to derive the input-values and output-values, and hence the value-added, in international prices. The ERP estimates are thus based on these implicit tariffs.

2. For the analysis of 1963–65, the input-output coefficients of the 1964–65 table are used. The ratios of the domestic price to international price, for the period 1963–65, are derived from the following sources: (1) The unit values (producer's prices) are computed from the ASI Volumes of 1963 and 1965; (2) the corresponding c.i.f. unit values are obtained from trade data in several sectors whereas, in others (3) we have used market-interviews-based average premium rates during 1963–65 and price comparisons from various other sources and studies. Note that while the a_{ij}'s used are the *average* for 1963, 1964 and 1965, based on ASI information, in nearly all industries, the premium rates used to derive the international prices are taken anywhere from the period 1963 to 1965, as available.

3. The precise methodology consists in starting with the 1964–65 input-output table (at 1960–61 prices). In the first instance this has been upgraded to 1968–69 prices by using sectoral price indices for 1968–69 with 1960–61 as the base. These price indices are derived from the wholesale price index numbers published by commodity groups. Care is taken in building up correspondence between sectoral classification and the commodity groups of the price indices. In fact, price indices for the financial year are derived by using detailed monthly price statistics as published price indices refer to calendar years. However, it cannot be denied that correspondence between sectors and commodity groups may not be perfect and some imputations have been inevitable. Sectoral indices have been built by using the weights of the commodity groups as given in the published sources.

4. To the data thus derived in 1968–69 prices, ratios have been applied to get the values in international prices. These price-ratios for 1968–69, and 1963–65 are separately derived, from several sources. Those for 1963–65 are, for example, based on (1) published premium data (Vyapar), (2) tariff rates and (3) direct price comparisons (from ASI and trade statistics), etc. Since these are averages of 2 to 3 years of 1963–65, the results are described as 1963–65 results. The price-ratios of 1963–65 are applied directly to the original input and output values of the 1964–65 input-output table, i.e., the values in 1960–61 prices. Hence the estimates of 1963–65 are all in 1960–61 prices, though they are derived from 1963–65 price-ratios of domestic to international prices.

5. In deriving DRCs, value-added inclusive of non-traded inputs (railways, electricity and margin) is computed as the domestic resources. The official exchange rate used for 1968–69 is Rs. 7.50 per dollar and that used for 1963–65 is Rs. 4.75 per dollar.

6. In assessing the extreme variations in the DRC estimates in Tables 13–1 to 13–3, the reader must bear in mind the fact of variations in premia: these have to be personally observed to be readily believed. Also, in noting the rather dramatic shifts in DRCs between 1963–65 and 1968–69 in Table 13–1, for identical industries, remember that these can arise from changes in (1) the relative domestic prices of inputs and outputs, (2) the ratio of domestic to international prices of inputs and of outputs and (3) the exchange rate. These factors, for example, account for the drastic increase in DRC for gur and khandsari (sugar) from a negative figure in 1963–65 to the large figure of 259.2 in 1968–69. In particular, the exchange rate had increased from 4.75 to 7.50 and the ratio of domestic to international prices had fallen from 2.80 to 1.89 for one input while rising for the output in this industry, accounting for the dramatic shift in its DRC. For details on each industry's DRC calculation, refer to Dr. V. R. Panchamukhi, *Reader in Econometrics,* University of Bombay, Bombay, India.

7. It may be contended that, in reality, our DRC estimates are ERP estimates rather than (shadow-price-adjusted) DRC estimates. On the other hand, note two points. (1) An appropriate methodology is necessary to derive shadow prices of capital, labor, etc. Thus, *any* adjustment of factor prices by numbers which are asserted to be shadow prices is little more than "sensitivity analysis" and does not really elevate the resulting DRC estimates to a greater claim of legitimacy. Nor can one claim, for example, that pushing up interest rates from lows of 3–4 percent annually to 10–15 percent must necessarily be good as it is a move in the "right direction": the theory of second-best does not validate the claim that a move in the direction of the optimal solution is welfare-improving. To put it another way, nearly all the DRCs, adjusted for so-called shadow prices, suffer *in practice* from very much the same defects (as regards their worth as measures of social returns) as ERPs. For a detailed critique of the two concepts, and their relationship to more sophisticated cost-benefit analysis, see I. M. D. Little and James Mirrlees, *Project Appraisal and Planning for Developing Countries,* Heinemann Educational Books: London, 1974, especially Chapter 18, pp. 363–366. Thus our stress in the text that the ERP/DRC estimates in this chapter are only "broadly" indicative of the differential returns from different activities, thanks to India's QR-regime, has a sound basis. (2) Further, while the text emphasizes only the "returns" aspect of these estimates, it may occur to the reader to interpret the ERP estimates as showing, in the usual manner, the "resource-allocational" or "pull" effects (among different activities) of the tariff structure so measured. This is not so, however, and not merely for the theoretical reasons spelled out in recent contributions to the general equilibrium theory of effective protection and resource allocation (e.g., see the *Symposium* on this topic in the *Journal of International Economics,* May 1973, with particular reference to the contributions by Bruno, Bhagwati and Srinivasan, and Khang). Among the other reasons, we may particularly mention that, in a QR-regime where producers have access to part of their imported inputs *via* AU licenses and part *via* the market, and the former access implies getting imports at premium-exclusive prices while the latter implies getting them at premium-inclusive prices, the calculation of ERPs from an incentive viewpoint should also take into account this differential effect on input protection. In the estimates of ERPs in Bhagwati and Desai, *op. cit.,* calculated again by Dr. V. R. Panchamukhi, this distinction was indeed taken into account, using estimates of the fraction of imported-inputs requirements which were met by AU licenses in each activity. This has *not* been done in the ERP estimates in the text here because the focus there is not on the incentive effects but rather on the cost-benefit interpretation of the DRC variety.

Hence, if we wished to get our ERP estimates closer to the "true" incentive-oriented measure, we would have to adjust them for the direct access to imports under AU licenses. And, if we wished to get our DRC estimates closer to the "true" cost-benefit-oriented measure, we would need to compute systematically a set of appropriate shadow prices—a major analytical and empirical enterprise in itself—and utilize these instead of the actual market prices.

NOTES

1. This work was carried out entirely, and with great care and skill, by Dr. V. R. Panchamukhi of Bombay University, India. He has co-authored this chapter.

2. Thus for example, Asit Banerjee, in a forthcoming paper in *Sankhya* (1974), has estimated the elasticity of substitution for cotton textiles, jute textiles, sugar, paper and the bicycle industries, indicating that this may well be close to unity (if we use the SMAC method of estimation) for all except paper.

3. This is clearly evident from Anne Krueger's recent, detailed study of the auto ancillary industry in India where, utilizing data gathered at the firm level, she has shown differences in DRCs among different activities of over 100 percent. Clearly, instead of permitting indiscriminate growth of nearly all ancillaries, by furnishing automatic protection to them, if the structure and degree of protection had been devised rationally, the net result could have been more social returns from the same resource utilization. See Krueger, *The Benefits and Costs of Import Substitution in India: A Microeconomic Study*, USAID, October 1970.

4. The methodology by which DRCs were calculated is the standard one and is therefore not spelled out here. However, see the Appendix at the end of the chapter for important details.

5. The coefficients of variation are included in Table 13–4.

6. The coefficients of variation are still high (though lower than in 1968–69) and are included in Table 13–4.

7. The enormous variations in import premia can result in "implausible" DRCs, given our methodology of computing DRCs by deducting the international value-added from domestic value-added. Thus, for example, for animal husbandry, in 1968–69, the implicit tariff rate for output was 125 percent and significantly larger than for the major inputs (where it was in the range of 50 to 80 percent). The net result was to make value-added negative at international prices during 1968–69. However, in 1963–65, the implicit tariff rate (determined by the import premium) was smaller on output than on the inputs, resulting in positive value-added at international prices. In this connection, it may be noted that very large variations in DRCs have been calculated also by Krueger, *op. cit.*, within the auto ancillary industry, even though international value-added was estimated by direct inquiries on c.i.f. and f.o.b. prices of inputs and outputs.

8. The DRCs are related to the ERP estimates as noted earlier in this chapter. Note also that our calculations of ERPs treat non-traded goods as part of value-added—the so-called Corden method.

9. The coefficients of variation are included in Table 13–4.

10. For negative value-added industries, the value-added in domestic prices is used as the weight because the ERP index is then calculated with the value-added in domestic prices in the denominator, when the formula is written as the incremental value-added divided by value-added at domestic prices.

11. The coefficient of variation is included in Table 13–4.

12. The conceptual and statistical difficulties surrounding the capacity statistics in

India have been discussed in numerous sources. See J. Bhagwati, "The Measurement of Excess Capacity," ISI Working Paper, 1962; and Nancy Slocum, *Underutilized Industrial Capacity in India: Exploration of Measures and Causes,* USAID, New Delhi, 1970.

13. Cf. Frankena, *op. cit.,* and Slocum, *op. cit.,* in particular.

14. The DGTD data on capacity utilization are also consistent with this picture.

15. These estimates are largely based on the official estimates but have been adjusted slightly. Also, estimates are based on "desirable" working conditions; i.e., using multiple-shift assumptions.

16. *Op cit.,* pp. 326–327.

17. This could happen through illegal purchases in the black market. It also became possible when the import entitlements, under the Export Promotion schemes, were made legally transferable since 1965.

18. In the paints and varnishes industry, reviewed in detail by Nancy Slocum, it is clear that the governmental allocational policies have enabled a number of units to survive, while excess capacity and shortage of materials persist. In fact, she even refers to "the black market sales which many of the small units engage in in lieu of production" (p. 57, *op. cit.*). This is known to have been a phenomenon prevalent in several industries.

19. Aside from interviews by us, the study by V. K. Ramaswami and D. G. Pfoutz, *Utilization of Industrial Capacity,* 1965, conducted jointly by the Ministry of Finance and USAID, confirmed the existence of serious bottlenecks in the system. The continuation of such difficulties as late as 1970 was confirmed by Nancy Slocum, in her *Underutilized Industrial Capacity in India: Exploration of Measures and Causes,* a study commissioned by USAID.

20. Cf. Nancy Slocum, *op. cit.,* on the railway wagons industry in particular.

Chapter 14

Export Policy and Economic Performance

As noted in Chapter 12, we can analyze the interaction between exports and economic performance in two different ways: (1) by assuming that the efficiency and choice of techniques, the available resources and knowhow are given and that the effect of improved export performance can essentially be captured in a planning-model framework by reworking the model with a revised export vector; and (2) by trying to examine whether an improved export performance could have led to larger savings, more technical progress, improved aid inflow and other benefits.

On the latter set of alleged, beneficial effects of improved export performance, our analysis has failed to turn up anything very convincing. In Chapter 15, we will note that the overall productivity change in the mainly exporting industries does not appear to be significantly higher than in the mainly importing industries; nor is there evidence that those firms that now engage in research and development are *either* export-oriented relative to those that do not *or* directing their research and development to better designing for export markets instead of directing it to processes for using locally available inputs. Nor is there evidence, as we will note in Chapter 16, that the mainly exporting industries save more than the mainly importing industries.[1]

On the other hand, the former approach does lead to positive and strong indications that an improved export performance would have promoted improved economic performance. We proceed to demonstrate this now, by exploring the implications of an improved export performance (already argued to be feasible) on long-term growth by undertaking a simulation exercise, using the Eckaus-Parikh planning model for the Indian economy.[2]

197

It should be emphasized at the outset that this exercise, based on the Eckaus-Parikh model, is no more than illustrative for a number of reasons, the more important of which are noted below.

1. The model (in the Guidepath I version we use) has no constraint relating savings to income generation except through the mild requirement that aggregate consumption in each period lies above a geometrically growing floor. Because of this, and the postulated high exponential growth rates subsequent to the planning period, the model results in a strikingly high marginal ratio of savings to GNP. An additional consequence is that the GNP growth over a fifteen-year horizon in the reference and simulation runs exceeds 10 percent annually, a rate considerably exceeding the actual performance managed by the Indian economy in recent years.

2. The fact that the data of the model, particularly the input and capital coefficients, are not only dated (in relation to estimates which may be made now) but that some of the capital coefficients have turned out to be very optimistic compared with experience (especially in agriculture), also accounts for the high growth rates of GNP turned up in the exercises with the model which exceed the actual performance of the Indian economy.

3. The aggregation in the model, resulting in only eleven sectors for the economy, also makes it impossible to draw comparative advantage implications meaningfully from the model. Thus, as will be noted below, we postulate a hypothetical, and very modest, increase in exports which is centered heavily on sectors other than agriculture, food and clothing. (However, even such a policy, more in keeping with the notions of the planners about the composition and feasibility of India's export performance, is then shown to be productive of a better economic performance.)

On balance, we still consider the present exercise to be instructive in its illustration of the growth potentiality of additional exports (in the manner precisely set out at the outset of this chapter), simply because any unhappy features of the model will affect both the simulation and the reference runs; and there seems to us to be no clear presumption that the *difference* between the two runs, attributable to the change in the export vector, will be significantly affected. We should also note, to avoid unnecessary confusion, that the Eckaus-Parikh model is a *planning* model and *not* an econometric (behavioral-predictive) model, so that the reader should not be surprised by discrepancies between the model's simulation runs and actual developments in the Indian economy.

The Eckaus-Parikh model is an intertemporal optimizing model, in which the economy is aggregated into 11 sectors. Further:

1. *The objective or criterion function,* which is maximized, is the sum of aggregate consumption in each of the plan periods, discounted by a social discount rate. The solution of each model achieves the highest value of this function that is consistent with all the constraints. This

particular objective is chosen because it reflects directly, through comparison with population levels, one of the major objectives of develment: improvement in the average standard of living. Other types of criteria, such as maximizing the growth of the industrial sector or expanding agricultural production as fast as possible, prejudge the means by which social welfare is advanced. It should be noted, however, that in a programming model, goals of economic policy can be stipulated not only by what is chosen to be maximized, but also by the content of the constraints.

2. *A consumption growth constraint* requires that aggregate consumption grow by at least a stipulated minimum rate. This rate, when compared to the population growth rate, indicates a required minimum rate of growth in the average standard of living.

3. *A savings constraint*, imposed in some of the models, relates the maximum permissible level of net savings to the net national product. It is yet another way of introducing social goals and a behavioral constraint into the models, for it describes, though indirectly, the limits on the willingness of society to sacrifice present for future consumption.

4. *Consumption proportions* are specified exogenously for each period in some models but are varied endogenously from period to period by means of consumption-expenditure elasticities in other models.

5. *Production accounting relationships* stipulate that the total requirements for each commodity in each period not exceed its availability in that period. The total demand consists of the requirements for the good as an intermediate input, which are determined by use of an input-output matrix, and of a number of final demands. These include the demands for inventories, new fixed investment, replacement investment, public and private consumption, and exports. The availability is the sum of domestic production and imports.

6. *Capacity restraints* insure by means of capital-output ratios that the output of each sector in each period does not exceed that producible with the fixed capacity available in the sector at the beginning of that period.

7. Capital accounting relationships determine capacity at the beginning of each period as the capacity previously available, less depreciation, plus the newly completed additions to capacity, plus that part of the depreciated capacity which is restored.

8. *New capital creation* takes place in each sector with a separate gestation lag for the contribution from each of the capital goods producing sectors. The different gestation lags for each sector are specified externally to the model.

9. *Inventory requirements* are determined by inventory-output matrices.

10. *Exports and public consumption* are estimated outside the model and supplied to it as data.

11. *Imports* are divided into two categories. "Noncompetitive" imports for each sector are determined by stipulated import-output ratios, but

the stipulations may change over time. "Competitive" imports are allocated by the model with limits set, in some versions, on the extent to which this type of import can be absorbed in any one sector.

12. *Balance of payments constraints* require that total imports in each period not exceed the foreign exchange availability as determined by exports and the stipulated net foreign capital inflow in that period. A goal of national self-sufficiency can also be imposed in this constraint through the time pattern stipulated for the decline and eventual elimination of the net foreign capital inflow.

13. *Initial conditions* are estimates of production capacities, stocks of inventories, and the unfinished capital-in-process actually available at the beginning of the plan period.

14. *Terminal conditions* must be provided in some manner, in order to relate the events of the plan period to the postplan period, so the model will not behave as if time stopped at the end of the plan. These terminal conditions are the final capital stocks on hand and in process of completion. They are either completely specified from some source outside the model, or they are partially derived in the solution of the model.[3]

The algebraic specification of the model is given in the Appendix to this chapter.

Among the various models considered by Eckaus and Parikh, we chose their long-term model, called *Guidepath Model I*. In this model, the time span is stretched to eighteen years, aggregated into six periods of three years each. Such aggregation was necessary to stay within the bounds of computational capacity. The terminal conditions of this model are determined by specifying that in the post-terminal periods, the growth rate of various elements of final demand such as consumption, government expenditure, exports, capital replacement requirement, and imports must exceed specified minimum levels. In the Guidepath Model I, the savings constraint referred to above was not imposed. Also, a process of modernization of the agricultural sector was built into the model, the details of which are not of interest in the present context.

The eighteen years covered were from 1966 to 1984; and the six periods were 1966–69, 1969–72, . . . , 1981–84. Of the eleven sectors of the model, four sectors (electricity, transportation, construction and housing) produced non-traded goods. Of the seven trading sectors, agriculture and plantations and, to a certain extent, food and clothing produced traditional exportables. It was decided that there was no point in postulating additional exports from these sectors. Thus the exports of the trading sectors were augmented in the simulation (compared to the reference run) as shown in Table 14–1.

Thus, in the simulation run, total exports in the final period were higher than in the reference run by about 6 percent.[4] Of course, the increase in exports of non-traditional sectors was considerably higher than 6 percent.

TABLE 14-1
Exports in Reference and Simulation Runs
(Rs. millions, 1959–60 prices)

Sector	3-yr. totals, 1966–67/1968–69			3-yr. totals, 1981–82/1983–84		
	Reference	Simulation	Difference	Reference	Simulation	Difference
1. Agriculture and plantations	6,961	6,961	0.00	12,367	12,367	0.00
2. Mining and metals	3,838	4,018	180	17,052	18,132	1,080
3. Equipment	1,833	2,193	360	10,657	12,817	2,160
4. Chemicals	647	782	135	7,251	8,061	810
5. Cement and non-metals	75	165	90	1,767	2,307	540
6. Food, clothing and leather	13,376	13,421	45	22,403	22,673	270
7. Electricity	—	—	—	—	—	—
8. Transport	—	—	—	—	—	—
9. Construction	—	—	—	—	—	—
10. Housing	—	—	—	—	—	—
11. Others and margin	4,146	4,146	0.00	9,632	9,632	0.00
12. Total	30,876	31,686	810	81,129	85,989	4,860

The impact of this order of increase in exports on macro-economic variables such as gross national product, consumption, investment and the savings/GNP ratio is shown in Table 14–2. The impact on gross outputs of the eleven sectors is shown in Table 14–3. The changes in shadow price of foreign exchange between the two runs are depicted in Table 14–4.

The results reported in Tables 14–2 through 14–4 are consistent with *a priori* expectations. It turned out that, in the reference run, only the outputs of sectors 1 and 2 were limited by capacity in the first period. As such, when higher export targets are set in the simulation run, including in particular for sector 2, these are met by scaling down consumption. The additional foreign exchange earned by these exports is utilized to increase investment. However, because of the monotonicity constraint (see model description), consumption can be pushed down only to its lower bound. For these reasons, an increase of Rs.810 million in exports during 1966–69 leads only to an increase of Rs.570 million in GNP and an increase of Rs.676 million in investment. Also, because the monotonicity constraint on consumption becomes binding, its shadow prices goes up from zero in the reference run to 3.92 in the simulation run in the period 1966–69. The change in gross output of each sector other than the first two which are constrained by capacity is greater than the increase in its exports, reflecting the direct and indirect requirements. The shadow price of foreign exchange, reflecting as it does the cost of additional exports, goes up compared with the reference for the reason mentioned earlier that the additional exports are made at the expense of consumption.

However, the increase in investment in 1966–69 made possible by the availability of extra foreign exchange from additional exports, eases the capacity constraints in subsequent periods. Since, in subsequent periods, exports are further increased, the question arises whether the extra capacity created by larger investments in earlier periods is sufficient to meet the additional export demands. It turns out that up to and including the period 1972–75, the extra capacity created is not enough and consumption has got to be sacrificed relative to the reference run. This is also reflected in the higher shadow price for monotonicity of consumption (in the simulation run) in these periods.

For the last three periods, extra exports result in extra consumption and investment. Thus in the final period, increase in exports is Rs.4,860 million while the increase in GNP is Rs.17,325 million, of which Rs.10,580 million is additional consumption and Rs.6,744 million is additional investment. With production capacity increasing over time in each sector, it becomes less expensive to raise exports and hence the shadow price of foreign exchange falls below that of the reference run up to 1972–75. It becomes nearly equal in the two runs from 1975–78 on, because exports do not run into capacity constraints in the simulation run from this period.

TABLE 14-2
Macro Variables in Reference and Simulation Runs
(Rs. millions, 1959–60 prices, except row 6)

	3-yr. totals, 1966–67/1968–69			3-yr. totals, 1981–82/1983–84		
	Reference	Simulation	Difference	Reference	Simulation	Difference
1. Gross national product	775,901	776,471	+57.0	3,108,605	3,125,930	17,325
2. Consumption	510,616	510,510	−10.6	1,313,880	1,324,460	10,580
3. Investment	186,036	186,712	+67.6	1,568,975	1,575,719	6,744
4. Exports	30,876	31,686	+81.0	81,128	85,988	4,860
5. Imports	45,876	46,686	+81.0	81,128	85,988	4,860
6. Savings/GNP	0.22044	0.22114	+.00070	0.50472	0.50408	−.00064
7. Sum of discounted consumption				2,218,474	2,226,239	7,765
8. Sum of undiscounted consumption				5,215,294	5,242,540	27,245

TABLE 14–3

Gross Outputs in Reference and Simulation Runs

(Rs. millions, 1959–60 prices)

Sector	3-yr. totals, 1966–67/1968–69			3-yr. totals, 1981–82/1983–84		
	Reference	Simulation	Difference	Reference	Simulation	Difference
1. Agriculture and plantations	29,156.80	29,156.80	0.00	73,485.11	74,892.34	1,407.23
2. Mining and metals	4,829.08	4,829.08	0.00	69,858.86	69,869.69	10.83
3. Equipment	7,779.58	7,824.08	44.50	75,528.56	76,663.93	1,135.37
4. Chemicals	4,131.38	4,157.28	25.90	29,683.00	29,971.20	288.20
5. Cement and non-metals	2,547.88	2,561.39	13.51	18,243.21	18,383.26	140.05
6. Food, clothing and leather	10,530.96	1C,537.45	6.49	29,080.43	29,313.75	233.32
7. Electricity	630.02	631.39	1.37	6,414.85	6,446.18	31.33
8. Transport	4,455.95	4,463.42	7.47	29,770.99	29,914.44	143.45
9. Construction	10,328.04	10,335.27	7.23	78,756.82	79,099.27	342.45
10. Housing	2,338.09	2,338.09	0.00	5,746.73	5,790.70	43.97
11. Others and margin	23,608.31	23,614.01	5.70	86,777.29	87,397.27	1,619.98

TABLE 14–4

Shadow Prices in Reference and Simulation Runs

Period	Foreign Exchange		Monotonicity of Consumption	
	Reference	Simulation	Reference	Simulation
1966–69	6.12	9.19	0.00	3.92
1969–72	11.85	2.73	0.03	0.78
1972–75	1.38	1.33	0.01	0.10
1975–78	0.73	0.72	0.00	0.00
1978–81	0.39	0.38	0.05	0.05
1981–84	0.54	0.54	0.15	0.15

NOTE: Figures represent the change in sum of discounted consumption over six periods per unit change in foreign exchange availability or the lower bound on consumption in any period.

In conclusion, we can state that additional exports in earlier years, even if they are made by pushing domestic consumption down, more than pay for themselves by increasing investment and growth in the future. Computable planning models such as the Eckaus-Parikh model are necessarily cumbersome; they build in a number of parametric assumptions and functional relationships that are less than accurate, and work with objective functions and related constraint-specifications that presuppose an accurate reflection of what the planners have in mind. In the nature of the case, therefore, any "runs" with such models can only be broadly suggestive; and, in this case, they do underline rather strongly—given the very moderate nature of the export increase specified—that a policy of promoting exports more energetically would have produced better economic results.

Appendix:

The Eckaus-Parikh Model

The variables and contraints of the so-called Guidepath I version of the Eckaus-Parikh model are given in this appendix. First we list in Table 14A–1 the variables occurring in the short-term "Target and Transit" models. Then, we list in Table 14A–2 the additional variables occurring in the Guidepath Model I. Table 14A–3 lists the constraints of the model. Some comments on the structure of this model have been made in Chapter 14 already.[5]

TABLE 14A–1

Symbols Used in the Target and Transit Models

Variables and Parameters*		Dimensions for n sectors, k activities T periods
$A(t)$	net foreign capital inflow in period t	T
$a(t)$	matrix of interindustry current flow coefficients appropriate to period t	$n \times k$
$b(t)$	diagonal matrix of capital-output ratios	$k \times k$
$c(t)$	column vector, each term of which indicates the proportion of the sector's output in total consumption	n
$C(t)$	aggregate consumption in each period	T
$D(t)$	vector of the amount of fixed capital (components) in each sector that is completely depreciated in period t	k
d	diagonal matrix transforming depreciation into capacity immobilized, each of whose terms d_{jj} is the maximum of $\left(\dfrac{r_{1j}}{p_{1j}}, \dfrac{r_{2j}}{p_{2j}}, \cdots, \dfrac{r_{nj}}{p_{nj}} \right)$; (r's and p's are explained further on in the list)	$k \times k$

(continued)

TABLE 14A–1 (continued)

Variables and Parameters*		Dimensions for n sectors, k activities T periods
E(t)	column vector of exports by each sector	n
F(t)	column vector of deliveries by each sector for private consumption purposes	n
G(t)	column vector of deliveries by each sector for government consumption	n
H(t)	column vector of deliveries by each sector for inventory accumulation	n
I	identity matrix	$n \times n$ or $k \times k$
J(t)	column vector of deliveries of intermediate inputs by each sector	n
K(t)	column vector of fixed-capital capacity in each sector	k
M(t)	column vector of total imports	n
M'(t)	column vector of noncompetitive imports	k
m'	diagonal matrix of import coefficients relating non-competitive imports to sectoral output	$k \times k$
M''(t)	column vector of competitive imports	n
m''	column vector of coefficients indicating in each sector maximum use of the foreign exchange available after competitive import requirements have been satisfied	n
n	number of sectors	
N(t)	column vector of deliveries by each sector of investment goods for new capital formation	n
p' p'' p'''	investment lag proportions matrices for capital; elements p_{ij}', p_{ij}'', and p_{ij}''' indicate the proportions of fixed capital in sector j supplied by sector i for new capacity 1, 2, or 3 periods ahead, respectively	$n \times k$
p	capital composition matrix where each element is $\Sigma_k p^k{}_{ij}$, and $\Sigma_i p_{ij} = 1.0$	$n \times k$
Q(t)	column vector of deliveries by each sector to restore depreciated capacity	n
qη	$[I - a(T) - (b(T)p'(T) + S(T))\eta - b(T)p''(T)(1 + \eta) - b(T)p'''(T)(1 + \eta)^2\eta]$ for $\eta = \phi, \delta, \gamma, \epsilon,$ or ν	$n \times n$
R(t)	vector of depreciated capital capacities that are restored	k
r' r'' r'''	matrices of coefficients, each of which indicates the proportion of depreciated capacity in each sector j supplied by sector i for restored capacity in period $t - 1, t - 2,$ or $t - 3$, respectively, to become effective in period t	$n \times k$
r	depreciation composition matrix, each element of which is D_{ij}/D_j, where D_{ij} is the ith type of capital depreciated in sector j	$n \times k$
s	matrix of inventory coefficients, each element S_{ij} of which indicates the deliveries for inventory purposes by sector i to sector j per unit of additional output in sector j	$n \times k$

(continued)

TABLE 14A-1 (concluded)

Variables and Parameters		Dimensions for n sectors, k activities T periods
T	length of the plan in periods	
t	time, in periods	
u	unit row vector $[1, 1, 1, \cdots, 1]$	$1 \times n$
V(t)	column vector of capacities lost in each sector due to the depreciation of some component of its capital stock	k
W	value of the objective function, which is equal to the present discounted value of aggregate consumption over the plan period	1
w	social discount rate applied to aggregate private consumption	1
X(t)	column vector of gross domestic outputs	k
Z(t)	column vector of new additions to fixed-capital capacity in each sector	k
ϕ	postterminal growth rate for consumption	1
δ	postterminal growth rate for depreciation	1
γ	postterminal growth rate for government	1
ϵ	postterminal growth rate for exports	1
μ	postterminal growth rate for imports	
$\rho(t)$	minimum rate of growth of aggregate consumption $C(t)$ over $C(t-1)$	1
α_0	diagonal matrix of growth rates used in calculating inventory investment in first period and maximum new investment in second and third periods	T
α_τ	diagonal matrix of growth rates used in calculating terminal capital requirements	$k \times k$

*Variables in capital letters; parameters in small letters.

TABLE 14A-2

Additional Variables and Parameters for the Guidepath Models

$X_1(t)$	output of the Incremental Agriculture activity in period t
$X_{12}(t)$	output of the Traditional Agriculture activity in period t
η	diagonal matrix for expenditure elasticities of consumption of each sector's output
$\lambda(t)$	population growth rate between periods t and $t-1$
τ	growth rate of cultivable land available to Agriculture
$y_1 y_{12}$	yields of output per unit of land in Incremental and Traditional Agriculture, respectively
$P(t)$	population in period (t)
U	activity aggregation matrix
*	variables marked by asterisks, e.g. $\overset{*}{X}$, apply only to first eleven activities

TABLE 14A–3
Guidepath I and Guidepath II Models

1. Objective Function

   (1.0) Maximize: $W = \sum\limits_{t=1}^{T} \dfrac{C(t)}{(1+W)^{t-1}}$

   Subject to:

2. Consumption Growth Constraints

   (2.0) $C(t+1) \geqq (1+\rho(t))C(t)$,   for $t = 0, \cdots, T-1$,

   Initial consumption:

   (2.1) $C(0) = \overline{C(0)}$,

3. Distribution Relationships

   (3.0) $J(t)+H(t)+N(t)+Q(t)+F(t)+G(t)+E(t) \leqq M(t)+UX(t)$,   for $t=1, \cdots, T$,

   where $U = \begin{bmatrix} 1 & 0 & \cdot & 0 & 1 \\ 0 & 1 & \cdot & \cdot & 0 \\ \cdot & \cdot & \cdot & \cdot & \cdot \\ 0 & \cdot & \cdot & 1 & 0 \end{bmatrix}$

   Intermediate products:

   (3.1) $J(t) = a(t)X(t)$,   for $t = 1, \cdots, T$,

   Inventory requirements:

   (3.2) $H(t) = s(t)\{X(t+1) - X(t)\}$,   for $t = 2, \cdots, T$,

   (3.3) $H(1) = s(1)\{X(2) - (1+\alpha_o)\overline{X(0)}\}$,   for $t = 1$,

   Private consumption:

   (3.4) $F(t) = \eta c C(t) + \left\{ \prod\limits_{t=1}^{t} [1+\lambda(t)] \right\} (1-\eta)c\overline{C(0)}$,   for $t = 1, \cdots, T$,

   Government consumption:

   (3.5) $G(t) = \overline{G(t)}$,   for $t = 1, \cdots, T$,

   Exports:

   (3.6) $E(t) = \overline{E(t)}$,   for $t = 1, \cdots, 2$,

4. Capacity Restraints

   (4.0) $b(t)X(t) \leqq K(t)$,   for $t = 1, \cdots, T$,

5. Capital Accounting Relationships

   Investment requirements:

   (5.0) $N(t) = pZ(t+1)$,   for $t = 1, \cdots, T$,

   Depreciated capital:

   (5.1) $D(t) = \overline{D(t)}$,   for $t = 2, \cdots, T+1$,

   Depreciated capacity:

   (5.2) $V(t) = dD(t)$,   for $t = 2, \cdots, T+1$,

   Restoration requirements:

   (5.3) $Q(t) = r(t)d(t)^{-1}R(t)$,   for $t = 1, \cdots, T$,

   Capital accounting:

   (5.4) $K(t+1) \leqq K(t) + Z(t+1) + R(t+1) - V(t+1)$,   for $t = 1, \cdots, T$,

6. Restoration Ceilings

   (6.0) $R(t) \leqq V(t)$,   for $t = 2, \cdots, T+1$,

7. Balance of Payments Constraints

   (7.0) $uM(t) \leqq \overline{A(t)} + uE(t)$,   for $t = 1, \cdots, T$,

(continued)

TABLE 14A–3 (continued)

8. Imports
Import composition:
(8.0) $M(t) = M'(t) + M''(t)$, for $t = 1, \cdots, T$,
Noncompetitive imports:
(8.1) $M'(t) = m'(t)X(t)$, for $t = 1, \cdots, T$,
Competitive import ceilings:
(8.2) $M''(t) \leq m''(t)[\overline{A(t)} + uE(t) - uM'(t)]$, for $t = 1, \cdots, T$,

9. Relationships Between Incremental and Traditional Agriculture Activities
(9.0) $X_{12}(t) - [1 + \tau]X_{12}(t - 1) \leq 0$, for $t = 1, \cdots, T$,

(9.1) $X_1(t) - \dfrac{y_1}{y_{12}} X_{12}(t) \leq 0$, for $t = 1, \cdots, T$,

10. Initial Capital Restraints
(10.0) $K(1) = b(1)(I + \alpha_0)\overline{X(0)}$,

11. Terminal Requirements in General
(11.0) $K(T + 1) \geq \overline{K(T + 1)}$.

12. Derivation of Terminal Conditions from Postterminal Growth Requirements
Postterminal growth rates of demands and imports:
(12.0) $C(t) = \overline{C(T)}(1 + \phi)^{t-T}$,
(12.1) $G(t) = \overline{G(T)}(1 + \gamma)^{t-T}$,
(12.2) $E(t) = \overline{E(T)}(1 + \epsilon)^{t-T}$,
(12.3) $D(t) = \overline{D(T)}(1 + \delta)^{t-T}$,
(12.4) $M(t) = \overline{M(T)}(1 + \mu)^{t-T}$,
(12.5) $X_{12}(t) = \overline{X_{12}(T)}(1 + \tau)^{t-T}$,

(12.6) $F(t) = \eta c\overline{C(T)}(1 + \phi)^{t-T} + \left\{ \overset{t}{\underset{t=1}{\Pi}} [1 + \lambda(t)] \right\} (I - \eta)c\overline{C(0)}$.

This implies

(12.7) $\overset{*}{X}(t) + X_{12}(t) = \overset{*}{a}(T)\overset{*}{X}(t) + [\overset{*}{s}(T) + \overset{*}{b}(T)\overset{*}{p}] \overset{*}{X}(t + 1) - \overset{*}{X}(t)$

$+ [a_{12}(T) + (s_{12}(T) + b_{12}(T)p_{12})\tau]\overline{X_{12}(T)}(1 + \tau)^{t-T}$

$+ \eta c\overline{C(T)}(1 + \phi)^{t-T} + \overset{T}{\underset{t=1}{\Pi}} (1 + \lambda(t)) (1 - \eta)c\overline{C(0)}(1 + \lambda(T))^{t-T}$

$+ \overline{G(T)}(1 + \gamma)^{t-T} + \overline{E(T)}(1 + \epsilon)^{t-T} + \overline{D(T)}(1 + \delta)^{t-T}$

$- M''(T)(1 + \mu)^{t-T} - \overset{*}{m'}(T)\overset{*}{X}(T)(1 + \mu)^{t-T}$

$- m'_{12}(T)\overline{X_{12}(T)}(1 + \mu)^{t-T}$, for $t > T$.

Define:
$q_\xi \equiv [I - \overset{*}{a}(T) - (\overset{*}{b}(T)p + \overset{*}{s}(T))\xi]$, for $\xi \equiv \tau, \lambda(T), \phi, \gamma, \epsilon, \delta, \mu$.

13. Particular Solution of (12.7)

(13.0) $\overset{*}{X}(T + 1) = [\overset{*}{q_\tau}]^{-1}[-I + a_{12}(T) + (s_{12}(T) + b_{12}(T)p_{12})\tau]\overline{X_{12}(T)}(1 + \tau)$

$+ [\overset{*}{q_\phi}]^{-1}\eta c\overline{C(T)}(1 + \phi)$

$+ [\overset{*}{q_{\lambda(T)}}]^{-1} \overset{T}{\underset{t=1}{\Pi}}(1 + \lambda(t)) (I - \eta)c\overline{C(0)}(1 + \lambda(T))$

(continued)

TABLE 14A–3 (concluded)

$$+ [\overset{*}{q_\gamma}]^{-1}\overline{E(T)}(1 + \gamma)$$

$$+ [\overset{*}{q_\epsilon}]^{-1}\overline{E(T)}(1 + \epsilon)$$

$$+ [\overset{*}{q_\delta}]^{-1}\overline{D(T)}(1 + \delta)$$

$$- [\overset{*}{q_\mu}]^{-1}M''(T)(1 + \mu)$$

$$- [\overset{*}{q_\mu}]^{-1}m'(T)\overset{*}{X}(T)(1 + \mu)$$

$$- [\overset{*}{q_\mu}]^{-1}m'_{12}(T)\overline{X_{12}(T)}(1 + \mu), \quad \text{for } t = t + 1, T + 2, T + 3.$$

14. Terminal Capital Stocks

(14.0) $\overset{*}{K}(T + 1) \geqq \overset{*}{b}(T)\overset{*}{X}(T + 1)$
        $K_{12}(T + 1) \geqq b_{12}(T)X_{12}(T + 1)$

15. Terminal Inventories

(15.0) $s(T)X(T + 1) \geqq \overset{*}{s}(T)\overset{*}{X}(T + 1) + s_{12}(T)\overline{X_{12}(T + 1)}.$

16. Consumption or Savings Constraint for the Guidepath II Model

(16.0) $C(t) + \mu G(T) \geqq \beta_0 + \beta_1\mu[(I - A)X(t) - \overline{D(t)}], \quad \text{for } t = 1, \cdots, T.$

NOTES

1. In fact, the recent evidence of the link between exports and domestic savings is based on macro-level regressions that would probably work equally well if imports were substituted for exports. See T. E. Weisskopf, "The Impact of Foreign Capital Inflow on Domestic Savings in Underdeveloped Countries," *Journal of International Economics* 2:1 (February 1972), pp. 23–38, where domestic savings are made a function of income, external resources and exports. There is no evidence in the published literature of differential savings rates *either* by industries in terms of trade orientation *or* by income classes in terms of their trade orientation.

2. R. S. Eckaus and K. Parikh, *Planning for Growth* (Cambridge: MIT Press, 1968).

3. *Ibid.*, pp. 9–10.

4. Though the intention was to postulate a considerably larger increase, in translating the intention to computation geometric growth was accidentally replaced by arithmetic growth with the consequent slowing down of the increases over time.

5. The tables in this appendix are taken from Eckaus and Parikh, *Planning,* Chapter 5.

Chapter 15

Investment, Innovation and Growth

Among the significant, but relatively intractable, issues in the study of QR-regimes is whether they have any discernible impact on the inducement to invest and the inducement to innovate.

The former question is of interest, because some LDCs presumably are in a position where the emergence of an adequate number of entrepreneurs to exploit economic opportunities is a prerequisite for industrialization. Hence if we can argue that QRs provide the economic framework needed to induce investment, that should be considered a merit of the QR-regime. On the other hand, we must also ask whether such inducement, if needed, could not also be provided by alternative policies; and whether such an alternative set of policies would not have resulted in a more efficient pattern of investments.

Closely linked to this is the question of the inducement to innovate. Efficiency in the pattern of investments is only one aspect of the problem. The quality of entrepreneurship and the inducement to innovate are recognized by economic historians and by economists estimating the role of technical progress in growth to be of at least equal importance. Can we then relate the QR-regime to these aspects of the economy as well?

These are interesting, important and difficult questions. In what follows, we attempt to answer them in light of the Indian experience, warning the reader that we are on relatively treacherous ground even as economic analysis goes.

INDUCEMENT TO INVEST

The notion that India lacked an adequate supply of entrepreneurship and that a system of automatic protection conferred by the QR-regime was necessary to induce investment is impossible to reconcile with the facts of Indian history up to the time that planning began in the 1950s.

The tradition of entrepreneurship in India has long been documented by economic historians.[1] Furthermore, this historic supply of entrepreneurship was not merely for trade but also for industry. In fact, the industrialization of India started in the nineteenth century and proceeded with moderate, and even negligible, tariffs during the first part of the twentieth century.[2] Furthermore, the leading industrial entrepreneurship tended to be economically rational and even "progressive." Thus, Jamshedji Tata, who set up in 1913 the first successful Indian steel mill, came from a background and fortune in cotton trade; and he built up an efficient and stable industrial force which was critical to performance in a steel mill. And Morris D. Morris has shown clearly how, in the cotton textile industry, where a stable and disciplined labor force was *not* critical to performance, the entrepreneurs were willing to accommodate quite different labor practices rather than invest time and money in changing them.[3] In Tata's case, the entrepreneurial activity even extended to setting up, from the beginning, a school to train Indian technicians to take over from the foreign personnel at the earliest!

It would appear to us, therefore, that in the Indian context it is not persuasive to argue that a QR-regime, with its automatic protection for indigenously produced items, was necessary to induce industrial investment. Furthermore, in the Indian case, the public sector has been an important investor in industry, thus weakening still further the argument for a QR-regime to provide automatic and indiscriminate protection to induce investment.

There is therefore nothing in the Indian experience to suggest that India could not have sustained the desired *ex-ante* levels of investment in industry by using a suitable tariff policy, the standard instruments of monetary and fiscal policy and her public-sector investment programs.[4]

INDUCEMENT TO INNOVATE

In point of fact, the QR-regime, as we have already noted in Chapter 13, only served to influence and, in conjunction with the industrial licensing machinery, to determine a pattern of import substitution that certainly appears to have been relatively chaotic and unmindful of economic costs. Did it also influence adversely (1) attention to quality and (2) technical progress? There is also the related question: does an export orientation produce better results in both these directions?

Adverse Effects.

1. Unfortunately, no meaningful statistical index of "quality" can be devised. On the other hand, it is manifest that in a regime which grossly reduces competition (as we have argued) and creates a captive market for many products thanks to the doctrine of indigenous availability, it would be "rational" and profitable for an entrepreneur not to pay attention to the quality of production. Thus, it is only the "quality-minded" entrepreneurs (like Tata, Mahindra and Mahindra, and Kirloskars, to take the most noted exceptions) who are known to produce products that approximate international standards of performance for similar products. For the rest, the effects of the economic regime appear to be evident, though impossible to quantify: products with faulty performance because of production defects or defects in the inputs of domestic manufacture. Even when one has allowed for the bias in evaluation arising from the fact that, in V. S. Naipaul's words, there is "a craze for foreign," there is so much general incidence of failure to improve quality of performance to satisfactory levels, and this is so precisely what one would expect as the result of the economic regime, that it seems fair to conclude that the regime has indeed aided in bringing about these adverse results.

2. Closely related to the failure of producers (even in the organized sector) to raise their output to satisfactory levels of performance, but shading into the problem of innovation which we discuss later, is the well-documented phenomenon of "design deficiencies," which Mark Frankena has studied in some depth for the engineering goods industry during the 1960s.

Frankena carefully explains that he is not discussing design deficiencies in the sense that Indian producers do not produce to the "latest," capital-intensive and automated designs, but rather that, even for designs that sell in the LDCs of Africa and Asia, the Indian are uncompetitive and "unpreferred" vis-à-vis those of rival producers. He also generally confines himself to examples that indicate that Indian designs are fully dominated by other designs, no matter what the shadow or actual prices of the factors of production. We must enter the caveat, however, that, while these examples establish a prima facie case that the Indian policy environment has produced incentives for a lag in adaptation to more efficient designs, they do not constitute a clear verdict to that effect. It is conceivable that the cost of buying or imitating these superior designs may outweigh the gains from their adoption, both privately and socially; only if the new designs were available without cost would these examples be, in themselves, complete proof of our contention. But the examples do remain strongly suggestive and supportive of our thesis. Let us therefore quote a few of the more telling ones.

For electric motors and transformers, Frankena notes that the Indian Tariff Commission Report of 1966 stated that:

> Indian motors were larger and much heavier than motors of the same horsepower manufactured abroad and that the excess weight was considered undesirable by users. It also estimated that adoption of foreign specifications would result in a reduction of 20 to 33 percent in material costs. The following differences in design and material specifications were noted: (i) foreign motors used aluminum die-cast rotors instead of rotors with copper strips; (ii) foreign motors used aluminum die-cast bodies instead of cast iron bodies, which resulted in a reduction of weight; (iii) foreign motors had class "E" insulation, which resulted in lower inputs of copper and electrical steel stampings than were required with the class "A" insulation used in India. In addition, class "E" insulation enabled motors to withstand higher temperatures.
>
> In the second half of the 1960's a number of Indian manufacturers adopted these design changes for part of their production. Nevertheless, in 1970 the Indian Electrical Manufacturers' Association reported that of 32 manufacturers in the organized sector and 170 in the small scale sector, only twelve produced motors with class "E" insulation.[5]

Again, with distribution transformers, the Indian manufacturers were continuing to use hot rolled sheets rather than cold rolled grain oriented sheets, with resultant energy losses up to 10 percent and an incremental cost in steel and copper of nearly 10 to 25 percent.

Among other examples of product-design improvement foregone, Frankena notes cotton textile machinery. The 1967 Tariff Commission Report mentioned ring frames abroad that incorporated several improved features enabling them to run at speeds up to 16,000 RPM without mechanical trouble whereas the Indian designs could not be taken beyond 12,000 RPM: "even at lower speeds the yarn breakages are sometimes heavy with consequent deterioration in the quality and evenness of yarn . . . there has been improvement in the quality of indigenous cotton textile machinery after 1963, but . . . the domestic products still lack proper designing, casting, standardisation and finishing. . . ."[6]

These examples relate to designs that appear to have been economically dominant over the ones still in vogue in India—in terms of the productivity of the output in user industry and/or the material cost of unit output itself.[7]

At the same time, problems of lagging designs were to be found in *consumer goods* industries as well: e.g., on electric fans Frankena quotes an Engineering Export Promotion Council Report on a 1959 exhibition in Singapore:

> Our (Indian) "Usha" and "Orient" table fans lacked the lustrous finish which was eye-catching in the case of (Japanese and Hong Kong) "Hulda" and KDK fans. If the revolving device and the finish of our table fans are improved, I see no reason why the sales should not improve. In the export

market, it is imperative that we should catch up with the latest design and construction of the Japanese fans.

and goes on to comment that:

A decade later Indian table fans were still out-dated and inferior in design, styling, and finish to fans exported by Japan and Hong Kong to developing countries. Japanese and Hong Kong fans had smoothly finished and bright-colored stands and plastic casings in modern shapes, nickel-chromium-plated fittings and protective mesh, and gadgets like time switches, variable oscillation-angle controls, and plastic piano-style keys for different speeds. The exteriors of Indian table fans were made of painted cast iron and steel, the fans were heavy, the styling, surface finish, and colors were not attractive, and there were no controls other than choice of speeds. Late in the 1960's, Jay Engineering introduced one model with variable oscillation control and piano-style keys but none of the other styling features. Indian fans were also noisier than Japanese ones.[8]

3. Next, we should also expect that the lack of competition in the Indian-type economic regime raises the possibility that firms may choose "leisure" rather than "profits."[9] If this takes the form of being simply sloppy about reducing costs and increasing productivity from the plant by better management, this is equivalent to "technical regress" and to social disadvantage. Unfortunately there is no technique by which we could have meaningfully detected this effect of the QR- and industrial licensing regime, and we must leave this purely as an *a priori* deduction.

4. We may also attempt to examine whether an estimation of technical progress for the Indian manufacturing sector shows any evidence of increase in productivity. We may hypothesize that the result of a framework of sheltered markets would be the absence of any noticeable trend toward growth in productivity.[10]

We should note initially that labor productivity did increase through the period of our study. Estimates by Banerjee[11] of the growth of labor productivity for 1946–64 are presented in Table 15–1. However, it is now clearly understood that such estimates have little relationship to growth of overall productivity, and that the superior approach is to proceed by estimating production functions and "technical change" therewith.

Recent studies of the growth of manufacturing in India have, however, come to conflicting conclusions on this issue, depending primarily on the nature of the adjustments made in the available series on capital. Using the Solow method of estimating Hicks-neutral technical change, but a capital series that shows a drastic decline in capital productivity from 100.00 in 1946 to 25.4 in 1964, Banerjee has estimated a trend rate of *decline* in neutral technical change of 1.6 percent in 1946–64.[12]

TABLE 15–1

**Indices of Labor Productivity
in Indian Manufacturing, 1946–64**

Year	Indices of Labor Productivity 1946–64	Year	Indices of Labor Productivity 1946–64
1946	100.0	1956	123.6
1947	94.9	1957	120.7
1948	98.7	1958	133.0
1949	96.6	1959	139.1
1950	91.8	1960	140.0
1951	97.7	1961	140.2
1952	96.1	1962	156.0
1953	107.8	1963	151.0
1954	107.8	1964	164.0
1955	134.3		
Trend rates of growth 1946–64	.033 (.0002)		

SOURCE: A. Banerjee, "Productivity Growth," Table 1.

On the other hand, Hashim and Dadi have used an adjusted capital series, estimating the purchase value of capital from the available written-down book-value data by more detailed and careful methods of adjusting for the age-structure of capital assets and rate of depreciation. Their estimates show an *increase* in capital productivity over the period 1946–64 and lead to a positive Hicks-neutral, overall productivity change at 2.8 percent annually.[13]

Quite aside from their adjusted capital estimates, it would appear to us that the Hashim-Dadi estimates are probably closer to reality because our hypothesis of the Indian sheltered-markets policy leading to negligible overall improvements in efficiency of factor use must at the same time allow for the fact that new investments in the new industries already embody the growth of know-how abroad. The estimation of (Hicks-neutral) technical progress, using the "disembodied" progress assumption, will thus tend to show positive, and even large, improvements in overall productivity even when there are no such improvements. Unless, therefore, the estimation of productivity change is adjusted for "embodied" technical change—a factor of obvious importance for India which imported the bulk of its capital goods through the period of our study—we cannot reach a firm econometric conclusion on whether the framework of Indian policies retarded the growth of overall productivity in the economy.[14]

Other Arguments.

There is therefore some *a priori* and empirical support, of different degrees of firmness, for the view that the Indian trade regime *in toto* led to, or accentuated, the lack of attention to quality, design and technical change. We may now push our analysis in other directions that bear on these issues equally.

1. If one considers change in overall productivity as the outcome of technical change (inclusive of managerial efficiency), and if one regards the degree of domestic sheltering through the import substitution strategy as the principal cause of decelerated technical change, then one should presumably expect the following two hypotheses to hold empirically:

(a) that the traditional, export industries (such as jute and tea) should exhibit higher technical change than the modern, new industries (such as chemicals and engineering goods); and

(b) that among the new industries, furthermore, the ones that have broken out more significantly into the export markets and over a longer period should also exhibit greater rates of technical change than the others.

These hypotheses imply cross-sectional differences, however, which may well be difficult to detect because of other differences among the industries that differentially affect the ability to invent and absorb technical change. For example, it may well be that, owing to the focus of research and development expenditures on modern industries in the West, the general rate of technical improvements that accrue in the new industries is vastly greater than that in the older industries such as jute and tea where the large Western expenditures on research and development have no impact at all. Hence our failure to find significant increases in overall productivity in the traditional industries may *not* mean that export orientation may not be an important factor in motivating technical change.[15] Similarly, the period during which several industries in India have been involved in serious export marketing may have been too small for any serious inferences from cross-sectional differences among the different new industries.

We should confess that we have not been able to secure the necessary estimates of technical change in enough industries, for the relevant time period, to cast any definitive light on the validity and import of the two hypotheses we have listed here. But they clearly are of sufficient importance to warrant a careful examination as more years lapse and data become available for a longer period to make time-series estimation meaningful (particularly with regard to our second hypothesis).

2. Yet another approach to the relationship of import substitution and export orientation to technical change is to examine the nature and incidence of research and development in Indian industries. We must note, in this con-

nection, the increasing evidence that research and development expenditures are finally beginning to emerge on the Indian scene, in a number of import-competing industries, that such expenditure is being undertaken by the very large firms, and that it is undertaken in the process of import substitution itself and reflects a quasi-Kennedy-Weizsacker process of search for processes that would avoid the use of scarce, imported materials and develop the use of cheaper, indigenous inputs. Of course, as stated earlier, this research and development activity may be expensive in relation to results: but it is certainly there now and is adding to the technological maturity and expertise that the country seeks as an objective in itself. Historically, one has only to recall Japan's transition from shoddy manufacture under bad imitation to decent manufacture under good imitation to excellent manufacture under outstanding imitation to innovative manufacture in recent years. In such a historical perspective, it would appear logical to entertain the strong possibility that at least *some* of the inadequacies noted earlier may be due to the difficulties of "first-stage" manufacture in a number of modern industries and that the growth of research and development in recent years may represent a growing transition to decent manufacture. What *is* the evidence of research and development in modern Indian industry?

Before we discuss research and development expenditure in Indian manufacturing industry, it is useful to note that the *total* as a proportion of GNP has been steadily rising, having more than doubled between 1958–59 and 1971–72 (Table 15–2); and that the private sector expenditure on research and development, while still a small fraction of the total, has increased during the same period so that it is now over 8 percent of the total whereas in 1958–59 it was estimated at 0.5 percent only (Table 15–3).[16]

There is also evidence that the bulk of this private research and development expenditure is inevitably concentrated in the larger companies, and that the level of expenditure generally rises with the size of the company.[17] Among the propositions of interest to our study, however, are the following which were the outcome of a sample survey conducted by Dr. Ashok Desai at our suggestion. Before we report on them, we should emphasize that the survey was primarily focused on chemical and dye (and a few engineering) firms in the Bombay region, owing to limitations of finance and willingness of firms to discuss the issues raised. Of the 18 firms interviewed, 4 were subsidiaries of foreign corporations, and of the remaining 14, 6 did not belong to the Large Industrial Houses. Further, of the 14 Indian firms, only 4 were joint ventures and the remaining were purely Indian in ownership. Thus, our sample managed to straddle all the important types of structure operating in Indian industry. Based on this survey[18] and drawing on the available literature on research and development in India, we can make the following qualitative observations which seem to suggest two principal conclusions: (a) that the

TABLE 15-2

R&D Expenditure in India in Relation to GNP, 1958–59 and 1965–66 to 1971–72

	1958–59	1965–66	1968–69	1969–70	1970–71[a]	1971–72[a]
(a) Total GNP at current prices (Rs. millions)	126,000[b]	217,990	302,320	330,190	363,210	399,530
(b) R&D expenditure (Rs. millions)	290	850	1,310	1,460	1,730	2,140
(c) R&D expenditure as % of GNP	0.23	0.39	0.44	0.44	0.48	0.54

SOURCES: *Report on Science and Technology,* 1969–70 and 1970–71, Government of India, Cabinet Secretariat, Committee on Science and Technology, New Delhi.

The GNP figure for 1969–70 has been obtained from Government of India, Department of Statistics, Central Statistical Organisation, National Income Unit, New Delhi. Similar figures for subsequent years are not available. The Planning Commission has envisaged growth of national income during the Fourth Plan period at 5.5 percent at constant prices. There was an average rise of about 6 percent in general wholesale prices during 1970–71, and the trend continued through the following year. Therefore, GNP for 1970–71 and 1971–72 is tentatively projected in this table at a 10 percent rate of growth.

a. Tentative, projected by the authors.

b. NNP

TABLE 15-3

Estimated R&D Expenditure in Central, State and Private Sectors, 1958–59 and 1965–66 to 1971–72

(Rs. millions)

	1958–59		1965–66		1968–69		1969–70		1970–71		1971–72	
	Expen- diture	% to total	Expen- diture	% to total	Expen- diture	% to total	Expen- diture[a] (Actual)	% to total	Expen- diture[b]	% to total	Expen- diture[b]	% to total
(a) Central sector (including uni- versities)	276.6	96.0	791.2	93.0	1,096.0	83.4	1,212.6	82.9	1,462.0	84.3	1,827.4	85.4
(b) State sector	10.0	3.5	35.1	4.1	119.9	9.1	122.2	8.3	125.8	7.3	138.4	6.5
(c) Private sector	1.5	0.5	24.3	2.9	98.5	7.5	128.1	8.8	145.9	8.4	174.6	8.1
TOTAL	288.1	100.0	850.6	100.0	1,314.4	100.0	1,462.9	100.0	1,733.7	100.0	2,140.4	100.0

SOURCES: *Report on Science and Technology*, 1969–70 and 1970–71, Government of India, Cabinet Secretariat, Committee on Science and Technology, New Delhi.

Adequate data for the State Sector have not been received. Therefore, figures for 1969–70 and 1970–71 have been repeated from *Annual Report on Science and Technology*, 1969–70. Figures for 1971–72 have been projected at a 10 percent rate of growth.

Increase in the expenditure by the private sector reflects receipt of information from some more companies. Where data for 1970–71 and 1971–72 has not been received, a 10 percent growth rate has been applied. Expenditure by the private sector also includes grants made by the CSIR Industrial Research Associations out of their own resources and included under CSIR expenditure.

a. Reduction in the expenditure for 1969–70 by the Central Sector reflects reduction in actual as compared with revised estimates as given in *Annual Report on Science and Technology*, 1969–70.

b. Tentative, projected by the authors.

import substitution strategy does *not* eliminate the incentive to conduct research and development but merely imparts a bias toward conducting it in a different direction, so that the really important question then is not whether it is eliminated by the import substitution strategy but rather whether the kind induced by such a strategy reduces or increases welfare in relation to the research and development that would otherwise be conducted; and (b) that orientation toward export markets does not in itself seem to increase the incentive to conduct research and development, so that it is difficult to sustain the argument that an export promotion strategy is superior to an import substitution strategy because it will lead to greater (and presumably welfare-increasing) research and development in the economy. Let us therefore turn to a series of propositions that emerge, somewhat tentatively, from our analysis.

Origins and Types of Research and Development in Indian Industry.

There are basically three types of activity that seem to have provided the impetus in Indian industry to set up research and development cells of one kind or another.

QUALITY CONTROL

Firms that started with quality checks often found that processing costs could be brought down by checking quality at a number of production stages instead of checking it after final manufacture. Thus, quality control led to process control, and process control often extended into a study of the processes and possibilities of improving them. Thus, one of the engineering firms surveyed by Desai used to check the quality of its castings from early on. During the 1966 recession, it tried to bring down the rejection rate by introducing checks at a number of stages—knockout, fettling, finishing, repairing and machining. It was thereby able to reduce the amount of work done on castings that were eventually rejected, and to bring down the mean fettling and finishing man-hours per ton from 110 to 80.

TECHNICAL SERVICES

The demand for some products, mainly chemicals, was not confined to one uniform quality; the quality demanded varied with the use for which it was required. Some tailoring of quality to customers' needs was involved. Hence technical services were associated with sales to develop qualities required by customers. Sometimes the demand for a particular quality demanded by a customer was too small, and the customer had to be persuaded and helped to use a substitute in greater demand. Thus, orders generated their own know-how requirements; and, as orders multiplied, the know-how developed to service them was often systematized into general product know-how and correlated with processes. This emergence of research and development out of servicing needs is typical of PVC compounds, which are sold to large numbers of technologically unsophisticated buyers for a vast variety of uses.

MATERIAL ADAPTATION

Often the policy of blanket import substitution forced firms to use indigenous substitutes; and where the domestic and the imported materials differed in quality, a firm had to work out processes to make the indigenous product useable. In a sense, material adaptation is a technical service to be given by the firm wishing to sell a substitute. But the principle of banning imports of anything that was produced at home relieved producers of the need to provide sales service; and often the indigenous producers were too small to solve technical problems arising in the use of their products. Thus, many chemical firms had to undertake research and development to standardize properties of indigenously available materials and to improve yields achievable with them. For instance, when one of the chemical firms tried to substitute Indian turpentine oil for European, it found that only 25 to 30 percent of the former consisted of alpha-pinene, the basic material for camphor, against 90 percent of imported oil. Thus, import substitution threatened to triple the turpentine requirements per kg. of camphor. Their technicians proceeded to analyze the remaining components of Indian turpentine oil, and developed a number of perfumery materials from delta-3 carene and longifolene, which were present in substantial proportions. Eventually, the market for these newly developed materials grew so large that a surplus of alpha-pinene became available beyond the requirements of camphor manufacture; new materials were then developed for manufacture out of alpha-pinene. A rival firm, on the other hand, solved the same problem by using camphene in place of pinene.

Clearly, the process of import substitution itself led to the encouragement of research and development activity in Indian industry, primarily through the creation of the need to adapt processes to the use of new, indigenous materials in many cases, thus supplementing the normal establishment of research and development-type cells for quality control and customer-service operations. In fact, this kind of impetus was also imparted by strict controls over the importation of plant and equipment; and, in some chemical and engineering industries, this led also to the creation of special plant-designing skills. Some well-known examples were the caustic soda plant expansion by Tata Chemicals from internal designing resources and the designing of the pigment plant by Sudarshan Chemicals.[19]

Of course, in only rare cases did the expansion of research and development activity in India lead to its orientation toward what is called "basic research." In the nature of the case, given the main concern of the firms to learn process and material adaptation, the research and development orientation was to be primarily of the nature of "operational investigations" and "development." Most of the research carried on seemed to be short term and focused on a specific process. For example, at one of the engineering firms surveyed 2,000 motor starters were held up on the production line for lack of silver salt, and the problem was given over to the research and development department. This department then proceeded to investigate what had been used prior to the use of silver salts, whether other firms used other materials for identical purposes, and whether the firm could adopt some alternative suggested by such investigations. The research revealed that the firm could use a compound that had been superceded in starter manufacture in other countries but still seemed to be the most economical substitute to use in India.

Research and Development and Exports.

The next set of propositions that seem to emerge from our survey relates to the interaction of exports with the type and level of research and development expenditure in Indian industry. It did seem to emerge from the survey interviews that several of the companies engaged in exporting as a *continuous* activity did consider that quality improvement was important, whereas those firms that engaged in exporting only as an *ad hoc* activity seemed to think that quality problems were not important and that the better production could be diverted abroad whereas the inferior products could be disposed of in the domestic market. It does seem, therefore, that export orientation did suggest greater preoccupation with quality of production.

On the other hand, the survey also showed that this export orientation did not seem to have led to any significant acceleration in research and development expenditures or to a more sharply focused research effort. This was because most research and development expenditure had in fact originated in response to the problems raised by the adaptation of processes to locally available materials and spares; and the solution to these problems generally meant also the solution to associated problems of quality. Hence, the export orientation of a firm did not seem to lend any significant edge to the solution of these questions. And indeed some firms even claimed that their need to engage in research and development had been reduced by expansion into export markets because they had had to undertake research and development to supply a variety of products to maintain a large sales volume at home whereas concentration on a few, standard items in the export market had reduced their need for research and development.

It also seemed as if many of the exporters were seriously worried about getting materials cheaply and readily rather than about quality of manufacture from these materials. This suggests that, in many cases, the basic research and development problems had really been those of getting familiar with the basic processes and then of adapting them to the use of available materials; and that once these had been solved, in the process of import substitution itself, the fact that the firm had begun exportation did not seem to lend any significant, further impulse to greater research and development activity or its redirection. In fact, this suggests rather strongly that the normal preconception that export orientation may be linked with the enhancement of research and development incentives may be true at a *later* stage of industrialization than that now characterizing countries such as India, Brazil and Mexico, i.e., a stage when exportation of *new products,* resulting from research and development, has become an important ingredient of a country's foreign trade, as is now the case finally with Japan.

Research and Development and Government Policies.

Finally, we must conclude that the *net* effect of government policies on research and development, in the Indian context, also reflects the impact of several other factors: (1) The strict industrial licensing policy meant that, if research and development was used to develop new types of outputs or new uses of given capacity, new licensing would be required, with its attendant delays and new uncertainties whether research and development would lead to any economic returns. Thus, any "excess capacity" for research that would result from the development of research and development cells normally deployed in the ways described earlier could not be profitably used to undertake *product-diversification* research, thus reducing, *ceteris paribus,* the level of research and development expenditure undertaken. (2) The early industrial licensing policy also had laid great stress on joint ventures under which foreign capital would come into India. This also frequently led to easy and repeated purchase of foreign technology, reducing, *ceteris paribus,* the need to undertake domestic research and development. (3) Recently, however, the government was to introduce liberal research and development incentives. Thus by 1971, research and development expenditure within the firm earned a 33.33 percent tax allowance; donations to outside institutions for such research earned a tax allowance of 27.5 percent; and research contract payments to associations, universities, and government agencies could be written off up to 10 percent of a year's corporate profit. There were also tax rebates introduced on sale of know-how: domestic royalties earned a rebate of 40 percent whereas royalties earned from sales of technology abroad were free from tax.

It is somewhat early to disentangle these different forces at work in determining research and development efforts in India. But we have clearly enough evidence now before us to be skeptical of some of the simplistic hypotheses in support of the export promotion strategy as being research and

226   GROWTH EFFECTS

development-stimulating and the import-substitution strategy as being research and development-inhibiting. Nonetheless, we can still argue, as we did earlier in this chapter, that the general incentives to reduce costs and to maintain quality cannot but have been reduced by the sheltered markets provided by policies of automatic protection and strict control over domestic entry. Thus, in this sense these policies impaired India's progress toward industrial efficiency at the speed that a framework providing for more effective competition would have made possible.

NOTES

1. For a long review of the literature on the subject, see Bhagwati and Desai, *India,* pp. 13–37.

2. *Ibid.* See also Padma Desai, *Tariff Protection and Industrialization: A Study of the Indian Tariff Commissions at Work* (Delhi: Hindustan Publishing Corporation, 1970).

3. Cf. Morris D. Morris, *The Emergence of an Industrial Labor Force in India* (Berkeley and Los Angeles: University of California Press, 1965). The "sloppy" cotton textile entrepreneurs were thus "economically rational."

4. In this context, it is also useful to refer to our analysis of "shortfalls" in industrial investment in the post-1966 period that have little to do with the QR-regime as such. See Chapters 8, 9 and 11.

5. Frankena, "Export," p. 4.

6. *Ibid.,* p. 10.

7. Note that it is *extremely* implausible that Pareto-dominant techniques would be "inefficient" because their "externality" or "second-best-type" (e.g., impact on savings *à la* Galenson-Leibenstein-Bator-Dobb) effects are inferior!

8. *Ibid.,* pp. 11–12.

9. Cf. Tibor Scitovsky's classic paper, "A Note on Profit Maximisation and Its Implications," *Review of Economic Studies* 11, no. 1 (1943).

10. We should like to acknowledge Solomon Fabricant for his valuable comments on an earlier draft of this subsection.

11. A. Banerjee, "Productivity Growth and Factor Substitution in Indian Manufacturing," *Indian Economic Review,* n.s. 6, no. 1 (1971).

12. *Ibid.,* Table 3.

13. S. R. Hashim and M. M. Dadi, *Capital-Output Relations in Indian Manufacturing* (1940–64), The Maharaja Sayajirao University Economics Series No. 2 (Baroda, 1973). See references there to earlier studies of productivity in Indian manufacturing and for details on the methods of adjustment to capital data. Note, in particular, that these authors (like the others) have not been able to adjust the capital series for under-utilization of capacity.

14. It would be useful to explore even this approach still further to see if any differential performance among different industries in the behavior of their total productivity indices can be observed and then related to the characteristics of these industries such as their degree of protection or their participation in export markets.

15. In the tea industry, moreover, the substantial British investment was being steadily pulled out and diverted to East Africa, so that there was no incentive to put resources into innovation and its implementation.

16. There are several conceptual and data problems with Tables 15–2 and 15–3, many of them discussed in the original sources. They should be regarded, therefore, as merely giving broad orders of magnitude.

17. See The Industrial Credit and Investment Corporation of India, Ltd., "Conference on Research and Development in Industry" (Bombay, 1971), pp. 10–12, for results of a sample survey conducted by the ICICI. The latter proposition, however, is only broadly true and is not corroborated by regression analysis.

18. The detailed results of this survey are reported in Ashok V. Desai, "Industrial Research and Development in India," mimeographed (New Delhi, April 1972). We have drawn extensively on this report here.

19. While we do not go into the expansion of design firms in India, which have developed extensive know-how in the design of Indian manufacturing capacity from indigenous talent and resources, this is a point of some importance in the present context. See Desai, *Bokaro,* for an analysis of the factors that interact with the development and deployment of such talent in the political and economic reality of national and international policies.

Chapter 16

Savings and the Foreign Trade Regime

In analyzing the impact of India's overall economic policies on the domestic savings effort, we will argue that:

1. there is little evidence that the marginal propensity to save in the Indian economy was significantly different between the 1950s, when the severity of exchange control (on the average) was less, and the 1960s, when it was more;

2. detailed analysis does not support the hypothesis that India's absorption of foreign aid has adversely affected her savings effort; this is a conclusion of interest, not merely because of widespread concern with this problem in LDCs today, but because the 1966 economic policy changes toward "liberalization" were partly motivated by the desire to continue aid flow from the consortium members who had virtually made these policy changes a precondition for continuation of aid;

3. there is no evidence that the more recent, import-substituting industries which have grown up primarily during the years 1956–70 under the economic regime we have been describing are significantly higher savers than the more traditional industries; and

4. we do not have adequate data to test the further hypothesis that "organized" industry *in toto* is a better saver than "agriculture." Thus we cannot argue convincingly that the exchange control regime, which buttressed the increasing industrialization, led to greater saving; nor can we establish any other strong links between savings and the Indian foreign trade regime although we consider several possibilities.

228

DOMESTIC SAVINGS AND STRINGENCY OF QRs

It is well known that the data on which Indian national income estimates are based are inadequate and even the methodology of computation is not necessarily the best that could be adopted given the data. The situation regarding savings and investment estimates is even worse: there are no "direct" estimates for either. In brief, aggregate investment is estimated as the value of goods and services used in investment activity. Savings estimates are obtained as a residual from investment estimates by subtracting therefrom the estimated external capital inflow. This is not to suggest that direct estimates are not available for some components of savings and investment—indeed, relatively accurate direct estimates are available relating to the savings and investment activities of the public sector as well as the large-scale manufacturing sector. But a large proportion has still to be estimated indirectly.[1]

Given the nature of the data, therefore, it was decided not to attempt to build an elaborate simultaneous-equation model of the Indian economy but rather to work with single-equation regression relationships. The idea is not so much to estimate the marginal propensity to save with great accuracy as rather to obtain some useful insights into overall savings behavior.

Let us begin, therefore, with the simplest possible relationship:

$$S_t = a_0 + a_1 Y_t + u_t \qquad (16\text{--}1)$$

where S_t stands for aggregate savings, Y_t for national income and u_t for a random disturbance term, all variables relating to year t.

In estimating equation (16–1), we had a choice in defining savings and income (1) in either gross or net terms, (2) at either nominal or real value, and (3) in either per capita or aggregate terms. Since the basis on which replacement of capital expenditures is estimated is extremely weak, we decided to define the variables in gross rather than net terms. Again, we decided to concentrate on the relationship between real magnitudes, though in a more elaborate model the impact of monetary factors should be brought in. Finally, to a limited extent we experimented with both alternatives in (3).

The period of our analysis was 1951–52 to 1969–70. There is a belief among some Indian economists that the period since 1965–66 is radically different from the period before, both politically and economically: politically, because the system was exposed to the deaths of Prime Ministers Nehru and Shastri in quick succession in 1964 and 1966; economically, because of (1) the two successive droughts of unprecedented magnitude in 1965 and 1966, (2) aid stoppage during the Indo-Pakistan War of 1965, its resumption in

1966 and subsequent scaling down and (3) the devaluation and liberalization of June 1966. Since we have data only for a four-year period since 1966, we cannot adequately test this belief. However, we do estimate the relationships separately for the entire period and for the period 1951–52 to 1965–66 to see whether there is any sharp break in the income-savings relationship.

From the point of view of the present monograph, perhaps an equally relevant division of the period would be 1951–52 to 1959–60 and 1960–61 to 1969–70 since the exchange control regime was more stringent on the average through the 1960s (the liberalization associated with devaluation being short-lived, as we have seen already). We thus examine the issue whether any significant change in savings behavior can be observed between the decade of the 1950s and that of the 1960s.

For converting nominal investment to real terms, we had two alternative investment deflators available (denoted by subscripts 1 and 2): one developed by the Perspective Planning Division (PPD) of the Planning Commission and the other put out by the Central Statistical Organisation (CSO). Since savings were obtained as a residual from investment by subtracting the external re-source flow (i.e., the current account surplus or deficit), we had a number of alternative ways of obtaining real savings, of which the following (denoted by superscripts I and II) were used:

I: Deflate merchandise imports and exports by their respective unit value indices and take the surplus or deficit on non-merchandise account without deflation.

II: Deflate the entire current account surplus or deficit by the unit value index of imports, the idea being that, in this way, we capture the real import potential of nominal resource inflow.

Thus, we had four alternative definitions of real savings, $S_1^I(t)$, $S_2^I(t)$, $S_1^{II}(t)$ and $S_2^{II}(t)$ where, for instance, $S_1^{II}(t)$ represents the real savings in year t obtained by subtracting from real investment (defined as the nominal investment deflated by the PPD deflator) the real external resource flow obtained by using procedure II described above. The per capita variables are denoted by the same symbols, but in lower case: e.g., s, y, etc.

The results of our regressions are reported in Tables 16–1 and 16–2.[2] The fit as measured by R^2 is quite good in all the regressions. It appears that the estimate of the marginal propensity to save is not very sensitive to the choice of deflators or of the procedure by which the real external resource flow was calculated, though some sensitivity is seen in the period 1960–61 to 1969–70. As is to be expected (given that population, income and savings were rising over time), the marginal propensity to save in each regression involving per capita variables is higher than in the corresponding regression with aggregate variables. The goodness of fit of the per capita relationship is, however, somewhat poorer.

(Table 16–1)[3] *or* the 1960s period of relatively tighter exchange situation was characterized by a higher marginal propensity to save than the somewhat less stringent period of the 1950s (Table 16–2).[4]

DOMESTIC SAVINGS AND EXTERNAL RESOURCES

We have postulated so far that savings are a function of income alone. However, it has been argued recently that savings are a function of domestic expenditure, rather than income, so that we should instead write:

$$C_t = \beta_0 + \beta_1(Y_t + F_t) \tag{16–2}$$

where F_t is the foreign capital inflow, defined as the negative of the balance on current account and C_t is domestic consumption. We therefore estimated the following equation as well:

$$S_t = a_0 + a_1 Y_t + a_2 F_t + u_t \tag{16–2a}$$

Clearly, when $a_1 = (a_2 + 1)$, this equation will correspond to equation (16–2). A positive (negative) value for a_2 would be consistent with the hypothesis that external resources complement (substitute for) domestic resources.

The following version of (16–2a), with F_t lagged by one year, was also estimated:

$$S_t = a_0 + a_1 Y_t + a_2 F_{t-1} + u_t \tag{16–2b}$$

The idea underlying equation (16–2b) is that if indeed consumption is related to expected volume of resources available, then it may be reasonable to presume that such expectations for any year are formed on the basis of the actual resources in the previous year. This would suggest that S_t should be related to Y_{t-1} and F_{t-1}. Given that the correlation between Y_t and Y_{t-1} is very high (while that between F_t and F_{t-1} is not) the relation (16–2b) would, however, do just as well as one with Y_{t-1} instead of Y_t.

The results for both (16–2a) and (16–2b) are shown in Table 16–3. Only the results relating to the PPD deflator and the second procedure for calculating the real resource flow are reported here. We find that when used in conjunction with income, the explanatory power of contemporaneous external resource flow in explaining savings is virtually nil: the coefficients on F are statistically insignificantly different from zero. The lagged response equations also perform badly: with one exception, the coefficients on F_{-1} are also not significantly different from zero. Thus we infer that domestic savings do not seem to be influenced by external resources.

On the other hand, a mild skepticism toward this conclusion may be in order. For one thing, the introduction of F_{-1} generally seems to lead to

Let us now examine the results in Tables 16–1 and 16–2 for inter-perio comparisons of the marginal propensity to save. Clearly, there seems to b little evidence for the view that *either* the post-1966 liberalization years sig nificantly changed the marginal propensity to save from the preceding period

TABLE 16–1

Savings Regressions,
1951–52 to 1965–66 and 1951–52 to 1969–70

	1951–52 to 1965–66		1951–52 to 1969–70	
1. (a) $S_1^I = -1453 + 0.24\,Y$		$R^2 = 0.94$	$-1053 + 0.21\,Y$	$R^2 = 0.93$
(241) (0.02)			(212) (0.01)	
(b) $s_1^I = \quad -66 + 0.33\,y$		$R^2 = 0.87$	$-54 + 0.29\,y$	$R^2 = 0.86$
(12) (0.03)			(10) (0.03)	
2. (a) $S_2^I = -1476 + 0.24\,Y$		$R^2 = 0.93$	$-1323 + 0.23\,Y$	$R^2 = 0.95$
(253) (0.02)			(191) (0.01)	
(b) $s_2^I = \quad -68 + 0.34\,y$		$R^2 = 0.86$	$-66 + 0.33\,y$	$R^2 = 0.89$
(12) (0.04)			(10) (0.03)	
3. (a) $S_1^{II} = -1509 + 0.24\,Y$		$R^2 = 0.93$	$-1216 + 0.21\,Y$	$R^2 = 0.94$
(264) (0.02)			(207) (0.01)	
(b) $s_1^{II} = \quad -68 + 0.33\,y$		$R^2 = 0.85$	$-61 + 0.31\,y$	$R^2 = 0.87$
(13) (0.04)			(10) (0.03)	
4. (a) $S_2^{II} = -1532 + 0.24\,Y$		$R^2 = 0.93$	$-1486 + 0.24\,Y$	$R^2 = 0.96$
(260) (0.02)			(186) (0.01)	
(b) $s_2^{II} = \quad -70 + 0.34\,y$		$R^2 = 0.86$	$-72 + 0.35\,y$	$R^2 = 0.92$
(13) (0.04)			(10) (0.03)	

NOTE: Figures in parentheses are standard errors. Refer to the text for explanation of the regressions.

TABLE 16–2

Savings Regressions,
1951–52 to 1959–60 and 1960–61 to 1969–70

	1951–52 to 1959–60		1960–61 to 1969–70	
1. $S_1^I = \quad -815 + 0.18\,Y$		$R^2 = 0.73$	$-592 + 0.18\,Y$	$R^2 = 0.73$
(520) (0.04)			(698) (0.04)	
2. $S_2^I = -1087 + 0.21\,Y$		$R^2 = 0.72$	$-1271 + 0.22\,Y$	$R^2 = 0.87$
(607) (0.05)			(560) (0.03)	
3. $S_1^{II} = \quad -532 + 0.16\,Y$		$R^2 = 0.63$	$-834 + 0.19\,Y$	$R^2 = 0.80$
(563) (0.05)			(610) (0.03)	
4. $S_2^{II} = \quad -804 + 0.18\,Y$		$R^2 = 0.67$	$-1514 + 0.24\,Y$	$R^2 = 0.91$
(600) (0.05)			(741) (0.03)	

NOTE: Figures in parentheses are standard errors. Refer to the text for explanation of the regressions.

TABLE 16–3

Savings Regressions
Including Foreign Capital Inflow, Various Periods, 1951–52 to 1969–70

(1) 1951–52 to 1969–70	(a)	$S_1^{II} = -124 + 0.22\ Y - 0.08\ F$ $\qquad\qquad (0.02)\quad\ (0.30)$	$R^2 = 0.94$
	(b)	$S_1^{II} = -1487 + 0.24\ Y - 0.57\ F_{-1}$ $\qquad\qquad\ (0.02)\quad\ (0.33)$	$R^2 = 0.95$
(2) 1951–52 to 1965–66	(a)	$S_1^{II} = -1611 + 0.25\ Y - 0.18\ F$ $\qquad\qquad\ (0.03)\quad\ (0.45)$	$R^2 = 0.93$
	(b)*	$S_1^{II} = -1976 + 0.28\ Y - 0.78\ F_{-1}$ $\qquad\qquad\ (0.03)\quad\ (0.38)$	$R^2 = 0.95$
(3) 1951–52 to 1959–60	(a)	$S_1^{II} = -553 + 0.16\ Y - 0.02\ F$ $\qquad\ (747)\quad (0.06)\quad\ (0.49)$	$R^2 = 0.63$
	(b)	$S_1^{II} = -1262 + 0.22\ Y - 0.70\ F_{-1}$ $\qquad\ (665)\quad (0.06)\quad\ (0.42)$	$R^2 = 0.75$
(4) 1960–61 to 1969–70	(a)	$S_1^{II} = -641 + 0.19\ Y - 0.29\ F$ $\qquad\ (741)\quad (0.04)\quad\ (0.57)$	$R^2 = 0.81$
	(b)	$S_1^{II} = -862 + 0.21\ Y - 0.49\ F_{-1}$ $\qquad\ (626)\quad (0.04)\quad\ (0.62)$	$R^2 = 0.82$

NOTE: Figures in parentheses are standard errors.

* The coefficient on F_{-1} is significantly different from zero at 5 percent level; other coefficients on F_{-1} are not significantly different from zero, in this table.

higher (*not* lower) coefficients on Y than, for comparable periods, in Tables 16–1 and 16–2. In contrast, a different test suggests an opposite inference: i.e., that domestic savings are a function of $(Y + F)$ rather than (Y). Thus, recall that if we write equation (16–2) as follows:

$$C = \beta_0 + \beta_1\ (Y + F) \qquad (16\text{-}2)$$

and

$$S = Y - C$$

we then have:

$$S = -\beta_0 + (1 - \beta_1)Y - \beta_1 F$$

so that we have the relationship that the coefficient on Y is equal to one plus the coefficient on F (or F_{-1}, if we put in lagged response). We can therefore test whether the coefficients on Y are indeed significantly different from one plus the coefficients on F and F_{-1} in Table 16–3. This test indicates that the hypothesis of equation (16–2) is *not* rejected by the data in Table 16–3: thus we cannot rule out *altogether* the possibility that external resources substitute for domestic savings.

On balance, therefore, we would conclude that there is not enough evidence, and at best the evidence conflicts, to say whether the absorption of external resources has adversely affected India's domestic savings effort.

Note also that, in regard to our earlier conclusions in this chapter, the introduction of F or F_{-1} into the estimating equation does not significantly affect the conclusions reached (*via* inter-period analysis) regarding the impact of the severity of exchange control on the savings effort.

Sectoral Impact.

We may next examine the possibility that, even if the overall impact of the external resource inflow on domestic savings is negligible, the impact on certain components thereof may be rather large.

From this viewpoint, it is relevant to distinguish between public and private savings, relating the former to public revenues and the latter to private income alone. Since private income as well as public revenues (to a smaller extent) were in turn correlated with Y, we used Y as the explanatory variable in addition to the external resource flow to reestimate the equations separately for private and government savings. The results are set out in Table 16–4, for the period 1951–52 to 1965–66.

As in the case of total savings, the explanatory power of contemporaneous capital inflow is nil in explaining either public or private savings. The lagged capital inflow, however, has a significant negative coefficient in the case of

TABLE 16–4

**Private and Government
Savings Regressions, 1951–52 to 1965–66**

$$S_{1p}{}^{II} = -1135 + 0.19Y - 0.28F \qquad R^2 = 0.91$$
$$(304) \quad (0.03) \quad (0.36)$$

$$S_{1p}{}^{II} = -1433 + 0.22Y - 0.77F_{-1} \qquad R^2 = 0.94$$
$$(245) \quad (0.02) \quad (0.28)$$

$$S_{1g}{}^{II} = -476 + 0.06Y - 0.10F \qquad R^2 = 0.84$$
$$(158) \quad (0.01) \quad (0.19)$$

$$S_{1g}{}^{II} = -543 + 0.06Y - 0.01F_{-1} \qquad R^2 = 0.84$$
$$(160) \quad (0.01) \quad (0.18)$$

NOTES: Figures in parentheses are standard errors.

The subscripts p and g denote respectively private and public savings. Refer to the text for explanation of the regressions.

private savings but the marginal propensity to save in the lagged relationship is higher than that in the unlagged one. These results, however, are difficult to interpret, as we would normally have expected the external resource inflow to work primarily through the budget—in view of the larger component of foreign aid—by reducing *public* savings: the significance of the lagged foreign resource inflow in influencing private savings seems to us therefore to be mainly spurious.[5]

Thus we conclude that our analysis contradicts the thesis that incoming foreign resources have seriously interfered with the domestic savings effort. This is probably not surprising since the planning mechanism has, by and large, served to make the domestic tax-and-savings effort keep in step with the aid flow, both because of internal clarity on this objective and external (aid-donor-induced) pressure-cum-ethos in this regard.[6]

RETAINED EARNINGS BY SPECIFIC INDUSTRIES IN THE CORPORATE SECTOR

The manufacturing sector as a whole accounted for less than 14 percent of national income in 1969–70. The contribution of registered factories was around 8 percent. The non-financial private corporate sector which is included in the group of registered factories and is its predominant part is estimated to have contributed about 5 percent of total domestic savings in 1971–72. Thus this sector is not a major source of savings in the Indian economy. However, since the exchange control regime had a major impact on this sector, it may nevertheless be of some interest to see whether the industries favored by the import substitution policies were relatively higher savers.

The Reserve Bank of India publishes financial data relating to large public and private limited companies. The private limited companies account only for about 10 percent of total assets of this group. Since this is a relatively small group, we decided to confine our attention to the public limited companies. A number of alternative relationships between retained earnings (RE) and profits after taxes (PAT) were estimated, of which the following are of interest:

$$RE = \alpha + \beta \, (PAT) + u \qquad (16\text{--}3a)$$

$$\frac{RE}{N} = \alpha + \frac{\beta}{N} + \gamma \left(\frac{PAT}{N} \right) + u \qquad (16\text{--}3b)$$

(N is net worth)

$$\frac{RE}{N} = \alpha + \frac{\beta}{\sqrt{N}} + \gamma \left(\frac{PAT}{\sqrt{N}} \right) + u \qquad (16\text{--}3c)$$

The relationship (16–3a) is straightforward and needs no explanation. The relationship (16–3b) was suggested by the fact that the Reserve Bank publishes only pooled data relating to the companies operating in different sectors of the economy and *not* individual company data. Since the number of companies in each sector has changed over time, it is possible that some heteroscedasticity may be present in equation (16–3a). Equation (16–3b), with $\alpha = 0$, would then correspond to (16–3a) with correction for heteroscedasticity if one assumed that the residual variance in (16–3a) was proportional to the *square* of net worth. Similarly, equation (16–3c), with $\alpha = 0$, would be the correct estimating equation if the residual variance in (16–3a) was proportional to net worth. Note, however, that the coefficient α in the equations estimated was *not* specified to be zero so that the *data* could determine whether it indeed was significantly different from zero. Also, note that a positive (negative) α (in 16–3b or 16–3c) will imply that for any given level of profits after tax, retained earnings will be higher (lower) the larger the net worth.

The regression results relating to 10 industries, for the years 1950–58 and 1960–61 to 1968–69, are given in Table 16–5.

The first four industries in Table 16–5 are, by and large, long-established and "traditional" industries; the first two are also major exporters and none can be considered to have been "helped" by the foreign trade regime. Industries 5 to 10 did certainly "benefit" from such controls, however. If we now look at the results obtained by estimating equation (16–3a), we find that while two out of four "traditional" industries had marginal propensities to save exceeding 0.50, the corresponding figure is four out of six in the case of the remaining industries. The correction for heteroscedasticity [equations (16–3b) or (16–3c)] improves the goodness of fit and equation (16–3c) seems to yield a better fit to a certain extent in almost all cases though, in none of the cases is the increase in R^2 very large.

Confining our attention to estimated equation (16–3c), in Table 16–5, we find that, keeping net worth constant, an increase of a unit in profits after taxes will increase retained earnings by more than 0.75 units in all cases except jute, for which the figure is 0.74. Thus, our analysis suggests that all 10 industries considered were good savers.

In order to examine rigorously, however, whether the "non-traditional" industries are (on the average) better savers than "traditional" industries, we ran a number of statistical tests. These tests were performed as follows. We estimated a common marginal propensity to save [i.e., β of (16–3a), γ of (16–3b) and (16–3c)] for the two *groups* of industries while allowing the other parameters to vary among industries, using an appropriate (slope) dummy variable technique. It turned out that the coefficient of this dummy variable [i.e., a variable that had the value zero for all the observations relat-

TABLE 16–5

Corporate Savings Regressions in Selected Industries

	$RE = \alpha + \beta(PAT)$			$\dfrac{RE}{N} = \alpha + \dfrac{\beta}{N} + \gamma\left(\dfrac{PAT}{N}\right)$				$\dfrac{RE}{\sqrt{N}} = \alpha + \dfrac{\beta}{\sqrt{N}} + \gamma\left(\dfrac{PAT}{\sqrt{N}}\right)$			
	α	β	R^2	α	β	γ	R^2	α	β	γ	R^2
1. Cotton textiles	−707.43	0.77	0.890	−0.05	245.64	0.86	0.997	−14.48	1,227.07	0.85	0.987
	(−7.3)	(11.4)		(−26.7)	(7.4)	(76.2)		(−25.4)	(16.4)	(73.5)	
2. Jute manufactures	−139.77	0.73	0.986	−0.01	−71.27	0.74	0.986	−2.07	−2.38	0.74	0.986
	(−17.85)	(33.15)		(−1.03)	(−1.09)	(29.27)		(−1.08)	(−0.02)	(29.74)	
3. Cement	−73.40	0.48	0.773	−0.06	7.74	0.90	0.957	−7.13	225.27	0.86	0.960
	(−2.12)	(7.37)		(−11.32)	(0.96)	(17.72)		(−10.83)	(8.68)	(18.54)	
4. Electricity generation and supply	−57.29	0.50	0.897	−0.05	−2.16	0.91	0.798	−6.06	183.73	0.94	0.938
	(−3.42)	(11.83)		(−3.34)	(−0.13)	(6.60)		(−5.30)	(4.08)	(10.56)	
5. Aluminum	−16.83	0.59	0.955	−0.05	21.21	0.80	0.924	−4.77	84.40	0.96	0.984
	(−1.64)	(18.40)		(−4.47)	(2.75)	(9.75)		(−7.68)	(6.73)	(18.40)	
6. Iron and steel	−103.73	0.63	0.736	−0.04	−73.50	0.98	0.964	−6.88	238.31	0.94	0.929
	(−0.99)	(6.68)		(−6.83)	(−2.43)	(17.56)		(−6.25)	(3.75)	(13.85)	
7. Transport equipment	−21.93	0.48	0.917	−0.04	31.88	0.79	0.939	−4.87	142.01	0.78	0.969
	(−0.84)	(13.25)		(−5.45)	(5.36)	(12.25)		(−5.93)	(5.78)	(13.74)	
8. Electrical equipment	−29.80	0.57	0.934	−0.02	3.91	0.67	0.853	−4.95	103.28	0.89	0.982
	(−1.48)	(15.13)		(−2.14)	(0.90)	(8.16)		(−7.82)	(7.08)	(18.57)	
9. Other equipment	−96.41	0.65	0.793	−0.03	22.70	0.67	0.874	−4.30	150.98	0.76	0.929
	(−2.45)	(7.81)		(−2.93)	(1.10)	(10.21)		(−5.23)	(3.77)	(13.99)	
10. Basic chemicals	−19.92	0.44	0.868	−0.05	21.21	0.80	0.931	−7.21	196.47	0.93	0.977
	(−0.82)	(10.26)		(−4.46)	(2.75)	(9.76)		(−7.93)	(7.42)	(14.53)	

NOTE: Figures in parentheses are t values. Refer to the text for explanation of the regressions.

ting to "traditional" industries and the value of PAT for (16–3a), PAT/N for (16–3b) and PAT/$\sqrt{N}$ for (16–3c) corresponding to each observation relating to "non-traditional" industries] was negative in each case [i.e., for (16–3a), (16–3b) and (16–3c)], suggesting that "non-traditional" industries on the average had a *lower,* not higher, marginal propensity to save! However, the *t* values of these coefficients turned out to be insignificant so that the average MPS of "non-traditional" industries is *not* significantly different (at 1 percent level) from that of "traditional" industries, except in the case of equation (16–3a).[7]

After comparing the average MPS of the two groups of industries, we also examined whether there is any significant difference between the MPS of industries *within* each group. This is done through an analysis-of-variance test which compares the increase (after dividing by the appropriate degrees of freedom) in the residual sum of squares brought about by estimating a common slope for the group in relation to the sum of the residual sum of squares of the industries in the group when a separate regression is estimated for each industry. It turned out that the MPS of the "non-traditional" industries did not differ significantly (in a statistical sense) regardless of the form of the relationship (16–3a, 16–3b, or 16–c) estimated; the "traditional" industries had, however, significantly different MPS (at 1 percent level) except in the case of equation (16–3a).[8]

We must conclude therefore that it is not possible to argue, on the basis of the available and analyzed evidence, that any systematic differences in the marginal propensity to save can be discerned in different industries, or in "traditional" as against "non-traditional" industries. In fact, the only significant differences within any group of industries that are observed belong to the limited group of "traditional" industries, something that yields no comfort to those who look to the efficacy of the trade regime in raising savings as an offsetting argument against those who convincingly demonstrate its inefficiencies in other respects.

OTHER LINKS WITH SAVINGS

The previous section suggests that, in terms of both the average and the marginal propensity to save, the corporate sector is perhaps the best saver. Hence, if the regime led to "additional" industrialization which, in turn, expanded the *corporate* sector, this could have contributed to greater saving.

In turn, if the result was also an expansion of *urban* incomes, we have the additional evidence, however slight, that urban *households* have a higher marginal propensity to save than rural households. The National Council for Applied Economic Research conducted two household savings surveys, the first in 1960 covering urban households, and the second in 1962 covering rural households.[9] The Council has also conducted another survey in the early 1970s, the results of which are yet to be published. The earlier surveys, however, showed that the marginal propensity to save (MPS), net of rural households, was 0.168 when savings in the form of currency, consumer durables and livestock were included, and 0.145 if these were excluded. The MPS of urban households was higher, at 0.34, coming down to 0.24 if the top and bottom 10 percent of income groups are excluded on assumption that their incomes are affected by transitory factors, influencing excessively the estimated MPS.[10]

We may finally note that the urban sector is also a better saver, not merely because of the corporate sector and the urban households, but also because the government's tax net is more effective in the urban than in the rural sector (to a point where agricultural income has escaped with virtually no taxation so far). On the other hand, one may also argue that the inability to raise enough savings from the urban sector could well have prompted greater efforts in the direction of agricultural taxation; alternatively, a rapidly growing agricultural sector, as seems now likely in the post-Green-Revolution period, could well have led to a better perception of the need to tax this sector and hence perhaps to greater action in that regard.[11] We also need to note finally that higher savings rates may still imply lower growth rates if the investment needed to sustain unit growth of income increases sufficiently in the process owing to inefficiencies or misallocation of resources. In particular, in relation to the urban expansion, note that such an outcome of the economic policies, even if it leads to an increase in the savings rate, may well require additional investments in high capital-output ratio activities such as housing and related infrastructure in the cities and thus slow down economic growth on that account.

The frequent argument that a QR-regime enables the government to get away with inflation and thereby encourages inflationary policies that combine with low nominal interest rates and declining real interest rates to cause a reduction in savings does not seem relevant to India which, until 1962–63, had experienced only a moderate trend increase in prices. The post-1966 situation in particular has had less price stability, but the period is too short and disturbed in the end by the refugee crisis of 1972 and the emergence of Bangladesh and its associated strains on the Indian economy to make any reasonable evaluation of this hypothesis possible at the time this monograph was written. Needless to say, however, there is *nothing* about a QR-regime which *requires* that real interest rates be kept excessively low.

We may next note the argument that India's development strategy erred in permitting a skewed income distribution which resulted in an unnecessarily import-intensive consumption pattern that increased the foreign exchange constraint and reduced the feasible rate of savings and growth.[12] Admittedly, there is a grain of truth in this; but it may well be contended that this argument is a critique of inefficient and unjust income-distribution policies, rather than of the QR-and-industrial-licensing regime. But there *is* a connection. It was really the growth of consumer *industries,* often at a very low economic scale but nevertheless supported by the QR-regime and automatically protected, that enabled the government to claim that luxury imports were down while permitting and encouraging the consumption of similar domestically produced luxury items in the name of industrialization. An economic policy that would have forbidden the indiscriminate growth of such consumer and allied industries domestically would have made the cost of permitting such luxury consumption much more obvious by making it feasible only through importation in many cases. This might well have resulted in greater political pressure to pursue income redistribution more energetically. Of course, a socialist cynic might well argue that the result would have been merely to seek other subterfuges to avoid making the genuine left-wing shift implicit in a redistributive program with a real bite.

Finally, we must note the rents which accrued to those who were given access to the scarce imports carrying large premia through the bulk of the period we have been studying. This implies that an alternative regime, under which these premia had been siphoned off into the tax net, would have been productive of more savings. If we allow for an average premium of 40 percent on imports, and assume an average import bill of Rs. 18 billions (which is the approximate average for the import bill for the first four years of the Third Plan) and assume, in turn, that half of this could have been subject to this premium-siphoning exercise, we would have had an annual tax revenue collection of Rs. 3.5 billions on this account alone, representing nearly 10 percent of the tax revenue in India during 1969–70 of Rs. 39.9 billions. Thus, even if nothing else had been changed in the Indian economic regime, a shift to an exchange rate regime which eliminated this premium, by devaluation or by the use of adjustable tariffs or exchange auctions suitably designed, would have helped generate greater savings.

Needless to say, all the increase in taxation would not have implied a corresponding increase in savings in the economy. While we think that it is reasonable to assume that increased government savings would have more than offset the loss in savings from those deprived of the import premia, we must admit also that the resulting increment in total savings is likely to have been rather small. This is because most of the imports went to the corporate manufacturing sector as the AU import licensing became more important, and the profits of that sector were subject to the 50 percent corporation tax anyway,[13] and, as we have already seen, the corporate sector has a rather large propensity to save out of incremental retained earnings.

In conclusion, we can only say that the linkages between India's trade regime and her savings performance are many and diverse; they are also difficult to evaluate and quantify with the degree of success that would be necessary to arrive at a reasonably firm conclusion regarding the sign of the *net* impact. It is clear enough, on balance, at the end of our analysis that one *cannot* really justify, on the available and analyzed evidence, any claim that the QR-regime, while it may have led to several static inefficiencies and costs, had at least the saving grace to improve the savings performance and thus lead to higher growth in the long run.

NOTES

1. More can be learned about this subject from C. R. Rao, ed., *Data Base of the Indian Economy* (Calcutta: Statistical Publishing Society, 1972).

2. The statistical results reported in Tables 16–1 through 16–4 have been taken from T. N. Srinivasan, S. D. Tendulkar and A. Vaidyanathan, *A Study of the Aggregate Savings Behaviour of the Indian Economy* (New Delhi: Indian Statistical Institute, 1973).

3. Recall, however, our *caveats* in the preceding discussion about the lack of sufficient data for the post-1966 period to test this hypothesis effectively. Table 16–1 is only a weak way of learning about this issue.

4. Note again that the early half of the 1950s was very comfortable but the last two years of the decade were already characterized by the strict QR-regime, as pointed out in Chapter 2. Note also that if the marginal propensity to save tends to rise with increasing per capita income, its failure to do so in the 1960s may be significant as a possible shortcoming of the QR-regime.

5. In fact, we might as well argue that the resource inflow could have improved investment opportunities—in India, the inflow of private foreign investment leads to the same result since joint ventures are actively promoted by government—and could have led to increased private savings à la Hirschman to utilize these opportunities! The only "weak" argument in support of the negative coefficient on F_{-1} is that consumption is a function of available imports which, in turn, reflect foreign aid inflow. This argument would be justified to some extent by PL480 imports.

6. For relevant details on the tax efforts of the Indian government from 1950 to 1966, see Bhagwati and Desai, *India*, pp. 71–73.

7. The *t* values were:

Form of Equation	Degrees of Freedom	t
16–3a	168	−5.23
16–3b	158	−0.84
16–3c	158	−0.19

8. The *F* values were:

| Form of the Equation | Traditional | | Non-traditional | |
	Degrees of Freedom	F	Degrees of Freedom	F
16–3a	3,64	1.57	5,96	2.18
16–3b	3,60	5.92	5,90	2.26
16–3c	3,60	7.74	5,90	0.32

9. The methodology, the sampling design and the detailed results of these two surveys were published in a series of studies by the government of India, New Delhi: *Urban Income and Saving* appeared in 1962 and the *All India Rural Household Survey* was brought out in three volumes in 1964, 1965 and 1966.

10. The Reserve Bank of India used to publish time series data (discontinued after 1963) on aggregate savings of rural households based on an extrapolation of the benchmark estimates obtained for 1951–52 in its rural credit survey. Since the methodology of extrapolation is subject to criticism (see the chapter by A. Rudra on savings estimates in Rao, *Data Base*), and since data for the years beyond 1962–63 are not available, we do not report the RBI results here. Some fragmentary evidence relating to household savings in some regions of India is also available. See P. G. K. Panikkar, *Rural Savings in India* (Bombay: Somaiya Publications, 1970).

11. At the height of the tax effort in relation to national income in 1965–66, the shares of the public sector and the private corporate sector in net domestic savings were estimated at 22.9 and 4.2 percent. In the preceding year, when there was no drought and therefore no need to subsidize food primarily, these shares were 29.3 and 5.2 percent. See *Fourth Plan Mid-Term Appraisal,* Vol. I, 1971, Government of India, Planning Commission, New Delhi.

12. *The Approach to the Fifth Five Year Plan,* Government of India, Planning Commission, New Delhi, claims to demonstrate this point by contrasting the results of a planning-model exercise with two different consumption vectors, one in which income is redistributed to the bottom 30 percent and one in which it is not. The emerging plan, therefore, is likely to opt for the former course on grounds of *both* growth and redistributive justice. We should note, however, that the alleged contrast between the two variants depends on assumptions about feasible growth rates in agriculture. In case of feasibility constraints on agricultural growth, the redistribution variant could well require the importation of so much food as to reverse the growth ranking of the two variants!

13. However, note also that whenever these premia were "cashed" in the market by *illegal* transactions, they escaped the tax net. In contributing to the large amount of "black" money in circulation, the exchange control regime, which made the transfer of AU licenses illegal but not infrequent, was itself a major force in making the tax effort of the Indian fiscal authorities less effective than it might have been.

Part V

Concluding Remarks

Concluding Remarks

The analysis in this volume points to the conclusion that India's foreign trade regime, in conjunction with domestic licensing policies in the industrial sector, led to economic inefficiencies and impaired her economic performance. This conclusion follows not merely from the static analysis in Part II, but also from our analysis of growth effects in Part IV. The policy framework was detrimental, on balance, to the growth of the economy by adversely influencing export performance, by wasteful inter-industrial and inter-firm allocation of resources, by permitting and encouraging expansion of excess capacity and by blunting competition and hence the incentives for cost-consciousness and quality-improvement. The effects on savings and research and development expenditures were, at best, ambiguous and cannot plausibly be cited as having offset these inefficiencies.

Secondly, our analysis of the June 1966 devaluation-cum-liberalization policy package, far from showing that exchange rate adjustment is unworkable, suggests the opposite conclusion. We have also been able to draw lessons on how such a policy package may be better designed to secure more acceptable and lasting transition to a less restrictive foreign trade regime.

Our detailed analysis of the June 1966 policy package, the lessons spelled out for making such a policy change more successful and efficient and the conclusion that such a change is necessary to stimulate the increased efficiency and faster growth of the Indian economy—these three aspects of our analysis strongly underline the need for India to adopt a new economic policy and the feasibility of such a transition.[1]

---

1. The dimensions of such a new policy framework were spelled out in our joint paper, "Licensing and Control of Industry," given at the Prime Minister's Conference for Young Industrialists, March 1966. See also Bhagwati and Desai, *India,* pp. 477–496; and Bhagwati, *India in the International Economy.*

Appendix A

Definition of Concepts and Delineation of Phases

DEFINITION OF CONCEPTS USED IN THE PROJECT

Exchange Rates.

1. *Nominal exchange rate:* The official parity for a transaction. For countries maintaining a single exchange rate registered with the International Monetary Fund, the nominal exchange rate is the registered rate.

2. *Effective exchange rate (EER):* The number of units of local currency actually paid or received for a one-dollar international transaction. Surcharges, tariffs, the implicit interest forgone on guarantee deposits, and any other charges against purchases of goods and services abroad are included, as are rebates, the value of import replenishment rights, and other incentives to earn foreign exchange for sales of goods and services abroad.

3. *Price-level-deflated (PLD) nominal exchange rates:* The nominal exchange rate deflated in relation to some base period by the price level index of the country.

4. *Price-level-deflated EER (PLD-EER):* The EER deflated by the price level index of the country.

5. *Purchasing-power-parity adjusted exchange rates:* The relevant (nominal or effective) exchange rate multiplied by the ratio of the foreign price level to the domestic price level.

246

Devaluation.

1. *Gross devaluation:* The change in the parity registered with the IMF (or, synonymously in most cases, de jure devaluation).

2. *Net devaluation:* The weighted average of changes in EERs by classes of transactions (or, synonymously in most cases, de facto devaluation).

3. *Real gross devaluation:* The gross devaluation adjusted for the increase in the domestic price level over the relevant period.

4. *Real net devaluation:* The net devaluation similarly adjusted.

Protection Concepts.

1. *Explicit tariff:* The amount of tariff charged against the import of a good as a percentage of the import price (in local currency at the nominal exchange rate) of the good.

2. *Implicit tariff* (or, synonymously, tariff equivalent): The ratio of the domestic price (net of normal distribution costs) minus the c.i.f. import price to the c.i.f. import price in local currency.

3. *Premium:* The windfall profit accruing to the recipient of an import license per dollar of imports. It is the difference between the domestic selling price (net of normal distribution costs) and the landed cost of the item (including tariffs and other charges). The premium is thus the difference between the implicit and the explicit tariff (including other charges) multiplied by the nominal exchange rate.

4. *Nominal tariff:* The tariff—either explicit or implicit as specified—on a commodity.

5. *Effective tariff:* The explicit or implicit tariff on value added as distinct from the nominal tariff on a commodity. This concept is also expressed as the effective rate of protection (ERP) or as the effective protective rate (EPR).

6. *Domestic resource costs (DRC):* The value of domestic resources (evaluated at "shadow" or opportunity cost prices) employed in earning or saving a dollar of foreign exchange (in the value-added sense) when producing domestic goods.

DELINEATION OF PHASES USED IN TRACING THE EVOLUTION OF EXCHANGE CONTROL REGIMES

To achieve comparability of analysis among different countries, each author of a country study was asked to identify the chronological development of his country's payments regime through the following phases. There was no presumption that a country would necessarily pass through all the phases in chronological sequence.

Phase I: During this period, quantitative restrictions on international transactions are imposed and then intensified. They generally are initiated in response to an unsustainable payments deficit and then, for a period, are intensified. During the period when reliance upon quantitative restrictions as a means of controlling the balance of payments is increasing, the country is said to be in Phase I.

Phase II: During this phase, quantitative restrictions are still intense, but various price measures are taken to offset some of the undesired results of the system. Heightened tariffs, surcharges on imports, rebates for exports, special tourist exchange rates, and other price interventions are used in this phase. However, primary reliance continues to be placed on quantitative restrictions.

Phase III: This phase is characterized by an attempt to systematize the changes which take place during Phase II. It generally starts with a formal exchange-rate change and may be accompanied by removal of some of the surcharges, etc., imposed during Phase II and by reduced reliance upon quantitative restrictions. Phase III may be little more than a tidying-up operation (in which case the likelihood is that the country will re-enter Phase II), or it may signal the beginning of withdrawal from reliance upon quantitative restrictions.

Phase IV: If the changes in Phase III result in adjustments within the country, so that liberalization can continue, the country is said to enter Phase IV. The necessary adjustments generally include increased foreign-exchange earnings and gradual relaxation of quantitative restrictions. The latter relaxation may take the form of changes in the nature of quantitative restrictions or of increased foreign-exchange allocations, and thus reduced premiums, under the same administrative system.

Phase V: This is a period during which an exchange regime is fully liberalized. There is full convertibility on current account, and quantitative restrictions are not employed as a means of regulating the ex ante balance of payments.

Appendix B

Indian Terms and Units

Indian Units.

1 crore: 10 million.
1 lakh: 100,000.
Tonne: metric ton; 1 tonne is equivalent to 1.096 U.S. tons.
Indian fiscal year: runs from April 1 to March 31. When a year is given in hyphenated form (e.g., 1952–53), it refers to the fiscal year. The calendar year is referred to by just one number (e.g., 1952).

Political Institutions and Parties.

Lok Sabha: Lower house of the Indian Parliament.
Rajya Sabha: Upper house of the Indian Parliament.
Estimates committees of the Lok Sabha: These committees generally undertake an evaluation of the various ministries and departments of the Government of India. In practice, the reports of these committees promote the accountability of the executive branch of the government to the Parliament.
Communist Party of India (CPI): The Moscow-oriented Indian Communist Party.
Communist Party–Marxist (CPM): The CPM was formed after the Chinese invasion of 1962. Its orientation is neither Soviet nor Chinese.
Communist Party–Marxist-Leninist (CPML): The CPML is militant in its ideology and violent in its tactics. It is most active in West Bengal, especially in Calcutta. It is Mao-inspired.

249

Congress Party (Ruling): The faction of the Old Congress Party with a left-of-center program, which was swept to power under Mrs. Gandhi's leadership after the general elections of March 1971.

Congress Party (Organizational): The faction of the Old Congress Party with the older leadership.

Dravid Munnetra Kazhagam (DMK): The political party with a regional basis in the state of Tamil Nadu in South India with Madras as the capital.

Jan Sangh: The right-wing party drawing its inspiration from Hindu cultural traditions and nationalist aspirations.

Praja Socialist Party (PSP): The socialist impact of this party, formed in 1952, was nullified mainly as a result of the socialist program of the Congress Party under Nehru's leadership.

Swatantra Party: The right-wing party of private enterprise.

Samykta Socialist Party (SSP): The socialist party under the colorful leadership of the late Ram Manohar Lohia, with a largely agitational approach.

Abbreviations Frequently Used

ASI	Annual Survey of Industry
AU	Actual User (Import) Licenses
CCI&E	Chief Controller of Imports and Exports
CG	Capital Goods (Import) Licenses
CGC	Capital Goods (Import) Control
DAC	Development Assistance Committee
DGTD	Directorate General of Technical Development
DLF	Development Loan Fund
EI	Established Importer Licenses
EP	Export Promotion (Import) Licenses
EPC	Export Promotion Council
GOI	Government of India
IBRD	International Bank for Reconstruction and Development (World Bank)
ICT	Indian Customs Tariff
I&SC	Iron and Steel Controller
ITC	Indian Trade Classification
JCCIE	Joint Chief Controller of Imports and Exports
NDC	National Development Council
NDR	National Defense Remittance Scheme
PL 480	U.S. Public Law 480
RBI	Reserve Bank of India
PPD	Perspective Planning Division, Planning Commission
POL	Petroleum, Oil, and Lubricants

SITC	Standard International Trade Classification
SSMI	Sample Survey of Manufacturing Industries
STC	State Trading Corporation
USAID	U.S. Agency for International Development

Index

253

224–225; international prices for,
101–102
Industrial licenses: allocation of, 183; and
control of foreign investment, 225;
effect on productivity, 216–217; effect
on research and development expenditures, 225; and excess capacity, 190,
245; and import licensing, 21, 30, 45,
125, 162, 170; liberalization of, 29, 79–
80, 80n, 125–126, 157; scope of, 21;
under Second Five-Year Plan, 4, 5, 28,
29
Industrial production. *See* Production
Industrial targeting, 4, 21, 29
Inflation, 84, 111, 116–117, 118, 149n,
169. *See also* Prices, increases in
Inputs: subsidization of, 63, 101–102, 103–
104, 106–107; use of imported, 45, 46;
use of indigenous, 223, 224–225. *See
also* Import-dependent industries
Institutional features of Indian economy,
5, 21, 24–26
Interest rates, and savings levels, 239
Intermediate goods: domestic production
of, 16–18; DRCs for, 182, 184–185;
ERP for, 182, 184–185; imports of, 4–5,
19, 36, 80, 125; licensing of imports
of, 18, 19; tariffs on, 184–185
International Monetary Fund, 152
International Trade, Ministry of, 73, 152
Inventories, holding of large, 44
Investment, domestic. *See also* Excess
capacity
—effect on: of capital inflows, 241n; of
devaluation, 124, 125; of droughts, 124;
of export performance, 202, 205; of
foreign investment, 241n; of government
expenditures, 124; of import liberalization, 124, 125, 127; of industrial
licensing, 21, 24, 46, 190, 245
—estimation of, 124, 229
—and government savings, 126
—by large-scale industry, 126
—pattern of, 4, 21, 24, 27–28
—projected levels of, 4
—protection of, 24, 213
—by public sector, 5, 24–25, 126, 213
—in rural areas, 124, 126
Investment, foreign. *See also* Foreign aid
—composition of, 9, 12
—effects of: on domestic investment,

241n; on savings, 232–235; on trade
balance, 20
—by exporters, 104–105
—and industrial licensing policy, 225
—and preferential treatment of exporters,
104–105
—restrictions on, 5, 9, 25
—role of, in development, 9
Invisible earnings: effect of devaluation
on, 92, 97; inclusion in import entitlement schemes, 79, 92
Iron and Steel Controller (I&SC), 36, 37
Iron and steel industry: corporate savings
by, 237; DRCs for, 179; effect of
devaluation on, 93; exports of, 132,
134–135; import allocations to, 37, 44;
import duties affecting, 96; import
premia affecting, 159, 160; industrial
licensing of, 79; public investment in,
24; subsidies affecting, 92, 99; supply
conditions in, 101–102, 103–104,
106. *See also* "New" industries

Jan Sangh party, 26
Japan, 9, 219, 225
Joint Plant Committee, 106
Jute industry: corporate savings by, 237;
DRCs for, 180; effect of devaluation on,
87, 88, 93, 136; effect of drought on,
120, 144; effect of liberalization policies
on, 119–120; export duties affecting,
138; exports of, 54, 55, 56, 57, 58, 60–
61, 130–132, 136, 144–145, 149n; subsidies affecting, 103, 107. *See also*
Traditional industries

Khang, C., 194
Kidron, M., 31n, 32n
Korean War, 27, 54
Krishnan, S. N., 109n
Krueger, Anne, 3, 27, 84, 183, 186n, 195n

Labor productivity, 216–217
Liberalization policies (of 1966). *See also*
Devaluation (of 1966)
—effects of: on economic efficiency, 170–
171; on exports, 129–146, 157, 158,
162; on investment, 124, 125, 127; on
production, 118–123, 127
—elements of: export duties, 84, 87–88;
export subsidies, 29, 83–84, 86–87, 89,

DATE DUE

GAYLORD			PRINTED IN U.S.A.